TRUE FAITH AND ALLEGIANCE

JOURNALS OF A NAVAL OFFICER
THREE DECADES OF THE COLD WAR

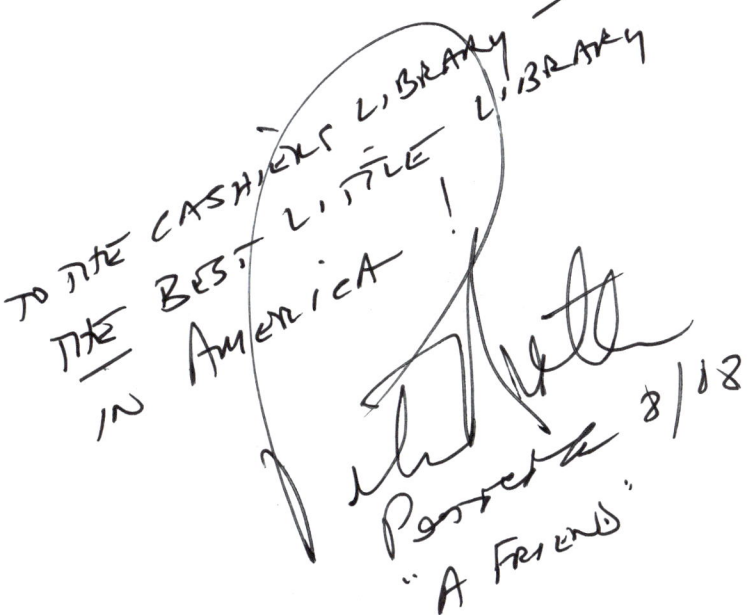

Rear Admiral Peter B. Booth
U.S. Navy Retired

DEDICATION

Dedicated to the tens of thousands of brave souls who gave their lives in the cause of the United States and to the millions who repeatedly did the tough jobs in hot war and cold over three decades — with **honor, heroism, sacrifice and allegiance to the flag** — and to those left behind on the home fronts in hometown USA including Carolyn and the girls.

Cover: A typical U. S. Navy fighter pilot at the ten-year mark ready for the tough job with a backdrop of the National Ensign.
Designed by Ashley Spears

Title: From the military oath of office —
". . . I shall bear true faith and allegiance to the Constitution of the United States of America . . ."

Other titles by Peter B. Booth:
Humble in Victory – A Novel

Copyright © 2004 by Peter B. Booth
Pensacola, Florida
pbooth@bellsouth.net
www.peterbbooth.com

All rights reserved
including the right of reproduction in
whole or in part in any form or by any means.
Excepting minor quotes for book reviews,
written permission from the author is required
for any reproduction, in whole or in part, of this book.

ISBN: 0-9728872-7-X

Published by:
CRB Publications
Pensacola, Florida
850.456.2400
www.peterbbooth.com
and
Trent's Prints
Chumuckla, Florida
www.trentsprints.com

CONTENTS

HOMICIDE —Fourteen months as an ensign on the destroyer Buck, C.N.G. Hendrix, JO's journal, titivation and learning in the Pacific.

WINGS — A year and a half of loops, spins, stalls, bombing, fun and girls as a student pilot in inverse order of listing.

DEMONS AND EXECUTIONERS — Two years with the F3H Demon, Hancock, red-shirt parties, all-weather fighter pilot and staying alive.

AARDVARKS AND PHANTOMS — The F4 Phantom joins the fleet, Kitty Hawk, Soviet Badgers, Hap Chandler and single-engine takeoffs.

STANFORD — MBAs, T-33s, Accounting II and a cross-country trek by small airplane.

INTERLUDE — F-111Bs, boredom, Washington, D.C. and bad eyes.

MORE PHANTOMS — Phantom instructor pilot, Key West, fire on the ground, air combat maneuvering and flat hatting.

COMBAT — One year with the VF-74 "Bedevilers," five days of Vietnam combat, the Forrestal fire and sadness.

DIAMONDBACKS — VF-102, the carrier America, combat, a Hong Kong hotel room and ten seconds of inverted flight.

DETACHMENT OCEANA — Neat job, more Phantoms and night bombing.

THE RED RIPPERS — Three years with a bunch of pig-headed, sausage-slinging, two-balled, he-men bastards of VF-11.

AIDES AND THE PENTAGON — Two years in the five-sided wind tunnel, blues in the summer, short skirts and the head guy's aide.

KING TUT, LOGS AND SYLVANIA — King Tut crosses the Atlantic, large supply ship gets lost in the North Sea, CO logs and Rickover.

FIRST IN DEFENSE — The carrier Forrestal, shooting down our own, some tough times and keeping the admiral waiting while I slept.

STAFFER — Battle Group training, soviet subs, 1,000-feet deep in ours', whales, McKee, Waller, P3s and the passive sonar equation.

PENTAGON REVISITED — Plans, policy, xerox machines, Foley-san, tanks and an inside look at a building that feeds on itself.

LOTS OF WINGS — Escape to reality, training the best of the best, the Blue Angels, getting your mind right and the will to win.

COLOR ME PURPLE — Chief of staff to an Army four star, jumping out of airplanes (not me), lots of generals, F-16s and purple suiters.

CAVEATS

As I grew within the Navy ranks, I always kept a folder within which were a collection of ragged, five-by-seven cards with anecdotes, names and places of each outfit I served with. Because I loved the world of the Navy and its incredibly fine people, I thought that one day, the experiences would make for interesting reading, if only for our kids and their kids. Finally, in the early 1990s, I stuffed the verbiage into my vintage Macintosh computer and printed out a four-inch-thick tome, took it to Kinkos for a few spiral-bound copies, gave one each to our daughters and put the remnants into a dust-gathering box. Included were a few photos and documents, mostly of those troops that bring this tale to life.

In my mind, this three-decade story weaves a real-life scenario of the thousands of real sailors and military folks — most all behind the scenes — who enabled our nation to defeat the Soviets and bring an end to the Cold War. My perceptions are central, but it is through the many lead characters in this tale that the reader may gain an insight into the inner workings of life on the deck plates, cockpits and higher-level staffs. Most of my friends and compatriots during this period served essentially the same as me (or tougher) and their families endured hard times, just as ours. By intent, I have downplayed the family side of this period; it could make a sequel of even greater interest. And, right or wrong, the perspectives, commentary and scenes are intended to be reasonably light and non-tutorial with no parsing of words or hidden messages; this is not a war-college thesis. And, I admit up-front to a modicum of embellishment on occasion.

Thanks go to the many real Navy folks and later, a few from our sister services, who so inspired me and countless others. They make this story and they are the heroes all!

So – this is just a collection of events, people, good times and hard from the mid-'50s to the mid-'80s. It is a story of *sacrifice, heroism, altruism, patriotism, courage* and *doing the tough job* on the part of so many. No one in this story got rich and few had cushy jobs. All, however, gave to their Navy and country and left legacies of service that few external to the culture of the military can match, or in some cases, understand.

PRELUDE

By intent, this tale of three decades as a Naval Officer begins with my first assignment as an ensign recently graduated from the U. S. Naval Academy in 1956. The twenty-one years preceding this event were heavily influenced by my parents and their lives in and about the Navy.

In fact, I flew for the first time in early 1934 while still firmly attached within my mother. Dad was a lieutenant (junior grade) at the time and took his pregnant wife for a ride in an old, U. S. Navy plane of some vintage at a field south of San Diego. My second flight was across the country in a Ford Tri-Motor at the age of three weeks, this time in the arms of my Mom while Dad went to sea as a float-plane pilot on a battleship.

Growing up, we lived in San Diego, Washington, Norfolk and a few others while Dad went from job to job afloat, in the air and ashore. On most of my birthdays, before blowing out the candles, I would secretly wish that I could attend the Naval Academy, and later, become a Navy pilot. Because both of my parents came from early-1900s, British-Scottish stock imbued with the flavor of study, hard work, ethical behavior, God-fearing and traditional middle-class values, so too did such mores impregnate my sometimes thick hide.

So it was, that in spite of many moves and occasional setbacks, I was able to enter Annapolis as a seventeen-year-old midshipman, raise my right hand and vow to ". . . bear true faith and allegiance" to the Constitution. Four formative years later, I became an ensign in the U. S. Navy and trekked half-way around the world to the USS *Buck*.

My dad circa 1936 holds me aloft beside his F4B Navy fighter.

My dad swears me in as a midshipman in Bancroft Hall in the summer of 1952.

HOMICIDE

Fourteen months as an ensign on the destroyer Buck, my CO, JO's journal, titivation and learning in the Pacific.

My first ship out of the Naval Academy was the U.S.S. *Buck*, a 2,250-ton destroyer with the call sign "Homicide." The first five minutes aboard were marked by two rather abrupt happenings: Reporting aboard in Kobe, Japan, I was greeted by a rough, not-too-pleasant, obviously-harassed Lieutenant (junior grade) — the Officer of the Deck (OOD). With no introduction, he uttered two sentences without waiting for a reply. The first was "What the hell are you going to use that sword for?" and, equally abruptly, the "Captain wants to see you — fast."

So, in my third-minute aboard, I was in front of a smiling Commander C. N. G. Hendrix, United States Navy, Commanding Officer of the *U.S.S. Buck* (DD 761), who wanted to know posthaste how my CRUDESPAC engineering school had gone. Unbeknownst to my new captain, that school had been cancelled. As to why, I explained it was because "I was scheduled for flight training at the end of a year on board." Because my new CO continued to smile, I did not realize what a big strike one this was at the time.

Strike two and right at plus five minutes on board was my new CO's query, still with a smile, the gist of which was, that if the Naval Academy graduation was on 1 June, 1956 and I did not attend the engineering school,

1

why had it taken 2.5 months to get to Buck? My lame and shaky reply had something to do with "60-days leave authorized, sir." Without batting an eye, Commander Hendrix continued to smile.

Such was my somewhat inauspicious start to an absolutely fascinating tour as a destroyer sailor that summer of 1956. As a new guy aboard, I was of course "George," sat at the end of the wardroom table and was the butt of many a sea story from our officer cadre.

We had fourteen officers on board, all of whom were ensign or lieutenant (junior grade) except the CO and Executive Officer (XO). Our XO was a mustachioed, mustang lieutenant commander named George W. Stubblefield. The XO and CO are central to this tale, for both had an enormously positive impact on me, though, not surprisingly, I was not smart enough to realize it at the time.

I was soon given three overriding assignments: Second division officer, completion of the CRUDESPAC junior officer journal and to "get qualified as Combat Information Center watch officer and Officer of the Deck Underway, ASAP."

The Junior Officer's Journal — the predecessor of today's Surface Warfare Officer training — consisted of a loose-leaf notebook about three-inches thick which covered the ship in detail including engineering, gunnery, supply, communications and so forth. By using reading material aboard, asking questions and with lots of snooping and probing on your own, you were expected to complete this in about three months.

One lesson comes to mind: "Trace out the 600 psi steam system." What a great way to learn at least a portion of the engineering plant steam cycle. Because our ship had two separate boiler rooms and two main engine spaces — producing a total of 100,000 shaft horsepower — this entailed a good bit of dirty and hot work in and amongst valves, pipes, cross-overs and the like. One thing was a given as I would work the journal: Ask a question of anyone and they were always more than willing to spend the time to share their piece of the action with the new ensign.

The journal had a side benefit too, in that it forced an interaction with the troops and the Chief Petty Officers. Heretofore, my association with the enlisted side of the Navy had been limited to playing the part as a youngster midshipman on a two-month cruise. The journal served to break the ice with the sailors and, if you were lucky, get an invite to the Chief's mess far forward for a cup of coffee.

The second division was a piece of absolute work and I remember it well! My leading petty officers were BM1 Louderback, BM2 Nolan and BM3 Crowder,

A real sailor! BM1 Louderback at ship's picnic.

2nd Division: l to r: Louderback, Crowder, Booth, Nolan, Moses A. Celestine. Top right note missing five-inch gun.

all boatswain's mates, who collectively led some twenty non-rated seamen. In effect, Louderback was the Chief. Our job was to take care of the after half of the ship from the quarterdeck to the stern.

My boss was the JG whom I met my first day. He was the operations boss, the gunnery officer and the first division officer. He was also the third senior aboard, physically a big fellow, wore a really seasoned bridge cap and was the senior watch officer. He cut a wide swath aboard Buck, and I soon learned that in order to make myself feel good, I needed to make my boss feel good first. In me, he saw but three things, read: 1) JO's journal, 2) neat and clean spaces aft and 3) rapid progress towards my OOD quals so that he could take himself off the watch bill as befits the status of the senior watch officer.

I'll come back to the Officer of the Deck (OOD) part later, because this is a major chunk of being a junior officer (JO) on a destroyer — eight hours per day in port and at sea, seven-days per week.

True Faith and Allegiance

There accrued also, a batch of collateral duties that were fitted in and amongst watches, journal, divisional duties and sleep. Mine happened to be as the "ship's secretary."

Our ship's office consisted of a tiny space off the amidships passage big enough for two equally-minute desks, one manual typewriter, an ink-fed mimeograph machine and one yeoman and one personnelman striker. My CO had a very pragmatic philosophy when it came to reports and paperwork: "You are judged in large part up the chain of command by the quality of your paperwork." Typos were simply not in his vocabulary — it was letter perfect or it was a non-starter. Woe be to the bearer of any paperwork that was not perfect! Because I was the intermediary between the CO/XO and the ship's office, I was the recipient of more visibility than I needed.

Another "spare time" effort concerned our somewhat crummy-looking 26-foot motor whaleboat. I soon learned that its condition was a continual sore point with my captain and that what he wanted, was the "Best boat in the division! Do you understand, Mr. Booth?" This clear verbal guidance was backed up by a letter-perfect memo to me via my equally concerned lieutenant (junior grade) boss. This was the first time I had heard the word "titivate" applied to an inanimate object. More on boat and titivation later.

My first two months aboard were a blur of watches, learning, junior officer journal, being a division officer, checking paperwork, watches, boat, and more watches. We were at sea almost the entire time in and about Japan, mainly working with a two-carrier task group and always with the other three destroyers in our division. I did my token engineering watches, got qualified as CIC watch officer and stood JOOD bridge watches. I was on a steep learning curve, knew a little about a lot and thought I knew a lot more than I really did.

A short digression is in order as regards my educational prelude to destroyer duty: The captain, my boss and I were the only Naval Academy types aboard, the others being NROTC, OCS or Mustang (up through the ranks). My impressions of non-USNA officers prior to reporting aboard were not overly positive, my only exposure having been on midshipmen cruises.

I soon learned that my impressions were poorly-founded because all of our officers were most

Buck's officers ... l to r: Speltz (MPA); Witucki (Chief Eng); Shannon (my boss); Cocking (Supply); Booth; Simmons (Elec).

Homicide

professional and talented. Each had been to extensive schooling prior to reporting aboard. The Supply Officer, John Willis, had been to a year-long supply school; the combat information officer had been to a comprehensive CIC school; the MPA and DCA (engineering) had been to the demanding type commander engineering school and so on. These young officers were knowledgeable and hard charging and soon earned my respect. In fact, I was scrambling more and more to make that respect mutual.

Our bridge watch teams underway consisted of two lookouts, a messenger, a boatswain's mate, a quartermaster, a helmsman, a lee helmsman, a phone talker and an OOD (Officer of the Deck). We normally had an after lookout on the stern and a man in after steering as well.

Because we spent a goodly portion of our time in complete emcon (electronic silence) and often times totally blacked out, one imperative was a good lookout doctrine. As a result, my CO wanted his OODs out on the open bridge and not inside the cozy and warm wheel house because ". . . you can't see anything from in there!"

On the bridge, we normally had three radios patched in, including two tactical circuits and a CIC net. During task group operations it could sometimes be intimidating with three radios crackling, squawk boxes bleating and phone talkers relaying info that two minutes prior had been over the radio and one minute before had come over the squawk box. The radar (singular) was, of course, all manual.

Personnel Inspection underway: Captain Hendrix with XO, Lcdr. Stubblefield and Ensign Booth.

Even on transits the watches went quickly. On quiet nights I would work the flashing light with some modicum of success, do "tacsits" with the other ships, be continually changing stations and so forth. There was seldom a boring watch.

I soon qualified as officer of the deck underway by virtue of lots of underway time and a senior watch officer that was getting tired of standing watches. I also thought quite highly of myself, my steaming cap had become well salted, my shoes were always salt encrusted (meant I was doing my job as second division officer), a blond mustache had germinated (after two months), and I no longer sat at the extreme end of the wardroom table. Most importantly, my boss, the JG, acquiesced to talk to me in a civil tone of voice.

True Faith and Allegiance

My "come-uppance" occurred one dark, rough and stormy night as our four destroyers approached a rendezvous with Task Force 77 with its two carriers, several supply ships, two cruisers and three divisions (four ships in each division) of destroyers. The call sign of the admiral in charge was appropriately, "Jehovah."

We steamed into the fray with four boilers on the line, full superheated steam, 25 knots, all three radios, squawk boxes and phone talkers going at once and Mr. Booth as officer of the deck. How I loved it — this is what it's all about!!

Our assignment from "Jehovah" over the primary-tactical radio was to form a horseshoe screen with a certain orientation to the guide, which was one of the carriers. It was an execute-to-follow vice immediate execute for which the combat information officer (snug in his warm domain one deck below) and I were thankful, as it gave us time to assimilate the somewhat complex order. In the school house it was a relatively simple evolution. At the time though, and given the circumstances, it was a bit more involved, but nothing a seasoned-destroyer team could not handle.

After a time frame some ten-times shorter than the classroom, the execute came and I answered in my most assertive and confidant radio voice, "Homicide, roger out." Off we went pitching and bucking at twenty-five knots on what I thought was a good course to station. Nothing was heard from my buddy in CIC who was supposed to be providing me his recommendations.

My captain was on the bridge and had not said a word. Midway through this black-night evolution, the carriers changed course to conduct night-flight operations, and the confidence built-up over the preceding 2.5 months started to wane. It was the type of feeling one gets when starting an exam you know you are not really ready for — kind of in your gut and knees.

My captain came up behind me and in a quiet voice, asked if I would "like some help?" By this time Mr. "Pride" was ready for anything, because in fact, he had totally lost the bubble. The captain made a couple of suggestions which I copied ver batim and the Buck coasted smoothly into station. The CIC watch officer — my buddy — was impressed, told my boss who in turn gave me a pat on the back for handling a tough situation so well. The captain just nodded with the hint of a knowing grin.

Mr. "Ensign" Booth learned his first real-world fleet lesson which was to never get confident to the point where you don't know when you are being backed into a corner. It was at this stage in my destroyer incarnation that I started to really dig-in and become a professional naval officer.

Destroyer Sailor!

Homicide

The lighter side of our overmanned and formal bridge structure had to do with some pet peeves of my CO, one of which was engaging in non-essential conversation with the watch. On one particularly cold winter night in the Western Pacific between the hours of midnight and 0400, BM2 Nolan was the boatswains mate on watch and wanted to tell sea stories. His entree was always an offer for a cup of coffee to which I politely refused, but one night acquiesced. Nolan went to the little coffee mess aft of the bridge and brought me a cup of real-black destroyer coffee. I thanked him and added that I would be most appreciative if he could go back and bring me some cream and sugar. With a note of genuine shock, my 100% Navy boatswains mate looked me square in the eyeballs from six inches and with great dismay, said, "Mr. Booth, real sailors don't use cream and sugar." I haven't used cream or sugar in coffee since.

Buck's coffee pot.

Like most destroyer COs, my Commander Hendrix wanted to know of any ship that would pass closer than two-to-three miles from us. The problem from the junior officer OOD perspective was that he was extraordinarily tough to wake up, particularly on the mid-watch. Us junior officers would regale ourselves in the wardroom with CO tales, as JOs are sometime wont to do. Upon calling the Captain one night on the hand-cranked, sound-powered phone about a very close contact, I got the standard "call me if he gets any closer." We JOs thought that his responses were hilarious, though unbeknownst to us, he knew exactly what the action was and, most probably, what all the guffawing was about at the end of the wardroom table.

And the boat — back to the ship's boat. Understand that this boat (one gong for ahead, two to stop, three for astern and four for full ahead), was the officer's boat, the liberty launch, the rescue boat and the Captain's gig. As much as we tried, it just looked sad, until one day, BM1 Loundermilk boondoggled a new fiberglass top to replace the tattered canvas top. I asked him where he got it and he opined that I really did not need to know. My boss was pleased and had the sense not to ask me where the Bos'n got it. For awhile at least, the Buck had the best-looking boat in the division, and Mr. Booth's star was a couple of degrees above the horizon.

Commander Hendrix, my CO, if you had not already gathered, is the central player in the saga of Homicide. He paid me great attention, very little of which was complimentary. But always it was prodding, questioning, pushing, testing and stretching. He really let me have as much rein as I could handle and then some. And occasionally he would really let loose when in his eyes, I had let him down. Bottom line, though not realizing it at the time, was that he

Commander C. N. G. Hendrix, U.S. Navy Commanding Officer, U.S.S. Buck (DD761)

was a great teacher and mentor for which, in years to come, I was most grateful. My first Commanding Officer had a marked and positive influence on my life and career.

Although we were at sea about 80% of that first four months, we had some great liberties and equally great fun ashore! Yokosaka was my first exposure to the A-33 Navy Exchange where I bought a Nikon camera for $88 which consumed my entire two-week pay check. Kobe, Japan was the home of a small steak house with the phonetic name of Arragowas and which seated but ten customers. Sasebo is where I first learned to play liar's dice and try to drink martinis, the latter of which came close to landing me in hack. Hong Kong is where I bought a cashmere/wool topcoat from Mohans and still have. Auckland is where I learned the difference between real beer and American beer, and almost landed in hack again.

And we had fun at sea! I recall one day, after having been at sea for about seven-straight weeks, our CO authorized a "beer call" and two beers for each man. The beer was left over from a ship's party in Kobe, was ice cold and was called Pabst Blue Ribbon. I never figured out if our skipper got permission to do this or did it on his own. I suspect the latter, for though he didn't drink or smoke, nor was he overly friendly, he did care for his troops — and his troops knew it!

Pabst Blue Ribbon wile underway in South China Sea.

Homicide

After a long at-sea period, we pulled into Sasebo, Japan for a few days. One day, I received an unfriendly summons to the XO's stateroom just forward of the wardroom. Without smiling, the XO handed me an official paper indicating that one of our crew had not paid his lawful bills when ashore. The culprit was one of my stalwart non-rated men, gregarious, very short and one of the few blacks we had aboard during that era. Though I remember his name well, that is not important. His problem:

One of my guys on watch.

He had bought a "small house of ill-repute" and was in arrears on the agreed amount. The XO got one-foot from my eyeballs and directed me to "take care of it, Mr. Booth!" Without hesitation, I walked aft to my leading boatswain's mate in the second division, stated the problem and, collectively, the problem was solved. Suffice to add, that on the deckplates, the miscreant became an unofficial hero of the ship. The next time we visited Sasebo, my guy stayed aboard.

Smoking — cigarette sea-stores cost ten-cents a pack and most of the crew smoked. One dark and quiet night, my friend Nolan sidled out to the open bridge and asked me for the umpteenth time if I wanted a smoke to which I always replied, "no thanks." This night though, I got the distinct impression that I ought to try one because that's what "real sailors did." You know the rest of that story — and you wonder how I remember his name!

In spite of some rather routine and unremarkable watch standing, we had lots of excitement. One night steaming into Hong Kong we heard a distress call from a burning freighter a hundred-or-so miles from us. Four-hours later we were alongside a 500-foot merchant ship the sides of which were cherry red. My CO put the bow of Buck close alongside the stern and, having been selected to lead the rescue party by virtue of a) being available and b) enroute to flight school and therefore presumably expendable, prepared to jump onto the burning vessel. I wish I could report that my team and I leapt aboard, rescued the crew, doused the flames, got some sort of an atta-boy and had a great Hong Kong liberty, but alas, the only part that happened was the liberty. Wiser heads prevailed and Buck backed away and left the ship for the salvage tug. So much for being a near hero.

We did have a tough accident, when our five-inch gun mount forward of the bridge blew up and killed two of our guys in the ammo handling room below. At this time I was the battle-station OOD (so the CO could keep an eye on me). Because the guns were pointed on our port beam, the shrapnel went

True Faith and Allegiance

in a circular plane which included the port side of the bridge. This shrapnel plane narrowly missed my rear and fortunately, the rest of the bridge team; not so for the good sailors one deck below.

This next vignette has nothing to do with being a hero, excitement or fun, but everything to do with being dumb. We were chasing a carrier as plane guard in good day-time weather, but with a long and very deep Pacific swell. Because the wind was blowing about 25 knots, the carrier was only doing about five knots. Turning into the wind, the big bird farm ordered us to follow which we did with about five degrees of rudder. As the ship entered the trough, we started to roll and then <u>really</u> started rolling. My response was to put on more rudder — wrong! Before I knew it, my nice peaceful and squared-away watch had generated into total disaster, as the ship went to a 36-degree roll. Desks, files, dishes, books, equipment and one totally unglued CO in full afterburner hit the bridge deck plates. My Captain did not even have the courtesy to say he had the conn to those on watch, but his "all ahead full and 30-degrees rudder" command left no doubt as to who was in charge. I was the dual recipient of a real fine lesson in grade-school seamanship and an even finer lesson in the CO's sea cabin later as to the inherent dangers of being complacent.

My first report of fitness as a naval officer was a beauty. The Captain called me into his sea cabin, showed me my "marked right down the middle" report of fitness and opined in his three-sentence narrative that ". . . if Mr. Booth would work harder and apply himself more diligently, he has the potential to become a productive officer." He told me that I was only measuring up to half of his expectations and that he, my CO, expected more. He read and said all this while looking me eyeball-to-eyeball and with only a hint of a grin. I got the message and was always grateful that he let us JOs know where we stood. Another lesson in leadership 101!

After five months in the Western Pacific, Homicide and I headed home to San Diego and Christmas of 1956. We did our obligatory full-power run between Midway and Pearl Harbor and for thirty hours or so, held 35 knots with a huge rooster tail behind us. The fuel-required versus horsepower and speed-generated curves so studiously studied the previous year at the Naval Academy, came to life in this real-world lab as we burned most of our on-board fuel in that short, max-power run.

During a two-week standdown in San Diego, we started to have problems with some of our enlisted men while on liberty in town for being "rough and rowdy." Because some of the problem guys were in my division, the word filtered down through our chain of command, "to find out what was going on!" Interesting, because my guys said they were not unruly. So, I left the ship in the standard officer liberty uniform of civilian coat and tie, headed for the bar in a moderately tough part of town and had one beer with a few of my guys. Literally, within minutes, the San Diego police (not Navy shore patrol) appeared and gruffly lined me and my guys up outside the bar. Though I tried to explain, I was unpleasantly reminded that if I kept talking, I too would

Homicide

end up in the slammer. Simply put, back then, San Diego, like many Navy towns, expressed the sentiment that "Dogs and sailors keep off the grass." Happily, this attitude departed the scene within a few years. Another lesson learned for one lone ensign.

Homicide and her three buddies soon set sail for San Francisco, Hunters Point Naval Shipyard and an every-four-year major overhaul. All four destroyers nosed into a huge drydock for what was to be a 2.5 month — yes, 2.5-months overhaul. My memories of the ship and shipyard are meager and more than likely transcended by the awesome animate attractions of San Francisco!

During this period, my CO ordained that he wanted new lockers for the crew and assigned me the project. After conversing with the Supply Officer who just laughed (habitability was not in the destroyer-Navy vernacular), I timidly told the CO via my boss and XO that there were no lockers to be had. My CO gave me another of those eyeball-to-eyeball exercises and with only the hint of a smile, said "Mr. Booth . . . I said I wanted lockers for the crew!"

We had a chief (top of the enlisted rates) by this time in second division and I recalled a long-ago leadership lesson at the academy along the lines that often-times the solution to a tough problem was to ask the chief. In short order, the chief asked me to order up a 2.5-ton truck, get a working party of eight men and meet him later in the day at 1900. The Chief, me, the troops and one large truck drove up to a huge flat-topped ship in an adjacent drydock, appropriated the requisite lockers and drove off.

This taught me some lessons: 1) Always watch out for what belongs to you or your guys, 2) If it's going to help your guys, bending the rules may be OK, 3) The Chiefs really run the Navy and 4) It's normal to feel guilty in a scenario such as this.

We worked hard in the shipyard, but had fun in nearby San Francisco. One of the animate attractions was a cute nurse who soon became front and center in my brain. We had a good time, I learned some collateral lessons and when we left the shipyard, I hoped to continue our budding relationship. As we cast off and slipped out of the monster drydock, one of my best friends and Naval Academy company and classmates, stood on the pier and waved to me, his arm closely about my love! Alas — the life of a sailor!

Our captain made me navigator for our post-shipyard refresher training in San Diego and for our subsequent voyage to WestPac. I still spent my eight hours on the bridge at sea, but no longer had the press of the junior officer's journal. But, because our only electronic navigation equipment was the Loran "A" (as big as a bedroom dresser), I spent a great deal of time in truly basic navigation; sun lines, LANs, DRs, bottom contour (my CO was big on this) and just sniffing the wind. Loved it!

Ship handling in and about docks and mooring buoys was always an arty endeavor. Homicide would rather have been in the scrap heap than have used a tug. In my entire time aboard, we never used a tug in spite of some pretty tough winds, currents and strange ports. The ship had a great deal of power and destroyer sailors were expected to use it in a prudent and professional manner.

During our workups, prior to departing on our second deployment, we practiced shooting our five-inch guns at sleds and aerial sleeves, evading mine fields and hunting subs in the deep waters off San Diego. One of these evolutions, was working our four destroyers against the new submarine Nautilus, the first of the nuclear-powered subs. Traditionally, 99% of the time hunting subs found the subs on battery power and very slow — like less than five knots. The Nautilus though, was just the opposite and ran underwater at speeds much faster. Though the sub was noisy when going fast, we had to slow in order to hear and see him on our underwater gear. Bottom line is that the Nautilus ran circles around the four best destroyers in the Pacific Fleet, much to the chagrin of the collective COs.

On my final voyage on Buck, we steamed some 10,000 miles from San Diego to Guam via Pearl Harbor, Pago Pago, Auckland, Manus and Subic Bay in the Phillipines. Pago Pago (pronounced "pango pango"), was a two-day refueling stop replete with dusty roads, a nurses residence and a few inter-ship softball games. As we were getting underway for Aukland, New Zealand, I noticed my Naval Academy class ring was gone — I had removed it at the ball field when playing a game earlier in the day. Standing on the quarterdeck as the lines were being singled up, I borrowed a ring from the nearest shipmate, held up a five-dollar bill and pointed in the general direction of the recent game. Literally, as the last lines were being cast-off, a little brown boy ran up and tossed the ring to me. What a day. What a great little boy!

Auckland was fun because: I met a neat young lady; drank too much real beer; gave a pint of my meager blood (anyone who did so got liberty that morning); watched my first soccer match; drove a car on the wrong side of the road; and met a ton of folks who absolutely loved America and American sailors. When we departed for the island of Manus some 2,000 miles closer to Guam, there were lots of tears, hugs and sincere handshakes.

Farewells in Auckland, N.Z.

While inport in the harbor of Manus in the Soloman Islands, I received word that my top assistant navigator, a quartermaster and prince of a sailor, had

Homicide

abruptly been removed from the ship. This particular sailor and I had worked closely for many months as the art of navigation was almost a full-time job back then including full celestial work in the mornings and evenings. It turned out that he was homosexual. No one bothered to explain the circumstances nor did they need to. Navy policy in this area was zero tolerance and unforgiving. Interestingly, in the following three decades, this was never repeated to my knowledge.

At this point, I had been on Buck for a bit over a year and, though still a lowly ensign, cut a modestly-wider swath than at my shaky initial introduction. Commander Hendrix was still the skipper, we had a new XO, my boss had moved to shore duty and I was still the second division officer with my great boatswain's mates — Louderback, Nolan and Crowder — continuing to do the tough jobs. Because we were close to a family on this small combat ship, most everyone knew one another. Guys (officers included) who did not pull their weight or thought too much of themselves, were simply tolerated. Fortunately, they were few and far between. Lesson learned, of course, was that respect is a two-way street!

It was in Guam that I threw off the last line and, with unseen tears, waved sayonara to Buck, my CO, a phenomenally-competent wardroom, Louderback, Nolan and Crowder, Homicide and a productive and fun introduction to the real Navy.

Last line off in Guam with a lumpy throat.

EPILOGUE I

Some 30-years later, I learned that my CO (now deceased) was to have an oceanography lab at the Naval Academy dedicated in his name. I sent the following message to the Superintendent, Rear Admiral Chuck Larson:

1. Chuck. Just received the invite to the oceanography lab and regret that I cannot be with you. I would be most honored if you could find your way to include the below comments in the program in some way.

2. Captain Hendrix was my first CO on board Buck (DD 761). I joined her and met my Captain in Kobe Japan some 29-years ago. What a leader and teacher he was and how in later years when I was in command, did I hearken back to the lessons he taught me. One stands out: I had been on board about two months and by virtue of almost continuous underway time and a shortage of officers, had been qualified OOD. My opinion of my own professional competence was quite high as Captain Hendrix had allowed me great latitude and a long leash. Unbeknownst to me at the time, I was a long ways from being a professional mariner. It happened one dark, stormy night as our four destroyers were joining a TF 77 three-carrier, horseshoe screen at 25 knots. The radios were barking out commands, the ship was rolling and CIC was rendering rather half-hearted recommendations. My confident bubble slowly became smaller and softer and it wasn't long before I totally lost the picture. Captain Hendrix had observed all this and asked me softly if I needed any advice. He quietly suggested a course of action which resulted in us smoothly sliding into our ordained spot in the screen in short order. It was at this point in my junior-officer longevity that I really buckled down to work and started paying attention and asking the right questions. Twenty-years later on the bridge of a carrier, when the going got tough, Capt Hendrix would

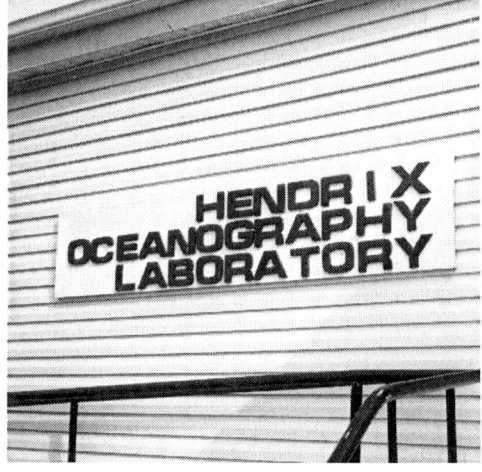

be beside me, for I thought of his incredible professional competence often. He was a stickler for doing it right the first time and for always putting forth a quality effort. The ship and crew reflected his leadership and pride for we were clearly the best in the fleet. On the squash court as well, he was tough and demanding. Right or wrong, he would tell me that it's not how you play the game, it's whether you win or lose. And a winner he was — as a leader, a teacher, a prodder, a professional. All of the above.

EPILOGUE II

Only recently, I unearthed a letter Captain Hendrix had written me in 1972, fifteen years after our tour together on Buck. It's content is unremarkable; the leadership lesson though comes through loud and clear:

On Buck, when you stepped aboard, I sized you up, saw in you an alert, dedicated, intelligent "potential admiral" material, tried to give you all responsibility possible, tried to teach you personally based on my own experience, and considered you then, and still do now one of the most outstanding naval officers I've had pleasure of teaching, serving with. As navigator and GQ OOD, you had one hell of a lot of responsibility for a young Ensign just out of USNA. I see in you a lot of things I've tried to be or had in my life in Navy — and now at USNA. But you earned it all — and deserved it — based on your bringing up at home, USNA indoctrination and own experience.

So, Pete, Jane and I are and always will be mighty proud of you — for these and many other reasons. Our Navy and country need outstanding men and professional leaders like you. There are too few around.

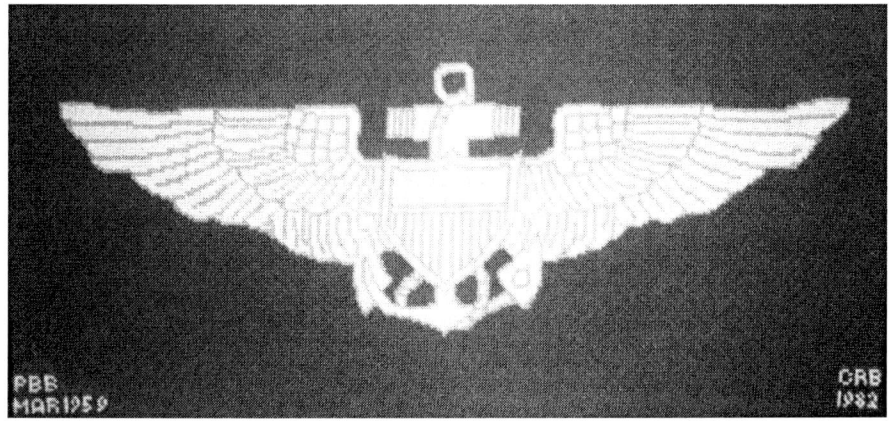

GOLD WINGS

A year-and-a-half of spins, loops, stalls, bombing, dumb-dumbs, fun and cute girls in inverse order.

I could not believe what was happening! After finally arriving at the starting gate to be a Naval Aviator, here I was, puking my guts out. It was a simple physical exercise that fall of 1957 — called a step test. All we had to do was step up onto a bench and back down for five minutes to a preset cadence. Sounds easy and it was, if you weren't smoking, if you hadn't stayed out late the night before and if you had had breakfast like we were supposed to do. What an ignominious start to becoming a Naval Aviator!

I had been on the road for a couple of weeks, having detached from my destroyer some 10,000-miles away in far-off Guam. This was our first day on the job to be followed by two-months of ground school. Lots of study and physical work and more fun in the ensuing sixteen months than most folks have in a lifetime. Here I was, about to fly airplanes and getting paid to do it. What a deal.

There was no doubt in my military mind that I wanted to fly. My Dad had been a long-time Naval Aviator and my Mom and I had flown all the way from San Diego to Baltimore in a United Airlines tri-motor transport when I was three-weeks old. Flying was in my blood. Dad had taken us up for short flights each year as was allowed in those early days, one of which was six weeks before I was born, in an open cockpit something or other. And, when I was in high school, I was a ditch digger for the state of New Jersey and made $1.67 per hour (more than some of the pilots in Dad's all-weather fighter squadron), all of which went to flying lessons with a phenomenal instructor pilot named Mae Berhinger with her own little Cessna 140. By the time I got to Pensacola, I probably had about 100 hours of boondoggle flight time, which stood me in good stead, at least initially.

Naval Aviation was riding tall in the saddle in those late 1950s. Jets, big aircraft carriers, solid reputations built on WWII and Korea and lots of great press. The image could not have been better. To serve your country as a warrior was a great honor; to do so as a front-line Naval Aviator was to me the ultimate achievement. Records were being broken monthly by Navy pilots and young guys were standing in line to join the action. When we saw the Blue Angels perform in their sleek F-11 Tiger Jets, they weren't just a class demonstration team, they <u>were</u> Naval Aviation.

We junior officers lived in "splinterville," a collection of old WWII barracks with two to a room, adjoining heads and no air conditioning. After spending over a year in a much smaller and hotter destroyer stateroom, I thought the digs were great. We ate in the same complex, just like aboard ship and walked a couple of blocks to class. Nobody complained.

Before coming to Pensacola the only thing I had heard about it was, "It's not very exciting" and "don't buy a car from Jarrard's used car lot." Wouldn't you know, the car bug bit and the first thing I did was call Mr. Jarrard and tell him I'd like to come out and look around, but had no way to get out there. He said, "Son, don't worry about that, I'll come pick you up." When I chose a classy 1952 Pontiac convertible, I told him "I didn't have enough money" and he said, "Son, don't worry about a trifle like that." I didn't and was soon the proud owner of my first car. It served me well

and I did some good PR for old Mr. Jarrard and his used car lot.

Pensacola had to be the absolute mecca for sea stories involving aviation. Most were told and embellished over big pitchers of cold beer, some of which was made locally, and always with an excellent level of receptivity. The stories were usually accompanied by gusty song, which got more vocal as we came closer to actually flying. One day we were issued our leather flight jackets (used and refurbished by the Florida prison inmates — true story) and old APH-4 hardhats. No stopping us now, and we started walking just a little taller.

On the day for our first flights at nearby Saufley Field, I looked up on the flight schedule board which had simply chalked in, "Jones/Booth." Across the hanger strode Lieutenant (junior grade) H. P. Jones, USNR. Mr. Jones looked me in the eye, shook my hand and asked if I knew what "HP" stood for? Without waiting for an answer, he said, "It stands for hot pilot and don't forget it." What brass, what BS and how true it symbolized the world we were stepping up to!

H. P. Jones was terrific. Enthusiastic, a good aviator, loved flying, lived the Navy and did his best to imbue this spirit into those around him. If we were pumped up before, we were on a rocket now. And what fun we had — loops, rolls, stalls, landings and even one prohibited snap roll. And lots of stories of how to stay out of trouble in the air, with an occasional embellishment for effect, as more seasoned aviators are sometimes wont to do.

The airplane was a piece of cake. It was the militarized version of what was to become the Beech Bonanza. The T-34 sported a big 225-hp engine, was stressed for six Gs and was an absolute delight to fly. A typical hop took off from Saufley and went to one of a dozen outlying fields for whatever was required for that particular flight. About 1+20 later, we would return to home base.

Student Naval Aviator in new leather flight jacket ... T-34 trainer in background.

As much as the airplane was a delight, getting in and out of Saufley was an incredible adventure. It had the most complicated procedures in the annals of aviation. To begin with, there were three separate runways, the first half of which were for landings and the second for takeoffs. Entering the field took the intellect of a Ph.D. for there were at least a couple-dozen crucial actions to be done before your wheels touched down. Prop, airspeed, goggles, canopy, RPM, radio, trim, brakes and a bunch of others had to be just so, as you wove your way into the pattern.

One story we learned early-on has a frustrated instructor pilot telling his student over the intercom system (he thought, but actually it was going out over the radio), that " You're all f------ up."

The tower operator immediately came up on the air and said, "Aircraft that just transmitted you're all f----- up, identify yourself."

Our flustered instructor regained his composure and in his most debonair manner, transmitted for all to hear, "I'm not that f----- up."

The top student for each week was rewarded with a hop in the station T-28, a big, single-engine trainer and the airplane we would fly in our next stage of training. Each morning, if the weather was questionable, the big R-1820 radial engine of the Trojan would crank up and go off to check the flying area. I never quite made it, but on occasion, would get up early to watch it warm up and take off with a deep-throated roar.

True Faith and Allegiance

My solo wasn't a big deal; I recall it as being quite routine. My instructor pilot was Lieutenant (junior grade) Manny Vierra, who simply had me stop the machine on a grass field, hopped out, walked 50-feet away, lit a cigarette and pointed to the sky. I remembered to come back and pick him up, and, after debriefing, walked just a little taller.

We had a T-34 land wheels up one day — no one hurt, but lots of teeth gnashing by all sorts of grim-faced officials. I remember my Mom warning me as I left home enroute to Pensacola "not to fly too low or slow" and "be sure and put the wheels down before you land." Well, landing wheels up is really hard to do, but having said that, there's not an aviator in the world that doesn't check his gear down at least several times on final approach. In the case of our Saufley hero, he really had to try. When asked why he didn't heed his warning horn, he simply stated he could not hear the horn because the tower was making too much noise "telling someone to wave off because his wheels weren't down." (True story!)

Whiting Field was a huge two-airfield complex about thirty miles from Pensacola and was to be our next stage of training in the big T-28s. Four of us drove over in caravan, and, when just inside the front gate, saw four T-28s taking off with a ten-second interval. Stopping our cars as if on signal, we watched in awe as the four, big and noisy machines flew directly over us at full power at about one-hundred feet. What a phenomenal introduction to the world of T-28s, Whiting Field and intermediate flight training!

T-28s in formation at Whiting Field near Pensacola.

The T-28 could pull 52.5 inches of manifold pressure on takeoff, but us student pilots were only allowed to go to 48 inches for our first few hops. It really was a lot of airplane for new aviators and an absolute delight to fly. It felt like, smelled like and flew like an airplane — solid, loud and with rudder pedals that seemed three-feet across.

We did our familiarization stage, intro to instruments, night flying, formation work, lots of acrobatics, gunnery and field carrier landing practice — about 80-hours worth and all challenging, fun and a series of finite and never-ending adventures into the realm of flight. Not only were we getting paid to do this, but flight pay was added to the base. And, we began to understand from whence came the sea stories, for we were adding new chapters of our own as we progressed.

Like Pat Henry, who lost an engine on takeoff, put it straight ahead into the trees, demolished the airplane and walked away with an "I can hack it" swagger. Or the instrument instructor I had who kept walking me down in 20-foot increments while under the hood (can't see out), had me pop the bag, and we weren't more than fifty feet above the ground. "Confidence builder" says my IP. And night flying. Of all the hops we had, the ones I don't need again are the once a month "follow-the-leader" night-flying episodes in the Panhandle of Florida. They were simply hairy and kept the strategically placed "space patrol" instructors busy in a "get-'em-home-alive" mode.

Barin Field, over in Alabama, was our next waypoint — for gunnery and carrier practice-work. Of all my flying over the ensuing decades, this was the most fun. There was no brass around, little ground school, no protocol, and lots of grass-roots flying. Our practice carrier hops were flown in a flat pattern about 125-feet above the ground under the watchful eye of our LSOs (landing signal officer) whom I would soon learn to be most influential and important in the business of carrier aviation. The name of the game was to follow his visual "paddles" instructions precisely and to maintain your airspeed at 78 knots — not 76 and not 80. Canopy was always open, goggles down, flight suit sweaty, right rudder the order of the day and really precision flying. What a trip!

Just to show us how slow the airplane would go and still fly was the objective of our first hop at Barin Field. All we had to do on this solo flight, was climb to 5,000 feet, lower the gear and flaps and record the point at which the engine torque over-powered the rudder available. What a kick. A lot of power to hold level flight, more and more right rudder and stick and finally, "wham," the airplane would abruptly roll off to its left. Usually, the recorded airspeed was right at 48 knots!

Sadly, our carrier qualifications were cancelled because the training carrier was in overhaul, so it was off to Phase IV training in Memphis, Tennessee and jets.

What a difference the T2V jet was from the hot, noisy and heavy controls of the T-28. The airplane was the heavily-modified successor to the Navy's TV-2 (T-33) and was used only for instrument training. As we were the nucleus class of students, we were really given the red-carpet treatment. The instructors were all seasoned veterans from the carrier Navy and, for the first time, we really felt we were getting close to the fleet. We were also having a lot more fun than we ought to have been having or deserved.

Phil Issacs was our one-man advance contingent in Memphis and was detailed by about ten of us to "line up a snake ranch and welcome party." Well, Phil was a real PR guy and not

only rented a perfect old house near the base, but produced a ream of printed flyers having something to do with ". . . student naval aviators arriving at new jet training base and sure would like you all to show up so we could get acquainted . . ." motif.

It was quite an arrival party and welcome and we were greeted in grand style to the Memphis variety of southern hospitality and friendship. I met a cute girl there who worked in town at the Toddle House head office, didn't know one end of an airplane from another, spoke real southern, and whose name was Carolyn. Memphis was no longer just a name; it was an event which kept me coming back for the next five decades.

Carolyn lived on a farm about 100 miles from Memphis on the way to Nashville. If there was ever a contrast to my upbringing and present fast-moving life style, it had to be that fourth-generation Tennessee farm. Quiet, slow moving, no drinking or carousing around and a trip to Memphis was a big deal. One weekend, we went over to Garnertown — the confluence of two county roads and four houses in the Tennessee farmland — and purchased a potion of genuine moonshine from "back yonder in those woods." I really liked Carolyn and fell in love with the simple lifestyle on the 080-degree radial and 97 miles off the Navy Memphis air navigation tacan.

It was with a heavy and mixed-up heart that I left Memphis after three months and caravaned south with my compatriots to Beeville, Texas and advanced flight training. Beeville was a town of 14,200 friendly people nestled in gently-rolling hills, home to a bunch of quietly-producing oil wells and an absolute jewel of a Naval Air Station, with 80 jets and a charter to produce two-hundred Navy jet pilots per year.

Our jets were single and dual-seat F9F-8 swept-wing versions of the venerable Grumman Cougar series and as nice an airplane as I've ever flown (that's three for three, I know, but each one gets better!) It looked like a jet and flew like one. On my first hop, my instructor said "do anything you want." Well, we had heard we might be given just this chance and, of course, everyone wanted to go supersonic. The F9 would go past the speed of sound, but really had to be coaxed to do it like: Climb to 43,000 feet, push the stick forward to zero G until pointed straight down and maybe, just maybe, the mach meter would flick past 1.0 indicated mach number. It really was no big deal, and like all supersonic flight, felt exactly the same as non-supersonic. Sorry.

But, I also wanted to do a vertical victory roll a la World War II and

F9F-8Bs in air over South Texas

the instructor pilot said, "Have at it." So, with max speed at about 15,000 feet, up we flew to the vertical, eased off the G load and rolled with maximum stick deflection going straight up! What a feeling and how totally exhilarating! Great that is, until the airplane started to run out of airspeed and me out of ideas as to what to do next. "No problem, I've got it," says my spring-loaded-to-the-let's-fly-the-pants-off-this-jet, equally-exuberant instructor. The airplane flipped and flopped a few times, and, like all airplanes will do with the controls neutralized, finally decided to stick its nose earthbound and down we went. How I loved it!

That training squadron at Beeville really had talent in its instructor-pilot ranks. Most all were the cream-of-the-fleet crop of seasoned aviators returning for a tour of shore duty. Among them were a generous smattering of WWII and Korea combat veterans. Two exceptions were Danny Michaels and Bill Miller, both Naval Academy classmates of mine and both recently designated as Naval Aviators. They would serve as instructors for 18 months and then join a fleet squadron.

Early on in the syllabus of about 100 hours, we really got into serious instruments and night flying, much of which was accomplished on extended cross-country flights. Danny was my primary instructor and did two things for me: First is that because of his tutelage and lessons back in the Texas skies, I'm probably alive today. I was a good pilot and even better on instruments, much of which I owe to Danny's quietly professional techniques. Flying off carriers and knowing how to fight your airplane, demands top-notch instrument instincts, so it was kind of a 1+1=3, synergistic scenario.

Danny also took me to Memphis on a few occasions and each time the bonds between Carolyn and me got tighter. I was dividing my time more and more between study and writing letters. One of these training flights was to Norfolk via Memphis.

After a great liberty in Cotton City, off we went for a night cross country to Norfolk in beautifully clear weather. I did all the obligatory evolutions, and, about half-way into the approach to Navy Norfolk at about 10,000 feet and coming down, Danny shook the stick and said, "I've got it." I was busy in the back seat cleaning up all the approach plates and charts, popping the hood and turning my brain to the flight-idle position, in that order. I mean totally relaxed! We smoked into the break that night at an easy 350 knots, broke downwind, down came the gear and flaps and Danny called "abeam with gear down and locked."

The tower radioed, "Not in sight but continue." Danny calls the 90-degree

Author with future roommate.

One of my great instructor pilots and classmate ... Danny Michaels.

position. The tower says, "...still not in sight." "Clank, clank," up comes the gear, flaps slide up, full power and off we went to Navy Norfolk, not Norfolk International Airport!

Unbeknownst to either Danny or me, my Mom and Dad had been in the Navy tower during our brief foray to the wrong airport. My Mom simply could not understand why we weren't in sight and was worried silly. My Dad knew exactly what had happened and just grinned when he met Danny. Trouble was that my Dad was a full captain at the time, the Chief of Staff for the entire Naval Air on the east coast, and old Danny was really embarrassed.

Back in Beeville, we were deep into tactics and learning to use the airplane as a weapons system. We shot hundreds of 20MM rounds at towed banners, dropped bombs and fired rockets at the Texas countryside, practiced carrier landings on the field and were close to aviator's heaven, because the flying was absolutely spectacular. But, the lure of the fleet was beckoning; how we wanted to get out to the fleet and the carriers!

Jim Baker, John Dotson and I were a flight, so we flew most of our training missions together. Jim drove an old beat-up Volkswagen, didn't drink, wasn't in love, was in perfect (read perfect) physical condition and was one of those 5% who are naturally-gifted aviators. John Dotson, on the other hand, was spring-loaded-to-the-get-in-trouble position, good looking, easy going, instant party and a likeable young officer. In the air, on the deck or anytime or anywhere, we had fun.

Baker, Dotson & Booth.

One time we flew up to Memphis with five jets, as the weather was bad in south Texas. Our lead, John Thaubald, was a likeable, affable and excellent instructor pilot who didn't get excited at the drop of a hat. Once, at the Naval Air Station at Memphis, we refueled, briefed and went up in the night skies for a ground-controlled-intercept flight under the direction of a local Air Force radar site. The weather was good, but there was a high solid layer of clouds from 10,000 to 15,000 feet. After completing the flight, John briefed that we would form up our flight of four with Booth in the lead and return to base for landing practice.

It is a given that 98% of the credit for the Blue Angels' precision formation flying, not surprisingly, goes to the leader, for if he is smooth and reasonably predictable, the flight will look good and the wingmen's job will be easy. The reason our returning flight was so incredibly ragged, was because Booth was rough as a cob. We finally got the field in sight and came into the break at a 40-degree angle in an echelon left vice right, a real basic no-no in aviation. John, from his perch overhead, calmly suggested I reenter the pattern, not turn into the echelon (another big no-no) and smoked down to monitor the progress from the end of the runway in his jet. This time we were perfect and right down the center of the runway . . . only it was the wrong runway. John, sensing some premonition of impending disaster, and an inflection in his voice slightly more strident than before told us to "climb to 3,000 feet, orbit the field and don't come down 'till I tell you to!" Sitting in his still-turning machine at the end of the runway, he then vectored each of his chicks into the break and final landings. Our flight thought all this was hilarious, except John didn't and because John didn't, I didn't.

A postscript to this small saga was landing at Barksdale AFB in Louisiana for fuel after an exciting low-level "recee" flight with our five jets only to be surrounded by Air Force brass and tommy-gun-wielding guards. Seems we had landed at a brand new Strategic Air Command base, the home of fully loaded (with big bombs) B-52s. We didn't get further away from our Cougars than the nearest head!

For Baker, Booth and Dotson, the multiple challenges and good times of the Naval Air Training Command ended with a small ceremony in the office of the command's head guy, Rear Admiral "Jumping Joe" Clifton. It was a real honor, for "Jumping Joe" had a great reputation in naval aviation. The euphoria of it all was short lived as Booth and Dotson were enroute to Memphis at top speed for my impending marriage to the young lady named Carolyn in but 48 hours. Here were the two greatest events in my life, and they were packed into less than two days!

March, 1959 ... new wings from RADM Jump'n Joe Clifton and LT (jg) and Mrs. Booth.

EPILOGUE

• **John Dotson** became a helo pilot, chased Soviet subs, later became a successful Houston attorney and global businessman and still retains his love of Naval Aviation and the memories of those sixteen months as a student naval aviator.

• **Jim Baker**, the most talented of our group, was screwed by the system, got out of the Navy, became a medical doctor, did a stint in the Army, rejoined the Navy as a full-fledged test pilot, flew engineering test as a civilian, returned to the Navy at age 55 as a senior flight surgeon and was last heard from, in the front lines of Desert Storm as the head doctor for all Marine aviation in the gulf.

• **Pat Henry** went on to become the top test pilot for the McDonnell Douglas Corporation and was the chief test pilot for the F-15.

• **Manny Vierra** still lives in Pensacola, we have lunch occasionally, and he denies that he allowed me to solo at that outlying field just because he wanted a smoke.

• **John Thaubald** ended up as a highly-regarded wing commander in the Naval Air Training Command, still teaching the new guys to fly.

• **Danny Michaels** became a Phantom squadron CO and the commanding officer of a major Naval Air Station and to this day, he and his wife are best friends.

• **Bill Miller** was killed as the lead civilian test pilot for the swing-wing F-14 when, for reasons unknown, he flew into the water near Patuxent River, Maryland on a routine test flight.

• **Admiral Clifton** died from cancer after retiring, but his office in Corpus Christi where he pinned my wings on, was to take on a special significance to me 25-years later.

• **Mae Behringer** lives near San Jose, has her own airplane and still flies regularly. A recent flight with her 41-years after our initial forays into the skies at the age of sixteen near Atlantic City was a pleasurable deja vu in capital letters!

• **Beeville, Texas** still quietly pumps oil, maintains its population of 14,200, but its jewel of a Naval Air Station has been decommissioned, an economic victim of a Cold War no more.

Gold Wings

- The **Naval Air Training Command** still pumps out 2,000 aviators per year — the best Navy, Marine Corps and Coast Guard aviators in the world!

- Forty-five years later **Carolyn** is still wife #1 and the Tennessee farm has hardly changed. The moonshine was unbelievably bad!

NAVAL AVIATOR CERTIFICATION
CNATRA-1210/1 (REV. 7-57) PAT
DEPARTMENT OF THE NAVY

NAME OF AVIATOR		
PETER BLAKE BOOTH		
DATE OF BIRTH	APPOINTMENT DATE	NAVAL AVIATOR NO.
20 JUN 1934	9 MAR 1959	V-15011

THIS IS TO CERTIFY that the person whose name appears above, having fulfilled the conditions prescribed by the United States Navy, was appointed a NAVAL AVIATOR on the date indicated.

CHIEF OF NAVAL AIR TRAINING
Navy—PPO CNATRA, Pensacola

Hoover Dam & 1956 Chevy - Headed west with new bride.

DEMONS AND EXECUTIONERS

The McDonnell F3H-2 Demon was a giant, single-seat, single-engine, carrier-based all-weather fighter circa mid-'50s to mid-'60s. Though it provided the fleet with a modicum of protection at the height of the Cold War, its capability was overshadowed by a reputation tarnished with problems, a saga embellished somewhat over the ensuing years. This is a two-year microcosm of a few folks who flew the Demon and survived its checkered legacy.

At a late-Friday all-pilot's meeting at the Miramar Naval Air Station near San Diego in 1959, four of us newly-designated Naval Aviators stood up and volunteered to fly the Demon in the squadron across the hangar. All fifty or so fellow-attack pilots echoed in a crescendo of laughter, for the Demon, despite its size, its great afterburner, its awesome noise and all-weather fighter mission, was known as an accident-prone dog. But, it got us in the air and in that first month, I flew 54 hours compared to the two or three I might have gotten in my previous training squadron.

My new bride and I arrived in San Diego having leisurely driven the 2,000-or-so miles from Memphis in our pristine, blue-and-white 1956 Chevrolet convertible. Each day and night on that voyage was a delight as we got to know one another and relished the unknowns of our future lives together. Our tiny apartment was a palace. On my first day on the job to becoming a fleet aviator, Carolyn offered me a "good luck," to which I responded with a smiling hug and reminder that in Naval Aviation, there was no luck, just skill and training.

New Memphis bride at San Diego and Yuma.

My new fleet fighter airplane almost killed me several times, partially due to my own occasional meandering pilotage and sometimes the airplane itself. Its mission was to fly at night in all-weather conditions and protect the fleet from gremlins, evils and attacking Soviet bombers. This latter criterion was compromised somewhat, because its big J-71engine had a tendency to quit in rainy weather. It also used prodigious amounts of fuel and never went very far, very long or very fast. The Demon could be coaxed supersonic in a shallow dive, if it wasn't too heavy, too hot outside and had had a recent wash job.

The Demon's main battery were its air-to-air missiles and a radar that when well-tuned and operated, could see a big Soviet bomber at about 25 miles. Two of its four 20MM cannons and the in-flight refueling probe in our squadron were removed to allow a small increase in the jets' maximum landing weight which only allowed three or four passes at the deck at night.

Not atypical of this era, I was also one of those guys who most of his life had lived, breathed and eaten Naval Aviation, an obsession at least partially influenced by my Naval Aviator Dad. It was my secret ambition to be in a night, all-weather Navy fighter squadron flying off aircraft carriers, the ultimate in the world of aviation. I had finally arrived Wow!

My first cruise on the carrier Hancock to the western Pacific started one week after our number-one daughter was born in San Diego and ended 9.5-peacetime months later. Preparing for this deployment, our squadron of twelve brand-new F3H-2 Demons had lots of excitement and a bunch of accidents.

Laura at five-days old with new Mom ... left the next day and saw both 9.5-months later.

Demons and Executioners

Our first accident was by my good friend Tony Miller, a laconic, confident and good-looking junior pilot, who while flying into Miramar in low cloud one night, lost his airplane (#409) somehow, and thanks to our brand-new Martin Baker zero-zero ejection seats, just barely managed to shell out moments before the airplane crashed into a protruding San Diego mountain. The local TV news was on the scene in a heartbeat with a close-up view of #409, with my name on the side. My bride, knowing I was flying at the time, thought I had bought it. I was of course, OK and landed a few minutes later thinking all the while that accidents, lost airplanes, ejections and close-ups on the TV news were all a part of the world of fleet carrier aviation.

Our routine ashore was mostly involved with flying and small squadron administrative-type jobs, one of which was as defense counsel in the event we had a Special Court Martial. Tony was my designated assistant. Well, we had one on a young sailor whom everyone — the CO included — knew to be guilty. As the appointed defense counsel, my total knowledge of the Uniform Code of Military Justice was derived from an obligatory correspondence course. The only advice that came my way, were spurious notes or comments on the sly with the common theme of "hang the guilty illegitimous."

Perry Mason was big then, so Tony and I decided we would put forth a quality and fiduciary effort and try to defend him like we were supposed to and not give it lip service, which I think we were kind of expected to do. After all, the man was guilty — right? It so happened, however, that our next-door neighbor in our tiny apartment overlooking the San Diego airport was a real Navy lawyer. To make a long story short, he taught us how to defend our man complete with peremptory challenges, basic rules of evidence (hearsay) and a few other basic tricks of the legal trade.

On the appointed day, in true TV fashion, the president of the court (a squadron lieutenant commander, my boss) and his four cohorts filed in replete with blue service (dress up) uniforms. We pled not guilty, partially because that was in our man's best interests and also because the more we got into the case, the more we felt he was not guilty of the charge. We promptly got rid of one lieutenant on a peremptory challenge, another for cause (he had espoused a "hang the guilty . . ." once too often), and forced the president into a red-faced, hyper-torqued-off, "let's-get-this-over-fast," rage. Bottom line — you guessed it — Not guilty!

This was however, one of my first lessons in winning the battle, but coming close to losing the war, for my Skipper would not speak to Tony or me for several weeks. I also learned what "persona non grata" meant.

Tony survived another accident coming in to land on Hancock in the daytime. When the engine quit in the landing pattern off Hawaii, he ditched, and ended up crawling out through the nose (yes, the nose!) and barely made it.

I'm sad to say though, that Tony didn't make it the third time around. After leaving the squadron, Tony joined the reserves up in Alameda country and in low-fog conditions, failed to gain altitude in his T-33 jet trainer and crashed into the Oakland Bay bridge.

In spite of our close calls, we had a lot of fun. Friday afternoon happy hours were de rigeur and we were, in toto, as totally obnoxious as you can get. Our wives and brides always joined us at about 1800, most of whom rested their hands on very large midsections and listened to the bravado with knowing small talk. We would regale ourselves with song (". . . there are no fighter pilots down in hell," ". . . the B-36 carries one teeny-weeny bomb," in a high voice), and so on. I suppose that if we acted like most reasonably mature folks of our age and "stature," we would have been looked upon as kind of weird.

Driving home from Miramar one New Years' night with my formal mess dress (Naval Aviator wings, one medal and name tag) in our Chevy convertible, Carolyn and I were stopped by a state trooper who complimented me on my driving (for I was driving very carefully) and said, " Mr. Booth, your . . ."

Before he could get the rest of it out, I blurted out, "How did you know my name?" Talk about being spring-loaded-to-the-stupid position! I am today forever grateful to a California State Trooper who liked the Navy and who only wanted me to know I had a tail light out.

Roster board with squadron logo upon departure for Western Pacific; sadly, many changes took place in just ten months.

Demons and Executioners

Sam Gibbons was one of our pilots. Sam also had a girl friend in San Francisco and was forever boondoggling a flying machine to go see her on Friday afternoons. During this period, we had been flying our Demons from the beach for a couple of weeks and routinely took off in afterburner (AB) mainly because it impressed the local attack pilots who had no such noisemaker. The real reason for AB of course, was that the old Demon would hardly make it airborne on a 12,000-foot, sea-level runway in the summer without it. In AB though, it acted like a real airplane and, except for the fact it could only stay airborne for about fifteen minutes in this mode, would have been the greatest flying machine in the world.

Anyway, Sam borrowed the station T-33 (two-seat, single-engine jet, very poor take-off performance) to go see girl friend, started down the runway, lifted off smartly (wrong, the old T-bird didn't do anything smartly), sucked up the gear (wrong again) and promptly settled back on to the runway in a shower of sparks, dust and a scratched belly. Sam stepped out (didn't need a ladder) and strode purposefully back to base ops and asked if he could have another airplane! I am pleased to report that Sam didn't see his girl friend for a long while, did not leave the BOQ for several weeks and stood squadron duty officer for the next month.

Bob Gale was my best friend. We had gone through flight training together, had volunteered to fly the Demon at the same time and had new brides who were also best friends. Bob was too, a phenomenally smart gent (chemical engineering from Cornell) and a naturally-gifted aviator. Like most aviators, we were intensely competitive in our flying.

One day off San Francisco, we were aboard Hancock and a test hop for an airplane out of periodic heavy maintenance came up. These were fun and challenging flights, always flown in the day and eagerly sought after. Bob and I argued over who should fly it and, because it was the new #409 and had my name on it, I thought I should do the honors. A coin toss decreed that Bob would go.

Halfway down the port catapult, something happened to the engine and he lost most of his thrust. Because the Demon had a good reputation as a ditcher, I felt he could ride it in and would have done the same in his situation. But, the moment 409 hit the water, Bob's seat ejected and, although his chute streamed, it never fully deployed. (The accident board surmised that Bob did intend to ditch, but that upon impact, the nose gear slammed back into the cable for the secondary ejection handle under his seat

Bob Gale in #409 just after catapult shot and moments before fatal impact. Note abnormal afterburner flame pattern.

Impact.

and involuntarily ejected him). I escorted Bob back to Chicago, riding sadly in the cockpit of the civilian cargo airplane. Though I had lost a number of really good friends in the cause of Naval Aviation, this one really hit home and I walked with an imperceptibly reduced swagger.

Five days before our squadron deployed for the western Pacific on board the carrier Hancock in 1960, our daughter Laura was born. Nine-and-one-half peacetime months later I returned, the first of many such extended separations over the next few decades. Carolyn spent most of the time at home on the farm in Tennessee with her parents and her new little one with no phone calls and only sporadic mail.

Our deployed station on Hancock was normally far out in the ocean west of the Phillipines so as to be in range for our big bombers (the A3) and its diminutive side kick (the A4) should the nuclear button be pushed. The most notable quality of this "nowhere" station were the continual high seas, which on the Hancock, translated into a pitching deck. This, plus the fact that the "Hanna Maru" was a small carrier compared to her newer namesakes, Forrestal and Saratoga, made for some dicey and challenging night work.

The Demon on a night catapult shot barely made it into the air, so we always went off in full afterburner, particularly when it was hot. Well, one day we got a new ship's captain who would have none of this afterburner business, because it "blinded his OODs" (never mind the nearest ship other than our own destroyers was a hundred-miles away). So — you guessed it — we took off in basic engine, and it was a seat-of-the-pants adventure each time and an exercise in milking the angle of attack for all the lift that big wing could generate!

PR drawing of Demon in afterburner with ship below. We all got these just outside the gate at Atsugi in Japan

Demon just before launch. Note two Sparrow missiles and cocked nose wheel.

Demons and Executioners

Sometimes just getting to the catapult was hairy. When we manned up, the flight deck was absolutely black (we wore red night goggles for half-an-hour prior to manning up) — not even red lights. The only lights were the yellowish wands of your taxi director. Turning into the wind, the ship would roll and heel to the point where once in awhile it took a sustained 90% power to get moving uphill (seven-degrees nose up on the attitude gyro). It was not unusual to have a good solid case of the leans (vertigo) before ever getting on the catapult.

Our air wing had a bunch of accidents while deployed, myself included. We lost one F-11 fighter and pilot when he pulled off a strafing run astern of the ship, did an aileron roll with the G still on the jet and hit the water inverted and at high speed, all in two blinks of an eye. One of our propeller-powered ADs flew into the water at night, our CO had to eject due to low fuel and a big A3 attack bomber hit the ramp and lost all three crew members. (I happened to be on the LSO ramp that night and one of the LSOs almost lost his leg from flying debris). I guess we all felt that this was Naval Aviation and if you couldn't take the heat, go do something else. Fear had nibbled at me, but in all my flying, I was on top, liked what I was doing, was kind of cocky and in control.

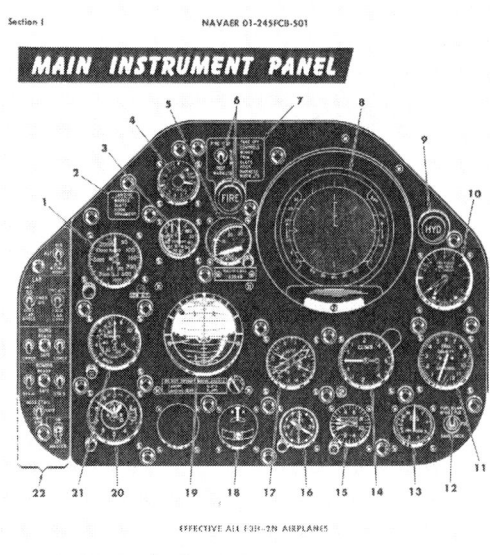

This came to a screeching halt one dark and blustery South China Sea night some 300 miles from the Phillipines, the Hancock rolling and pitching like an old barge. In some thirty night landings, I had never failed to trap or even waved off. This night though, my Demon and I hit the unyielding deck of the Hanna-Maru, missed the wires and with eyes-wide, jammed the throttle to the fire wall, came in with the speed brakes, jerked the nose up and boltered into the blackest nothing imaginable.

For the first time in my short flying experience, I was absolutely and unequivocally petrified; knees shook, hands gripped the stick and throttle with gusto, eyeballs tried not to look at the fuel gauge and the heartbeat was maxed-out. Whereas a few minutes prior I had fancied myself king of the mountain, now I would have been happy to get to the top of an anthill. I did make it, but with a shattering hit to my pride, ego and a bent nose strut.

True Faith and Allegiance

The accident was, I suppose, mild compared to the norm of the deployment (and pre-deployment). On my fourth or fifth pass with not much gas and no in-flight refueling, I did a "DFD," which in LSO parlance is "dive for deck" and is a 100% "no-no" in the business of carrier aviation. In so doing, I bent an incredibly strong and almost indestructible Demon nose strut and had to be towed out of the landing area.

This incident took its toll, for I was all of a sudden, somewhat demotivated, mainly, I figured, because of a fear of failure. I was however, given the opportunity to practice field carrier landings ashore and get back to basics, for which I am grateful and thankful to some senior folks in our squadron. It gave me the chance to get my bearings and confidence back. Never again was I to approach the very complex business of flying in a macho, sometimes casual, nothing-can-happen-to-me attitude.

My stateroom on the Hancock was just below the wardroom, not air conditioned and had curtains vice doors. I had two roommates, Ted Oliverio and Hugo McCauley. Ted was a Naval Academy company and classmate and Hugo and I had gone through flight training together. Both wore the wings of a Naval Aviator, but had been permanently grounded to a non-flying status and spent the long deployment tending to minor ground duties with no flying.

PR shot before come-uppance. Bob Constans to left.

I came close to buying the farm again on this cruise, and once again it was my doing. Coming in to land on a totally-dark and no-horizon night, at 600-feet and six-miles astern of the carrier, the ship told me to change radio frequencies to a manual setting. Because the radio was down, aft and to the right, and the dials quite small, it took some dexterity to do this simple task. I fiddled for what seemed like a few seconds and then noticed the reflection of my lights on the water! I was deadly low and barely pulled up in time. A sad sequel to this tale is the loss of a good friend of mine two-weeks later in an F8 Crusader, Terry Emory, six-miles astern of the Ranger at night. I wonder?

"Tiny" Granning was at least 220 pounds; a bear of a man with a great flying reputation. He took over our squadron when our CO had to eject and hurt his back with our canon-shell activated ejection seats. Tiny was a kick the tire, light the fire, brief on guard type aviator of the old school. His first hop with the squadron was a fly off to Kadena AFB on Okinawa with four Demons. Once airborne, our leader kicked his tail back and forth indicating that we were to get in a tail-chase position. At 15,000 feet, 350 knots and about three Gs,

Demons and Executioners

up we went for a loop in Demon basic engine and full of fuel. Well, lead barely made it over the top, two fluttered over, three ended up in a zero-G recovery and four (me), exercised the "what-do-you-do-at-90-degrees-nose-up-and-no-airspeed option."

Normally, prudent radio discipline and only necessary talk is the norm, but our new skipper was unglued and couldn't understand why "you bunch of turkeys were unable to do a simple loop" and ended up with the admonishment to, "Let's look good at Kadena."

Getting a grip, we smoked into the break at Kadena AFB on Okinawa at 400 knots and nicely tucked in. We'd show these Air Force types a lesson or two in crisp carrier naval aviation airmanship. Well, Tiny slowed his Demon way down on final, touched down 50-feet past the threshold, held the nose way up and #2 to his right and aft did the same. #3 and #4 though, were close behind (let's look good) and fighting turbulence, should have waved off (need to look good), didn't, elected to land and blew both main mounts on both jets as we gallantly attempted to miss hitting one and two dead in front of us. Because the coefficient of friction goes way up with flat tires, we did indeed manage to stop. However, it took half the base to get us clear of the runway. There were more Air Force colonels out there than pilots in our squadron. What a disaster! Old Tiny, of course, smiled later on, but I can promise, he wasn't smiling that day.

Tiny was great on liberty too, but as big as he was, he simply could not hold down more than a couple of drinks before crashing. In Yokusaka, Japan one Saturday night, the "Executioners" had a red shirt party (we had red shirts for special occasions), and sure enough, Tiny went down hard. Three of us junior officers were detailed to take him back to the Hancock moored near-by. We got a cab, poured Tiny in, and, under the watchful eyes of a rather bored ship's Officer of the Deck (non-aviator), tried to wake him up. No joy. So, we took him to a local hotel (BOQ full), kept his ring and wallet and told mama-san we'd pick him up in the morning. You guessed it! Tiny woke up early, didn't have his wallet, had lost his ring, couldn't remember the night before and was totally frantic. Mama-san just smiled. Our only real tactical mistake in retrospect, was in taking our sweet time to pick him up the next morning.

After one particularly rough three-week at sea period out in the South China Sea, it was decided to have a "red shirt" party which is a euphemistic way of "lets have a gentlemanly social." On very rare occasions, we would overdo it and this was one of those nights at the Cubi Point O'Club. It turned out the local supply folks were having a rather sedate affair in honor of a rather senior visiting pork chop (supply officer) in the club's main ball room. One of our guys in his tell-tale red shirt and short pants, wandered into the party. The senior officer, seeing the "not-allowed-here" short pants, told Mr. Red Shirt to "take off those pants, Mister" which our intrepid Demon driver most obediently did — on the spot. That was the fastest two weeks in hack any of us had seen, notwithstanding the fact we were at sea the entire time.

Back to my friend Tony. Tony was an adventuresome junior officer who loved his liberty. One morning, as the entire Hancock crew was on the flight deck at quarters preparing to get underway from Cubi Point in the

True Faith and Allegiance

Phillipines, here came Tony bounding across the vast tarmac — late! By this time, the gangway was up and lines cast off. Two things happened: First, some enterprising soul lowered the starboard aft elevator to the hanger deck level and secondly, Tony commandeered a bus and had it drive up under the over-hanging aircraft elevator. All lines were now in, the tugs were pulling the ship off, the entire ship was cheering and hollering and Tony climbed aboard over the elevator safety-net. No one ever bothered to ask why he was late and not surprisingly, he never went in hack. It's the classiest entree to an aircraft carrier we'd ever seen and Tony got a lot of attaboys from the whole ship, his flamboyant reputation garnished with one more hash mark.

Carrier landings were a central focus of life on Hancock and with the "Executioners" of VF-114. And, notwithstanding the Navy's substantial helo and land-based maritime air contingents, carrier aviation had always been the epitome of any type of aviation, particularly night carrier flight operations.

U.S.S. Hancock in daylight and calm seas ... note slightly high meatball in both port and starboard mirrors and big A3 bombers just abaft the island.

Normally, a key element in the training of a Naval Aviator before he joins the fleet, are day carrier qualifications in two types of aircraft. In my case, the training aircraft carrier was in overhaul, so a whole host of new aviators got their wings without ever even seeing a carrier. As a result, my first catapult shot and arrested landing were in the Demon on Hancock. I can remember well my first attempts, because that's what they were — attempts.

Demons and Executioners

The first time I rolled into the groove far behind the ship, I absolutely could not believe it, and only made it halfway down the glide slope before waving off. The next time, I got to "in close" before having second doubts. When my hook finally grabbed a wire at 135 knots on the comparatively small deck, it was the greatest feeling I've ever had. In fact, I felt ten-feet tall — I had arrived and was I ever hooked!

Catapulting to me was equal to any landing and I always marveled at the tremendous forces that took that big machine with 10,000 parts and hurled it airborne in about 170 feet. Once you salute the catapult officer or turn your external lights on at night, you are going flying — there's no changing your mind. The thrill, the excitement, the slight unknown, the power and the cleanness of a catapult shot is something that never gets old.

But nights are a different story. Once on the catapult and at full power, the signal for your willingness and readiness to go aviate is to turn on your external lights (dim and steady, please). Your head is firmly back against the headrest, your left arm has an immovable hydraulic lock on the throttle, your right is gripping the stick, the eyeballs peer ahead into an absolute black nothingness and your brain is asking the question of why I am doing this at 0300 on a cold and overcast night, 7,000 miles from my new bride.

Once airborne though, the answer comes, for the soft lights of your instruments tell a familiar story: Attitude, angle of attack, rate of climb, airspeed, engine instruments (particularly in the Demon) and so on. And you mutter to yourself how you love it all!

Demon just before trap, well short of #1 wire.

True Faith and Allegiance

We had a covey of really good LSOs (landing signal officers). Many thought the new angled deck of the carriers and the equally innovative mirror landing system, would prove the demise of the LSOs, as the British Navy had proved some years prior. In the late '50s though, the airplanes were really ahead of the carriers and the accident rate was sky high. Were it not for guys like Fred Hoerner (our squadron's LSO) and Skip Furlong (the F-11s'), we would most likely had lost more airplanes and pilots.

I mention Fred and Skip, because they were in that 5% of all Naval Aviators one could characterize as gifted. Both were exceptionally cool under pressure and superb LSOs. One time, in solid cloud, Skip lost his gyro horizon, went partial panel and, just like driving to the grocery store for milk, flew his "Tiger jet" down to a good landing in low overcast.

We shared a ready room with Skip's squadron, which flew only in the daytime. Very crowded, no privacy, pungent from the multitude of sweaty flight suits and hardhats and the site of the every-evening movie. The trusty Demons though, continued into the wee hours, we "Executioners" relegated to movie calls on occasional non-flying nights.

The Demon didn't exactly leap into the air, ever. When we did use AB, it flew off quite nicely. The problem was that the Demon's big J-71 Allison engine ran OK so long as you didn't disturb it, like deselecting afterburner. So after take off in AB, the pilots scan shifted to engine nozzle, temps and RPMs whenever changing the status quo. What a deal.

Hugo McCauley lines up too far left and ends up in port catwalk.

As you may have deduced, the Demon's engine was its nemesis. The airplane was really quite advanced and functional. Mute testimony to its early underpowered engine problems, were the many static displays and maintenance trainers using the pre-fleet models. The J-71 was supposed to solve this, but never did. The Demon, to its credit, would have been a great all-weather airplane with a little more reliable and powerful engine. Back in those heady days of fighter development, however, there was always something on the come. The come in this case, was the Phantom, also a McDonnell product and much like the Demon in many design respects.

When Demon drivers converge three-and-four decades later, the sea stories flow, the lies grow and the feats of dare have already expanded beyond all logic. But to those of us that flew her and survived, there rest special memories of a gallant and spirited old lady.

Tiny Granning top center, Fred Horner top right, John Bull third from left in front, Sam Gibbons second from left top: Big F3H Demon jet top, left, center and right.

EPILOGUE I

• The trusty **Demon** was phased out in the mid-sixties in favor of the Phantom.

• **Tiny Granning** (now deceased) went on to command an air wing and ship and retired to Pensacola where he instructed in small planes and still thought us turkeys should have stayed with him in the loop.

• **Fred Hoerner** went to the Navy's test pilot school, made three consecutive long combat cruises on the Oriskany during Vietnam, left the Navy, but continued to work on aircraft cockpit instrumentation at the giant Navy test center at Patuxent River.

• **Tony Miller** is no longer with us, but his cheerfulness and smile live on in my memory.

• **Skip Furlong** commanded an aircraft carrier, made flag officer and has been instrumental in the development of the National Museum of Naval Aviation in Pensacola after retirement from active duty.

• **Bob Gale's** widow Anne, would come to various changes of command in which I was involved over the years, and treasures those few months with Bob in San Diego.

- The **Hancock** served her country well in one Cold War and three hot ones until, at the age of 32 in the mid-'70s, was cut up for scrap.

- The long separation of this cruise became the first of many, **Carolyn** symbolic of those who kept the home fires burning.

- To a **forgotten multitude** of flyers and fixers, the Demon was loved, defiled, stroked, kicked and bid good riddance, all rolled into one. A beautiful restoration was accomplished in Pensacola in 2001 and today it stands tall in the National Museum of Naval Aviation and is the museum's only displayed airplane that has its tailhook down and ready to trap!

EPILOGUE II

The foregoing chapter was put to paper in the early nineties, the sources for my meandering thoughts coming strictly from a few notes, a creaky memory and a few yellowing photos. Ten years later, I was cleaning out some old cruise boxes long in storage and ran across a package of some one-hundred letters I had written to my new bride and brand-new daughter who spent the 9.5 months of this carrier deployment in San Diego, with her folks in Tennessee, with my folks in Washington and a short two weeks in Chicago visiting Ann Gale, Bob's widow. Much to my surprise, the letters cast a totally different hue to the somewhat light and anecdotal tales of "Demons and Executioners." Here are a few unedited excerpts all of which take place aboard or close to the U.S.S *Hancock* (CVA 19):

24 July, 1960, off Hawaii: "*While ashore at Barbers, I ran off the taxiway along with a couple of others. No damage except my pride. The next hop my engine sucked up something it should not have and it needs an engine change. Back at the ship, I had a night hop and didn't do too well. The skipper was not happy.*"

2 August, 1960, South China Sea: "*Had a good talk with the skipper today. He hasn't been doing too well in his flying of late. In fact, the other night, he hit the ramp with his hook and it was the second time. I should talk though — I came in so hard the other night that I blew two tires which is hard to do in a Demon.*"

2 September, 1960, South China Sea: "*My division is really coming along fine. The guys have loads of spirit and are working very hard and doing a wonderful job. But the problems they have! Two were late returning from* *liberty, one got into a fight ashore, my chief broke a finger, one has to have an operation on his leg and one 18-year old with a 16-year-old wife found out he owes $200 because she borrowed a friend's car, had an accident and drove away."*

1 October, 1960, in port Sasesbo, Japan: "This is really a heck of a way to have a marriage. I've been doing a lot of thinking about the Navy and all. You and Laurie will always be first in my life. I love my little family a great deal."

15 October, 1960, in port Hong Kong: "Today has been most enjoyable marred only by the fact that liberty has been curtailed due to a large destroyer tender having just pulled in. It make no difference that Hancock has been operating 20 hours a day for twelve days and the tender has made an arduous high-speed run direct from alongside the pier in Yokusaka."

17 October, 1960, South China Sea: "Didn't get to write last night because I was night flying off this bouncing (as usual) ship in lousy weather. It took me about three hours to get back to normal; it was so dark that it seemed like an inkwell. I was kind of glad to get back aboard."

22 October, 1960, South China Sea: "I have some very sad news for you — Bob Constans is no longer with us. His accident was exactly the same as Bobs'. As if that isn't enough, the skipper had to eject last night due to many reasons, but I didn't help matters because I bent the nose gear on my plane and fouled the deck for a few minutes."

24 October, 1960, in port Subic Bay: "The morale of the pilots in the squadron is rock-bottom low. A lot of little things have been brought to a head by our two major accidents. A few of the pilots have not been doing too well. I'm in that category because of my night landings of late. Anyway, we really got our tails chewed out by the higher-ups and told to square away or else."

7 November, 1960, South China Sea: "I didn't write last night as I had some bad luck. Ever since the skipper's accident I've had even more problems at night. Well last night I pranged one in way too hard and really messed up the nose gear. I'm told it was pretty hairy. I'm OK except my pride."

11 November, 1960, South China Sea: "My little mishap will cost the taxpayers $17,000. Tell that to your Dad and he'll have a fit. I'm glad it wasn't any more."

26 November, 1960, in port Subic Bay: "Life on this cruise seems to be a bowl of worms. Perhaps it has to do with what has happened the past few weeks. I feel like a second-rate pilot."

2 December, 1960, South China Sea: "*Launched with six others and was no sooner airborne in the clag than my fire warning light started to blink brightly. I called for Sven to check me over, but in the few minutes it took for him to join up, I must admit I was concerned as the sea was very rough and windy. Landed back aboard with no problems and it turned out to be false.*"

17 December, 1960, ashore at Atsugi, Japan: "*Some bad news with a happy ending: John Bull had to eject and is OK. Don't know any details.*"

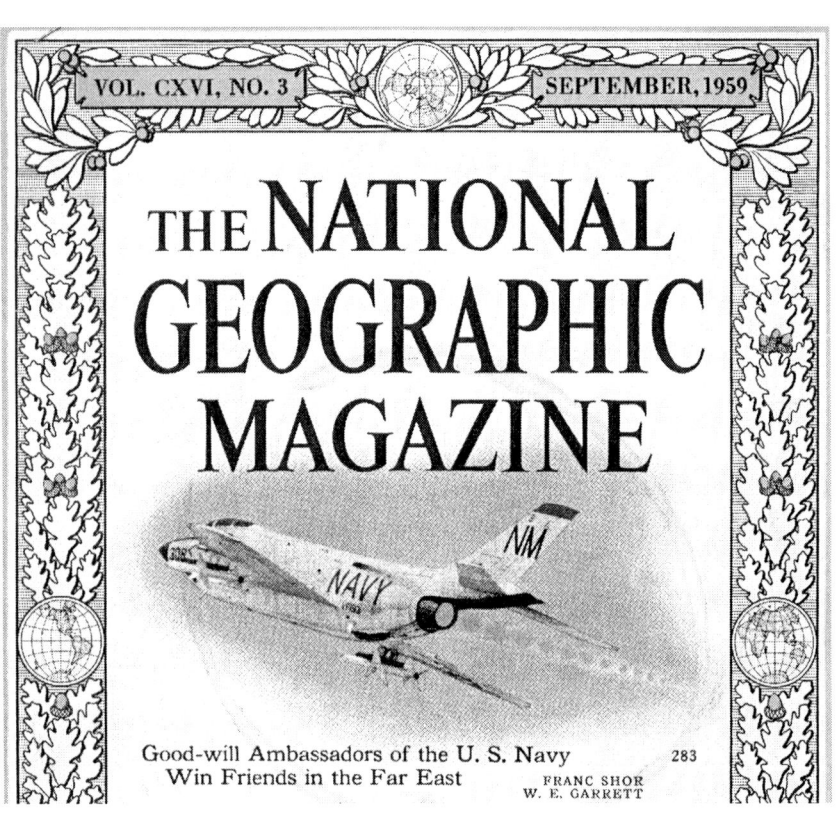

AARDVARKS AND PHANTOMS

The Phantom joins the fleet, mach two, the U.S.S. Kitty Hawk, Soviet Badgers, Hap Chandler and single-engine takeoffs.

In real Walter Mitty style, there I was at 45-degrees nose up in a sparkling, brand-new Phantom with Lieutenant Pete Conrad in the back seat trying to get me to go higher and faster. This, my 5th flight in the twin-jet Phantom, was a zoom climb to about 70,000 feet. Pete, who was perhaps the most avid aviator I've known, was having a great time in the "no controls" back seat of our F4B jet. Had it not been for Pete, I probably wouldn't have looked outside. It was indeed a gorgeous vista.

The really hard part of the whole mission however, was getting into the full-pressure suit. We needed these because if you lost cockpit pressurization above about 50,000 feet, you turned into instant mashed potatoes. Besides costing the tax payers far more than ten years of my lieutenant's salary, they were the epitome of user unfriendliness. We spent more time getting indoctrinated into the pressure suit than we did in the airplane, or so it seemed. Once in the airplane, it was kind of neat, because your suit was air conditioned and you didn't have to wear the iron oxygen mask. (So-called because it generally fit like a pair of football shoulder pads on a five-foot-two-inch ballerina and in over 5,000-wearer hours, never remotely fitted the contours of my face).

Once airborne in our incredibly light and fast jets, we simply headed west over the Pacific, climbed to 38,000 feet, accelerated to 1.6 mach (about 1,000 mph) and pulled the nose up 45 degrees. From then on you were a rider. The afterburners blew out at about 65,000 feet and at idle, the engines were bumping 104%, near the limit.

The whole time, Pete was like a little kid in a candy store. I'm convinced he would have flown in the Navy for nothing so long as someone fed him three squares a day. I remember when I was checking out in the F3D Drut — a very-slow, twin-jet night fighter that was used for radar training. It was a Friday afternoon, which meant an imperative called happy hour at the Miramar Naval Air Station. Pete, who was checked out in the venerable machine, came up to me and said he had heard I was looking for a check-out pilot and without further ado said "let's go." We did all the obligatory maneuvers and ended up per the check ride at 45,000 feet over Los Angeles. We were then supposed to glide at idle power all the way to San Diego some 120 miles to the south. And that we did. Pete, who had recently finished a tour as a Navy test pilot at Patuxent River, filled me in with a steady stream of "Hey, did you know . . .?" What a pleasure to fly with. It was worth a missed happy hour!

In that summer of 1961, our squadron of F3H Demons changed planes, insignia and call signs, but kept our bright-orange-color motif. Everything was orange — flight suits, hardhats, tails of airplanes and even the ready room trash cans. Here we were, the Navy's first Phantom squadron on the West coast, and our color was a garish and bright orange!

We also changed our logo from the Executioner (a hooded executioner with black headgear and crossed swords — real class) to the Aardvarks — a long ant-eating something or other. Instead of the easily understood Executioner, we were now some unpronounceable Greek saying, the only persons who knew the meaning, being the CO and XO. That process of change is still a mystery and far be it from the power structure in those days to involve the ilk of junior officers like me in such momentous goings on.

My introduction to the Phantom had come a year before at Pt. Mugu Naval Air Station when Commander Don Engen was setting the world time-to-climb records. The scenario was really spectacular: His Phantom was poised at the end of the east/west runway facing east, in full afterburner, latched to the deck with a standard carrier catapult holdback (no brakes), only the pilot aboard and burning fuel down to about 3,800 pounds or some 600 gallons. The airplane, of course, was like a feather — probably about 28,000 pounds empty with no missile racks, missiles or extra avionics gear.

Well, when Don decided it was time to go aviate, he electrically cut the holdback and what a sight it was to us 800-hour pilots standing beside the runway. It was almost like a catapult shot, so rapidly did the jet get airborne. Even with the gear handle up at the moment of liftoff, I'm sure the 250 knot gear-down limit speed was exceeded. Booming out to 400 knots, up came the nose, fast climb to about 40,000 feet then out to 2.1 mach (twice the speed of sound) and then up he goes again, topping out in marginally-controlled flight at over 100,000 feet and both engines shut down. Then, with micro amounts of fuel left, landing was straight-in to Edwards AFB in the desert. Total time airborne — about 20 minutes!

Those were heady days in Naval Aviation. We had four large super carriers with a covey more on the way. The F8 Crusader was making its mark as a truly hot fighter. Huge A3 twin-engined bombers could fly to practically any target in the world with the big bomb. Its counterpart, the minute A4 light-attack jet, could carry the same bomb, albeit not always in a round-trip mode. The all-weather F4D Skyray and the F3H Demon were en route to the museums and county court-house lawns. And the Phantom was clearly the world's absolute ultimate in a flying machine.

To the consternation of many old-time Navy pilots, the Phantom had a two-man crew, with a pilot and radar intercept officer (RIO). Our squadron, VF-114, was stacked with really experienced pilots, half of whom had had a test pilot tour and all but four of us, second tour. The RIOs came to be known by lots of less-than-complimentary names, few of which could be put in writing. GIBs, guy in the back seat, was one of their more gentlemanly handles.

I was blessed to have paired off with Wes Barret who had served his first tour running the back end of Super Connie barrier patrols out of Hawaii. Wes, like every last one of our pilots and RIOs, loved to fly, was good at it, never got flustered and contributed a solid 50% or more of the weapons system when we were airborne.

Me, Wes Barrett and Phantom on board Kitty Hawk.

Initially, most of the pilots thought the GIBs were excess baggage except to work the radar. But it was amazing how quickly the two-man concept took hold. It wasn't long before our senior types were fighting over who would get the best RIOs. And, just as the pilots were a talented bunch, so too were our backseaters. Soon, we became a real team, notwithstanding the gibing comments of our single-seat A4 and F8 brethren about our "guys in the back seat."

Unlike subsequent models of the Phantom for our Air Force and other countries, the Navy's never had controls in the back seat. We did have eleven two-seat F4As early on which were essentially F4Bs in which a crude stick, throttle and engine instrument kit could be added as desired to the back seat.

True Faith and Allegiance

Never were there any rudders or brakes. No one ever liked the-controls-in-the-back-seat idea though, because with all the electronic gear, it was really hard to see out the front end. I think too, it had something to do with the ingrained single-seat mind set of the Navy. Since day one, with a handful of exceptions, Navy fighters had been single-seat aircraft. Eventually, of course, we got lots of dual control jet aircraft for training, but back then it really didn't make much sense to most of us to have two pilots in the same airplane.

As is the case with most Navy fighter squadrons, the Aardvarks were loaded with characters. If you were not a character or famous for something in the standard Navy fighter squadron, the system would do its best to make you one or the other.

The lead character of the Aardvarks happened to be our commanding officer, Hap Chandler, a Patuxent River type (read test pilot), good looking, debonair with his longish hair and generous smile and an avid aviator — he loved to aviate. Here he was, with twelve, shiny-new, absolutely gorgeous Phantoms and one night at Miramar when it was rainy and thundering (literally), he goes up in the station twin-engined Beechcraft (bug smasher) "to get some actual night instrument time."

Our number-two guy was just the opposite of our smooth CO. A rough, tough, mustachioed, spring-loaded-to-the-attack position, card-dealing, whiskey-drinking and a good aviator to boot, described Joe Konzen, our XO.

Our third senior was a bachelor, Lieutenant Commander T. Schenk Remson. Schenk (phonetically, Skank) would fly anything, anytime, anywhere and under absolutely any conditions, with no exceptions. In the air, Schenk was one of those 5% of Naval Aviators who were naturally gifted for flight. He was also his own man and like lots of fighter pilots in those days, didn't kowtow to "shore based staff weenies telling us what to do."

As Ops officer, Schenk was instrumental in many of our evolving tactics on how best to employ our new machines. Early on, we really focused on intercepts. In fact, we were much more of an interceptor than a fighter. On one short deployment to the Yuma desert east of San Diego, we would deck launch (always at night), run out to about 1.6 mach, launch our head-on Sparrow missile and then reattack with our stern-aspect heat-seeking Sidewinder missiles, all simulated, with one of our own airplanes as the target. We were lucky to get one intercept before we were low fuel! It was during this time that the Aardvarks got quite a bit of press because of the sonic booms in the desert. Hap loved this and announced this

Wes Barrett, me, Hy Dawkins and Sam Amons.

phenomenon to the local and San Diego papers, as, "The Sound of Freedom." We could do no wrong!

The opposite extreme was Schenk's push for low-altitude intercepts at sea. Because our radar could not look down, he figured we would look up at the target. The only problem was that Soviet tactics had them coming in to attack the carrier very low, so as to be below the ship's radar coverage. Some of us figured 400 feet to be a reasonable altitude at night. What Schenk had in mind though, was 50 feet in the daytime and a bit higher at night and he did it. Anything Schenk did, was done with a flourish.

And the characters go on — Archie Lane, another talented aviator, who one hot summer day in a fully-loaded airplane, took off from Cubi Point in the Phillipines and did three consecutive immelmens! And Dan McCormick, whose wingman I tried to be, jinking, climbing and diving through every South China Sea cloud he could find, "just to see if I could stay with him." I didn't. John Bull, Hy Dawkins, Pat Henry and I were the new guy "nuggets," fresh out of our venerable Demons.

VF-114 pilots, RIOs and ground officers aboard Kitty Hawk in full pressure suits. Top row from right: Schenck (6th); John Bull (8th); Booth (9th); Barrett (10th); Ross Terry (11th); Dick Rich (12th); Dan McCormick (13th); Archie Lane (15th); Joe Konzen (front 6th from left).

Because we had really hot new machines and the Navy had set all sorts of records in the past couple of years, we were really big on PR. Old Hap loved it! One day, President Kennedy had come to the Kitty Hawk to witness the latest and best in carrier aviation. Of course, there was to be an air power demonstration and night flying. Wes and I were to launch in afterburner (one Phantom on each of four cats), climb steeply (doubly impressive on a carrier because of the 30 knots of wind down the deck) and then shoot a night approach to an arrested landing, catapult again and land. All in the calm waters and good weather off San Diego. What a deal!

Well, we were spotted on the starboard elevator just forward of the bridge and really pumped up. It wasn't so much the president as it was an easy two night traps. Well, we could not get one generator on the line — the bus tie closed OK, but there was this bright warning light staring me in the face and reminding me that Hap had told us not to do anything "dumb." With some despondency, the tower told us to keep turning and that the spare would launch in our place.

End of story? No, for here comes the president — no life preserver, no hard hat or goggles and totally alone. He waves from the dark flight deck! Wes and I waved back and futilely yelled at him to get back inside followed immediately by a call to the ship's Air Boss to let him know that the president of all the United States was wandering about one of the most dangerous places known to man. In a heart beat, he was surrounded and ushered back inside, but not before waving to us again. What a guy!

John Bull's part of this presidential exercise was to drop 22, 500-pound bombs in a ripple mode. I don't know who thought this up because a) John had not dropped more than six practice bombs in his life and b) there was not even the slightest gleam in anyone's eyes at the time that the pride-of-the-fleet Phantom would ever be a "bomber." Anyway, John was detailed to take a clean (no fuel tank) F4B up to the factory in St. Louis from San Diego and get it wired for its 22-big bombs.

Landing at Albuquerque for fuel, John couldn't get the starboard engine started, a common problem in those days. So, exercising the "right-or-wrong, make-a-decision" philosophy of Naval Aviation and recognizing the operational importance of the impending mission, John took off at a field elevation of 5,000 feet — on one engine. As soon as he got airborne, he brought the throttle around the horn, hit the igniters and the starboard engine started right up. No big deal for a fleet Phantom fighter pilot!

Well, John came smoking into the break in St. Louis and upon being met by the senior naval aviator, a commander, downed the airplane because the "starboard engine would not start." John was really fortunate he didn't get a one-way bus ticket to the Naval Air Facility, Argentia, Newfoundland as the BOQ officer. We all thought it incredibly funny, made a lot of sense, couldn't figure out why all the hoopla and just went to show the unlimited versatility and initiative of the generic Naval Aviator.

The Phantom was perhaps the best carrier-landing airplane ever bought by the Navy. It was amazingly responsive to slight power changes and, of course, it had power like no other airplane had ever had. Its only drawback was that it couldn't come aboard the carrier with much fuel. With a 600-gallon center-line fuel tank, racks, sidewinder and sparrow missiles and a not-too-recent wash job, the jet could come aboard with about 4,000 pounds of fuel, enough for four or five passes at the deck at night. It could refuel airborne as well which was the good news. Bad news was that the tanker — a tiny A4 jet — passed fuel at a rate almost equal to what we were burning in the process. That said though, we usually had priority in the pattern, which was nice for us, but supremely aggravating to the rest of the air wing who, on some dark-night evolutions, were forced to "make way for the Phantom in the groove."

Two seconds to trap.

But one of the best things about the Phantom, was that it could not operate aboard a "small" carrier, like the Hancock. Not only was the deck bigger on the Kitty Hawk, but so were the catapults. Even in rough seas the big deck held the advantage, for, whatever the reason, it did not move up and down and sideways nearly as much as her smaller counterparts.

Having just settled into the Kitty Hawk, the Navy's newest big-deck super carrier, off went the Aardvarks to Alameda and night carrier qualifications on the carrier Midway. Three points: First is that the Alameda O'Club had the longest bar in the Navy; second is that the Pacific Ocean off San Francisco has the deepest ground swells in the world and third is that the tail end of the Midway, even in a smooth sea, moves with the combined vigor of an Hawaiian hula and Arabian belly dancer, which is to say, totally unpredictable.

Still on the mend from my Hancock/Demon night-landing setbacks, I approached this exercise with confidence, for I had worked hard and learned much about flying in the interim. One totally black, pitching deck, cold and blustery night, Wes and I went and banged out six reasonably-successful landings and were greeted like heroes in the ready room. In fact, us nuggets did well compared to some of the old timers who had not seen a night deck in a long while. I got to fly an airplane off to the beach from about one-hundred miles off shore, and what an incredibly lovely midnight sight was the San

Francisco Bay area on a crystal clear night. About ten feet of the world's longest bar was kept busy for a few more hours!

A portion of our workup training for the Western Pacific and the Seventh Fleet in early 1962 had us in Hawaiian waters, but due to impending H-bomb testing well to the south, our night flying was cancelled several times. This excerpt from a letter to Carolyn was a sobering reminder of the deadly nature of the Cold War:

> *For the last few nights, they have cancelled the big H-bomb blast and last night it looked like another delay again. But, I decided to go topside just for the heck of it. Right on schedule, it went off. Believe me, I've never seen anything to equal such a sight! Even though it was 750 miles away the ship was lit up like broad daylight. Twenty minutes later, the sky was still a dark red. When we start playing around with things like that, it's time to stop and take a long, hard look at where we're going.*

Catapulting in the F4B was kind of different because the airplane was slow to rotate at low gross weights and could have a very rapid rotation when heavy with fuel and ordnance and went like this: Once over the catapult

Catapulting from Kitty Hawk's #3 waist catapult. Note stick full aft and full flaps.

shuttle and into the holdback, the nose strut was extended about two feet, which actually gave the machine a more positive angle of attack once it left the ship. Even so, the book said to hold the stick all the way aft on the stroke, give the plane a chance to dig in and then ease off on the stick. On about one of ten cat shots, the pilot would underrotate and get the heart rate of the ship's Captain and Air Boss up a peg or two, or overrotate and get it up three or four pegs. Actually, it was really a function of your speed off the catapult and your gross weight. But, every once in awhile, at heavy gross weight launches with tanks and heavy with ordnance, an unwary pilot would leave the stick full back for a micro-second too long and the result was a spectacular wing-rocking, rudder-pumping, stick-forward, "I've got it," exercise in basic airmanship.

One day halfway through our first cruise on the Kitty Hawk, we received a message from the test pilot guys at Patuxent River telling us guys (the fleet) how to take off from the ship in a Phantom. To us, the effrontery of some shore-based staff weenies telling the fleet how to fly our airplanes was too much — at least according to Schenk's gospel.

Old Hap saw it differently and directed us to "keep the damned stick back like the Pax River guys (he was a test pilot as well — they all stick together) tell us to do!" So, the bull Ops Officer and the CO had a toe-to-toe, the upshot of which was that after about ten really tail-dragging overrotations, we went back to flying the airplane and not trying to do it by rote.

Christmas and New Years Eve of 1962 were spent far out at sea off Northern Japan on board the Kitty Hawk and, at the instigation of our hard charging XO, had a bit of medicinal brandy in our home-made eggnog. I needn't go into the gory details other than to suggest the emergence from sources unknown of some mighty fine compliments to the Doc's brandy. We had an agreeable time up there in forward officer's country in that far-away spot in a lonely ocean, and even sang a verse or two of Joe's favorite songs, the names of which are irrelevant and the meaning of which made sense only to those of the same professional persuasion.

One real glummy and snowy day far north in the Pacific in that winter of 1962, Wes and I were in the duty five-minute alert Phantom absolutely freezing and questioning our motivation to go aviate when we could hardly see the end of the bow catapult and knowing that no one would be dumb enough to launch in weather like this! "LAUNCH THE ALERT FIVE," booms the word over the flight deck PA system, and, four-and-a-half minutes after our untimely wakeup, were airborne and on top of the clouds heading for the Soviet who dared to trespass in our territory.

Our lead was Lieutenant Commander Dick Rich and his RIO, Ross Terry, both super naval officers and aviators. We soon joined on what was one of the very early Soviet Badger overflights of our carriers. They took lots of pictures of this new Navy fighter and we did the same. And there was some real solid aviator-to-aviator body language to wit: I was tucked in quite close to the big twin-engine bomber and the pilot of the Soviet motioned to us in sign language known to all aviators, to "move out." I moved in closer. He then very abruptly moved his big right wing down right over our tail, which forced us to pop a fast negative G or two on the Phantom. Well, it's one thing to fly close and another to pull a dirty trick like that on a fellow aviator! So, we came real close alongside and I shook my fist at him. He in turn, took off his oxygen mask and gave me a big toothy grin. Macho versus macho. Quid pro quo! The instant replay would have called it a draw.

Soviet Badger and friends in the far North Pacific winter waters. USS Kitty Hawk in background. Note smiling tail gunner.

    Ross Terry, not to be outdone, had the intelligence guys make up a sign in Russian that said "smile" and showed it to the forlorn tail gunner from his aft cockpit. The gunner, all alone and far from home as well, took his mask off, smiled and showed Ross and Dick a centerfold from Playboy. The universal language of aviators works again!

    The Badger was smart, as he didn't try to find the ship in that weather and headed for his Siberian home. Our first clue as to the conditions below the thick cloud layer was when the ship told the photo Crusader and a covey of A4s to head for a Japanese air field some 400 miles to the southwest because the "weather was below minimums." We had insufficient fuel to make the trek, so were committed to landing aboard. At 1,200 feet and six-miles astern, in solid snow cloud, we were told to be "careful coming out of the gear because the deck was icy." I recall thinking what an abjectly stupid thing to say, pressing on, breaking out with some LSO and back-seat help and landing behind Dick and Ross.

Aardvarks and Phantoms

Because we had the old-style bulky and terribly-hot exposure suits (poopy suits) and the water was extremely cold, we were wearing our full-pressure suits. One of these almost did me in during our initial training. This particular training exercise was to strap you in a seat suspended over a ten-foot-deep pool, put your gloves and hardhat on, drop you to the bottom and demonstrate how much fun and how easy it was to breathe with the self-contained oxygen in the seat pack. After a few minutes, the instructor would signal OK, you would release from the seat and scramble to the surface. Well, before the attendant could get my helmet on, the wire holding the seat broke and I went down like a rock. I could distinctly hear someone yelling to, ". . . get the SOB out of there," in a high-pitched and frantic voice. Of course, I slipped the seat belt, but by this time, was full of water with a very substantial overall negative bouyancy. Two guys pulled me out none the worse for wear, repaired the wire rope to the seat, drained the water out of my suit and back in I went. Enough said!

Flight surgeons were a big part of squadron life up forward in ready one aboard the Kitty Hawk. Affectionately known as "Quack," whenever one of these "Docs" ventured into the ready room, a resounding chorus of "Quack, quack, quack," would reverberate with gusto.

Actually, the flight surgeons were a somewhat anomalous lot. Full-fledged medical doctors, they had attended a three-month course in aviation physiology and received about 30-hours of basic flight instruction back in Pensacola. These guys assisted the ship's senior medical officer in ministering to the medical needs of the 5,500 folks on board as well as ships in company with the big carrier. They would also "bird dog" two or three squadrons each. By this I mean, hang out with, watch for fatigue, snoop out personal problems that could affect their performance and fly once in awhile in the squadron aircraft, if it had more than one seat. Only the "quacks" could dispense medicinal favors, such as brandy and would do so in moderation after a really tough or black-night mission.

We also had to endure a once- or twice-per-week lecture having something to do with aviation physiology such as, ". . . be sure to eat a good breakfast, don't fight with your wife, get lots of sleep, grunt when you pull Gs and, if the water's cold, wear an exposure suit. Always, before the poor guy could utter a word, the "quack, quack, quacks," were in a full-force chant.

One slow day, our guy was giving us a weekly dose on the subject of not flying when your blood sugar is low. "If you eat one doughnut for breakfast," says the Doc, "your blood sugar spikes and then goes right down after an hour or so." The message was obvious, that if only a doughnut was eaten for breakfast, you might just be incapable of shooting down the enemy due to some insidious internal chemical imbalance. He then asked, "Now, what do you need to do to be mentally alert in the air?"

"Eat more doughnuts," was the irreverent response from the back of the ready room. So much for the Docs.

True Faith and Allegiance

We had some spectacular accidents that cruise on Kitty Hawk, but nothing like those on the Hancock the year before flying Demons. Early on, we had an F8 hit the ramp at night and literally explode, an A3 big bomber did the same (really bad), an RF8 photo had a wing fold on cat shot and Schenk collapsed a main landing gear coming aboard in a rainstorm. They blamed Schenk 100% for that because it was only "light" rain, according to the high command. But, I was back on the LSO platform and could have testified it was raining hard, but no one asked. As all weather as the Phantom was, it was a handful in rain because the forward part of the windscreen became opaque in anything over light rain. Not too impressed, Schenk had some colorful language regarding the qualifications of the accident board.

Back in those peacetime days, we did a lot of PR work for visiting dignitaries, including fire-power demonstrations at the drop of a hat. Usually, our role was to 1) do an immelman (half loop) right off the catapult, including some at night, and/or 2) a supersonic flyby. Hap finally let us JOs in on the latter and we really had fun. The supersonic pass was really not a big deal, but nonetheless it had to be approached carefully. The limiting, not-to-excede speed down low for the Phantom was 750 knots (about 840 mph), with the altitude as close to the flight deck as was prudent.

Joe Konzen, Hap Chandler and Dan McCormick in ready one.

Commander Hunt Hardisty had recently set the low-altitude speed record in the Phantom after his predecessor's wings had shed doing the identical maneuver in what is euphemistically called a "pilot induced oscillation — PIO." What it translated to in the real world of flying Phantoms extremely fast and very low was, that if you moved the stick 1/16th of an inch the airplane would react violently, so only move it 1/32nd of an inch! Bottom line was to fly the airplane very smoothly and don't for an instant get complacent, for it could eat you alive in less than half a heart beat.

The Kitty Hawk spent about 40% of that seven-month cruise in port. Yokusaka, Sasebo, Hong Kong, Cubi Point and one visit to Manila in the Phillipines for the purpose of hosting a presidential visit. In this latter stopover, we were, of course, on our best behavior with a crystal-clear inference to the crew to toe the line and act accordingly. As a precaution, it was standard procedure in each port to put ashore a 50-officer-and-man shore patrol contingent to handle any problems our guys may have while on the "beach."

Aardvarks and Phantoms

One rainy and stormy night, I was assigned to police the landing area where our boats would load and unload for the 30-minute trip to the anchored carrier. Normally routine, this night would be difficult, for the seas kicked up, the boats were canceled and a bunch of enterprising young Filipinos were selling small, but potent bottles of homemade rum at $5 a pop under the fence enclosing our compound. The results were predictable: Tired, wet and anxious to bunk down, the troops became increasingly belligerent and vocal, including a pair of youngsters, one Navy and one Marine, who were about to square off after exploring the origins of their respective ancestry.

Seeking to maintain the peace at all costs, I stepped between the two budding pugilists replete in my crisp summer whites, lieutenant's bars and bridge cap, at the precise moment the Marine was rearing back for a swing at the Navy "swab," and caught the back of his fist full in my face. Down I went, hard on my back in the mud. Now, hitting anyone is a real "no-no," but hitting a commissioned officer is a triple "no-no!" The compound became deathly quiet. So, un-officer like as it was, I figured the longer I lay there, the more under control would be my temporary charges. It worked.

The next morning, a sheepish and contrite young Marine knocked at my stateroom door up forward on the 02 level, hat in hand, his Marine captain CO at his side, with a genuine offer of apologies to "the Lieutenant." I accepted with a handshake and a wink of my swollen eye to his CO.

On the appointed day to receive the Phillipine president, the ship was spotless and all were in the whitest of white uniforms with strict orders to be in the uniform of the day at all times. Two of us decided however, to sneak in a quick trip to the weight room, about 100-yards from our rooms. In order to limit our exposure on the way back, we ran, all dirty and sweaty. But, "whack!" I cracked my head on a hatch coaming with enough force to generate copious quantities of scalp blood. I mean really bleeding! Wrapping my sore head in a towel, off we went to sick bay. No choice. The Doc laid me out and started stitching and wouldn't you know, in walks the president of the Phillipines and his entourage. Well, instead of being torqued off, the ship's high command were delighted because the President was, for here was a real-life example of the ship's medical department in action! The moral is that life on a carrier is multi-dimensional.

We spent a lot of time in the ready room on that first cruise for, notwithstanding all the attributes of our fabulous new jet fighter, the Phantom had a poor record of combat readiness in those days, mainly due to a lack of spare parts. So we had time to think in addition to playing an occasional game of Acey Duecy. While others in less prestigious segments of Naval Aviation might falsely argue that the notion of thinking and fighter pilots to be somewhat of an oxymoron, John Bull and I were trying to figure out how to get back to the states and our brides before the ship docked in San Diego. It went like this:

John and I with our RIOs, would launch in two machines 1,000 miles from San Diego, get multiple in-flight refuelings and land on the carrier Saratoga off the east coast. This would fit in nicely with the advanced PR priorities of the

Aardvarks, bring great credit to Hap and Joe, get the Kitty Hawk in the news, demonstrate the versatility of the F4B Phantom and, most importantly, get the four of us home three-days early. Great story, great potential, but the bosses wouldn't buy it. Sorry!

John Bull in a pensive mood in ready one on the way home.

EPILOGUE

- **Hap Chandler** became CO of the big Miramar Naval Air Station in San Diego, retired to the Dallas area, has his own personal Citation jet and still goes up when the weather is bad to "get some actual instrument time."

- **Joe Konzen** became CO of the VF-114 Aardvarks, retired to the Seattle area and now lives nearby in Pensacola, Florida.

- **Schenk Remson** became a Phantom squadron CO, flies his own home-built airplane and to this day continues to cut a wide swath in the northern reaches of Idaho.

- **Dan McCormick** went on to squadron and carrier command, made flag, does seven knots on his sailboat and reminds all when I'm around, that "Booth never could stay with him."

- **Dick Rich** was killed over Vietnam in a Phantom.

- **Ross Terry** was shot down in Vietnam, survived six years as a POW and now lives near us in Pensacola.

- **Don Engen** retired as a three-star admiral, became head of the FAA and was extremely active in civilian aviation. Sadly, he lost his life in a high-tech glider over the Colorado mountains.

- **Hunt Hardisty** retired as a four-star admiral, still as impressive and motivational as when he was setting low-altitude speed records, only to pass away not long ago — one of the real heroes.

- The "staff weenie from Patuxent River" who told us how to catapult was my brother-in-law, **Bill Ramsey**, who went on to command a nuclear aircraft carrier and retire as a three-star admiral.

- **Pete Conrad** became an astronaut, landed on the moon and stayed active in matters aviation and space. Sadly, he lost his life in a motorcycle accident.

- **John Bull** left the Navy, earned his doctorate and became an astronaut.

- **Pat Henry** left the Navy, became the head test pilot for McDonnell Douglas and was a leader in the development of the F-15 Eagle and F/A-18 Hornet. He now lives not far from the Miramar Naval Air Station and plays an occasional game of golf.

- **Wes Barrett** became a financial planner near San Diego, having served his country with honor and beyond the call of duty as Booth's backseater.

- The **Phantom**, in the colors of the Mississippi Air National Guard and the U.S. Air Force, flew in the 1991 combat against Iraq, thirty-years after this tale. Amazingly, in 2003, it still flies with the German Air Force.

- **Archie Lane** left the Navy, became a test pilot for North American Rockwell and most recently, totally restored a vintage Beech Staggerwing airplane.

- **Kitty Hawk** fought in the first and second Iraq wars with a combat air wing that had a full mission capable rate of over 90% and continues to roam the oceans of the world with impunity and pride from its homeport in Yokusaka, Japan forty-one years after this tale.

- **Badger crew** unknown, but probably writing tales of dumb American fighter pilots who don't know how to fly formation and guys in the back seat who ask if they have any girly pictures.

STANFORD

MBAs, loops in a T-33, the Bugsmasher, Accounting One and a cross-country trek at 144 mph.

When I saw my report card at the end of my first semester at Stanford, I almost croaked. There it was — a big capital-letter "D" in accounting. For the second time in my life, I experienced the specter of failure.

We had moved, Carolyn and me plus one two-year-old daughter, to Palo Alto from the exciting, challenging and heady days of Miramar, Phantoms and flying. The reason I was here instead of in a flying job, like being an instructor pilot in the Phantom training squadron, was that Lieutenant Commander Dan McCormick had made me put down "Business" and "International Relations" in the "What post-graduate course do you want when you finish your first tour of sea duty." Not wanting aeronautical engineering for a number of really pragmatic and valid reasons, I put down three innocuous choices which I knew I had not a prayer of getting. One day, however, aboard the Kitty Hawk far out at sea, Dan said I had to take a test — the admission test for the Graduate School of Business at Stanford University. After he told me "times up" for the first section and my response that "I'm not half-done" and his "tough," I got down to work and, I guess, did OK.

Back at the farm, as Stanford was known, I was having problems with my big "D." I had it pretty well figured that accounting was a straight-forward,

True Faith and Allegiance

rather simplistic notion of adding and subtracting a few dollars and cents. Was I ever mistaken! To begin with, most of our class of 200 eager-beavers and ultra-high achievers, had had accounting, so the school assumed a working knowledge of the subject. Well, my point in all this, is that accounting was no different than the other "simple and non-technical" courses of that first of four semesters. Stanford did not teach per se: they provided the student with exposure to a wide variety of situations and case studies and from these lessons, resulted an incredible learning experience. I remember well our first day when the Dean succinctly stated, ". . . the school was not about to teach you definable skills from which you could barter yourself into a high-paying job. Rather, it would endeavor to expose you to the skills and lessons that would make you better able to perform as a CEO in the years to come." I figured that maybe this too, would be kind of heady. Absolutely no one there in 1963 could have cared a hoot about what a great aviator I had been or that I had single-handedly driven a destroyer about the Pacific Ocean. What did impress a few of them was the money that I made as a lieutenant in the Navy, which, compared to the zero income of most of my compatriots, was a lot. But, I missed the camaraderie and comparative freedom of my squadron and even sent them a telegram when they started the next cruise aboard Kitty Hawk. But what I soon began to miss the most was the lack of free time, because the longer I was resident at Stanford, the further I got behind and harder I worked. Why Stanford business types were so successful became readily apparent — they simply outworked the competition! An interesting credo, for I had never seen folks work as hard and long in my life.

Vespa with Laurie in Palo Alto.

We lucked out in finding a pleasant little house in Palo Alto, one bedroom of which was soon converted to my study command center replete with an old door for a desk. As parking at the school was impossible, I somehow found a used Vespa motor scooter which I would park amongst the thousands of bicycles, a stone's throw from the classrooms.

Nearby was the Moffet Field Naval Air Station and the most beautiful T-33 jet I'd ever seen and at least a hint of the real world I had left behind. One of the station pilots checked me out and what a pleasant respite from the worries and pressures of the school. It was another world. Our standard hop was to take off VFR (clear of clouds), do a tour of the San Francisco Bay area and head for the San Joaquin valley. By this time the tip-tank fuel tanks were empty and we could do some standard acrobatics. What a fun airplane was this little underpowered trainer. It was really basic; no stability augmentation between you and the control surfaces, no triple hydraulics, no radar, no fancy zero-zero ejection seats and no black-assed night cat shots! It even had a yaw string on the top of the nose so you could tell, without going through a myriad of electronics, when you weren't motivating straight through the air.

The best fun of all though were spins. Ever since I had left the T-28 trainer in flight training, no one did spins in any of the swept-wing aircraft, at least not intentionally. You would simply zoom to about 20,000 feet, hold the nose up about 60 degrees, let the speed bleed down to about 70 knots or just before a good stall and then come full back on the stick and kick hard on one rudder. For those non-test pilot, non-aeronautical engineers like myself, the aerodynamics of spins came alive in that dancing yaw string! In a real spin, the airplane of course, is fully stalled and yawing (turning) at a rapid rate. So, the trusty string sticks up in the airstream at about a 30-degree angle and is way off to one side. It's the best indicator of a stall/spin I've ever seen and totally fail-safe.

T-33 jet at nearby Naval Air Station, Moffet Field.

Before I get back to the farm, MBAs, Accounting II and Quantitative Analysis for Business Decisions II, there are a couple more sea stories. (I may never get back to the school). The station helo pilot was a neat guy named Buddy Larkins. Buddy wanted to fly a jet so bad he could taste it. One day he offered to check me out in the helo if I in turn, would check him out in the T-33. Well, flying and systems-wise the T-bird was as simple as you can get and it didn't take old Buddy long to ace it and do spins, loops and landings like a real "jet pilot." I wish I could say the same for the cantankerous HO4S helo. I had had a real humble pill one day back at Miramar when a salty old Chief AP (one of the last enlisted pilots), took me up in an HUP helicopter to pick up a Demon at a nearby air station. If ever there was a machine that was destined not to fly, it was the HUP! It wobbled, pitched, bucked and if

Me and Buddy Larkins

you let loose of the stick, it has what my test pilot buddies would call negative stability, which is a euphemistic way of saying "if you let loose for more than three seconds, you would crash." The HO4S was a bigger handful than the HUP and embraced all the HUP's wonderful flying qualities! One right hand, one left arm, a left hand and two feet were all in constant motion.

Fortunately, the call to studies prevented a serious foray into the ridiculous world of vertical aviation, fun though it was (with a highly qualified pilot at the controls). One of my flying buddies for a few hops in the T-33, was Dick Stratton who was later to return to combat, fly A4 light-attack jets, be shot down, become a POW and grace the cover of Life magazine in a low bow. We had fun as Dick really didn't enjoy boring holes for flight time (we had to get four-hours per month for pay) but did relish bending and stressing the machine and sharpening his flying skills in instruments and acrobatics. A real pleasure to be in the air with!

I also flew the T-bird with an ex-Blue Angel whose name I forget. Actually, I shouldn't forget it because we were almost buried on the same small mountain peak near Carmel. Notwithstanding this, Lieutenant Blue Angel was a joy to fly with. He really enjoyed aviating and was good at it and loved loops. Blue was up front one gorgeous San Joaquin Valley day and did eight consecutive loops — nice, easy and graceful maneuvers with the yaw string straight as an arrow, just the right amount of G and a slight easing on top so as to "make a good round circle." Over the top each time, as the opposite horizon came in to view, my friend Blue would utter with absolute sincerity, how good it felt and, as the nose was straight down, opine as to how this "really cleaned out your soul." I loved to fly with aviators who loved to fly and didn't mind showing it.

One day, my flying buddy, who was also at Stanford in the Aero course, and I met to get our 1.5 hour hop, but our friend the T-33 was down. Well, the station also had a small twin-engined Beechcraft used for short logistics flights. The "Bugsmasher" and I had had a few hops spread over several years, the most recent of which was as co-pilot with a station lieutenant commander who exclaimed after letting me try to land it once and damned near pranging me, him and the airplane, ". . . what in the hell have you been flying, Booth?" Blue assured me that he was fully checked out in the machine, so off we went. Well, Blue couldn't get the engines started and had to entice a plane captain to "start 'em up." Blue muttered something about hot weather, took off after a fashion and headed south for Monterey. Out over the Pacific, we decided to head east over the hills to the valley. The terrain was about 3,000-feet high, so we added power and started an easy climb. Clearly, the Bugsmasher is no Blue Angel F-11 or even a doggy T-33. In fact the old HO4S with a full load of Marines could outclimb our trusty steed. You can probably guess the rest of this story. Blue adds power, adds more power, drops flaps, slows down and all of the above again. The saddleback in the hills that looked so benign awhile ago is now about to eat us alive. Full power, full flaps, max RPM and hanging on the props just at the power-on stall point (stall being defined as that point at which the airplane ceases generating meaningful lift and takes on the flying characteristics of a flat rock). Some provident force gave us a few feet and two absolutely-ashened aviators emerged into the valley, turned north to Moffet Field, executed a straight-in landing with nary a word said. The only epilogue to this tale are two words: Survival and stupidity times two!

Back at the Stanford farm, life became a frantic quest for staying ahead of the continued challenge. It wasn't really grades as much as it was pride. Everyone worked hard; that was the ethic. But, it was still academia and those guys know how to cram the most days off into one year of any profession going.

We had summers off, long Christmas leaves and a couple of weeks free in the spring. Not all that bad. So, at the end of the first nine months, we had three months off; one month of leave and two months "to get a job where you'll learn some practical business savvy" so said the U. S. Navy. My fellow lieutenant, Ken Froelich, and I boondoggled stays at the nearby Lockheed plant (Polaris missile) and the big United Airlines maintenance base at San Francisco. The latter was fascinating and the lessons learned would stay with me for years to come. One of our mentors at United suggested we come by on a Sunday evening to watch a big Boeing 707 come in for its every 18-month overhaul. Within twelve hours (we stayed there), a swarm of some forty men descended upon the giant airplane, which one hour before had been carrying passengers and which had been logging hours at the rate of 11-hours-per day for almost 500 days. By 0600 all seats were out, two engines were off, half the avionics were out, one landing gear assembly was off, one flap gone and half of the airplane had been stripped preparing for a full paint job. Incredibly, it was back in the air Monday a week at 0800 with passengers! All this impressed me for I was used to a squadron airplane disappearing into the maw of a major overhaul, never to be seen again in my lifetime. An engine change would take several days, if you had a replacement engine. United, on the other hand had it together. The management techniques were quite unsophisticated. I expected to see banks of computers and loads of analysts. Not the case. The secret for this rapid and quality turnaround was having a team of extremely knowledgeable people who had done the requisite planning and who were motivated by the fact that if the big 707 was not back in the air to start its next 6,000 hours on Monday morning, they might be out on the street selling used cars. "Our" airplane flew its test hop as scheduled the next Sunday morning and had several hours to spare. Respite was short-lived however, as another 707 was already winging its way to SFO and a one-week major overhaul.

Lockheed, on the other hand, was a different story. The government-owned plant in Sunnyvale built the very complex and state-of-the-art submarine-launched Polaris missile and everything was quality control. The management scheme was structured to respond to Navy demands. In fact, the naval officers in the plant really ran the program. As students, Ken and I were privy to lots of top management meetings wherein we could observe and ask questions. Because we were students and Navy, we were really treated

True Faith and Allegiance

well. I don't mean this in material terms as much as everyone, it seemed, wanted us to know what and why they did what they did. Compared to the fast-moving fleet (and rapid feedback) and United (weekly results), Lockheed was a case history of precise and very-slow movement. Over the long run, of course, its submarine-launched ballistic missiles proved enormously successful, both operationally and technically, and were a decisive element in keeping the Cold War peace.

What to do on our one-months leave? Carolyn wanted to go to Tennessee and the farm where she grew up. But our austere Comet, which replaced my pride and joy, a 1956 blue-and-white Chevrolet convertible (burned while in storage while I was on the Kitty Hawk cruise), was a non-air-conditioned, super-economy, three-speed, stick-shift model and there was flat out no way we were driving 2,000 miles and back again! Ergo, lets fly! Advertising in the San Francisco Chronicle as "commercial pilot desires use of four-place single-engine airplane for the month of August," I received some really interesting responses including one fellow who would love for me to fly with him, but not my three females. And another, who had landed his beautiful retractable Commanche, wheels up on the east coast and wanted me to pick it up for him after it had been repaired. As it turned out, the Piper guy in Oakland offered me a great deal on a spanking-new Piper Cherokee 180 — four place, cruises at 144 mph true, a gorgeous machine and at a phenomenal price. So, one low-overcast Palo Alto day, one baby girl, one three-year old and one white-knuckled wife, stuffed into "Cherokee 7761W," and off we went to "on top at 1500 feet" and a gorgeous sunny day. What a trip that was! A total of 44 hours and all the way to Washington (my folks wanted to see the family too).

The Tennessee farm from 8,000 feet.

Our modus operandi was to fly about three hours, always clear of the clouds, at 7,500 or 8,500 feet and two hops a day. How pleasant it was compared to Route 66 below us. The girls would all take a mild dose of Dramamine, the purpose of which was to prevent air sickness, but which really made them drowsy. Soon all were asleep and it was me, my machine and my three girls all cruising along with great mutual contentment.

We were flying to Albuquerque that first day with a fuel stop at Winslow, Arizona. About noon, we were walking out to our 7761W, when a big guy comes up and asked where we were headed. Offering "Albuquerque," he opined that "wouldn't do that if I was you," and as to why, "It gets a mite bumpy in the afternoon." He was right of course, so we kind of hung out (one three-year old and one constantly wet or messy — no disposable diapers in those days — six-month old). Our friend and I walked out to our airplanes about four o'clock for the flight, him to his big twin and us to our little one. My new-found friend, who was also enroute to Albuquerque, couldn't get one of his engines started, so off we went. Well, about an hour out of the big A, here comes the big guy's twin up alongside us and booms out on the radio, ". . . where you all staying?" and to my ". . . don't know," he said "I'll take care of it," and off he went. Sure enough, as we taxied in about sunset, there was the courtesy car right beside us and we were in a neat motel ten minutes after shutdown. Our friend set the tone for the rest of the trip, for everywhere we went, we were treated like long-lost cousins. Enroute from the farm in Tennessee to Washington, we stopped in Knoxville to have lunch with some of Carolyn's kin and then on to the exciting world of Washington's National Airport on a beautiful and serene summer day.

Tuning into the approach frequency about 70-miles out, we were met with a steady stream of chatter. I was glad the girls were dozing because with all the radio talk, the high traffic count and trying to figure out if "landing north" meant on runway 33, 36 or 03, it was confusing. All worked out fine and we had a nice visit until time came to depart on the long trip westward. I noticed that the little rudder of 7761W was severely bent — someone had hit it and didn't bother to tell anyone. Here ensued another civilian business lesson in how to get parts fast. A phone call to the Vero Beach Piper plant had a replacement rudder enroute on the afternoon airplane and it was installed that night. Off we went into the calm blue yonder, headed back to the farm at Stanford via the farm in Tennessee.

Well, not quite; three minutes after taking off, with the Pentagon slipping beneath our port wing, my wife announced with absolute stark terror that her "door was not closed." She didn't buy the logic that as long as we were flying, Superman could not have opened the door. So, twelve minutes after lifting off from National Airport, we landed at the nearly deserted Leesberg airport, rolled to the end, closed the door and took off in the opposite direction enroute to Knoxville and another great lunch. Wrong!

Settling down at 8,500 feet, cool and peaceful, Dramamine just starting

7761W at National Airport with Dad and girls ... note new rudder.

to do its thing and this awful odor permeates the cockpit which no amount of outside air could dissipate. It was, of course, number-two daughter who had instigated a total disaster in the back seat. "We have to land" says Carolyn. It wasn't an invitation, a suggestion or idle conversation; it was an imperative! The nearest field in the foothills of the mountains was Hazard, Kentucky, with no navaids and with a one-way (literally) approach. We made it fine, said "no thanks,we didn't need gas," to a smiling attendant at the one-pump, one-small building (with HAZARD on it), did ask where we could put all the debris from the combat zone and took off in the opposite direction for the second time that day, with a much more content six-month-old baby and mother.

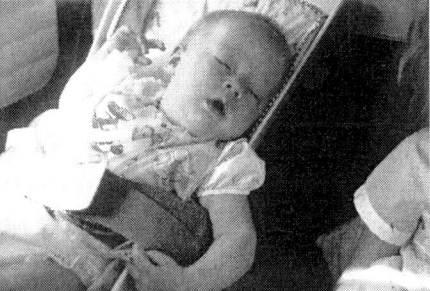

Emergency diaper change enroute.   *Renee with clean diapers.*

The second year at the big farm was almost pleasant. I had aced the accounting final at the end of the first year which was a typical Stanford non-traditional exercise: Two-hundred graduate students walked in with our little blue answer books (I never saw a multiple choice test in two years), and on a table in the center of the room were about 500 slick annual reports from several large public companies. The final exam was but fourteen words: "Using the annual report of your choice, analyze the financial health of the company." The Stanford heavies could have cared less if you knew the difference between a debit and credit or some fancy accrual method, but they darned sure wanted you to know how smart CFOs and CEOs could make a doggy company look like IBM in its heyday. More and more the lessons learned from Stanford began to relate to the Navy in terms of solving problems, generating teamwork, participation of the troops and impacts on the bottom line. Our classmates went off to all corners of the business world and many today are or have been leaders in their companies. I've often wondered how I would have been motivated to sell toothpaste, make annual reports look good, decide what to wear each day and maybe be a commuter to the same building for two or three decades.

Those were heady days for business, the country and the Navy. We had a new President with great charisma and an infectious enthusiasm.

We had too, the nibblings of a place called Vietnam and many of my friends were intensely involved. The reality of the uncertain world we lived in came thundering to life one gorgeous morning as we students were taking a break in the Stanford courtyard. Waves of B-52s at a lowish 5,000 feet circled the Bay area and the papers had made mention of an Alameda carrier underway for an emergency deployment. It was of course, the Cuban missile crisis. We were incredibly close to all-out nuclear war. It was a sobering time for lots of folks, including the Soviets who knew that the young President Kennedy meant business.

I wish I could have said the same for Vietnam.

EPILOGUE

- **Stanford's Graduate School of Business** still goes strong, gives the same accounting final, has 40% women students vice 2%, now has 400 students in each class and still produces a sizeable share of the nation's CEO cadre.

- Lieutenant **Blue Angel** is whereabouts unknown.

- **Ken Froelich** served with distinction in Vietnam and subsequent tours in the intelligence community before retiring from the Navy.

- Cherokee **7761W** was totally destroyed in a crash two years later, cause unknown.

- The quality-conscience folks at **Lockheed's** Sunnyvale plant contributed enormously to the winning of the Cold War with a succession of deadly-accurate and reliable sub-launched, nuclear-tipped missiles.

- Due to the efforts of the **Dick Strattons, Ken Froelichs, Blue Angels, Buddy Larkins** and **lots of others**, the political war of Vietnam came and went, the nuclear standoff known as mutual assured destruction never came as close again as it did in Cuba, and American business and the democratic process were provided the framework to function and prosper.

INTERLUDE

The shortest tour of all, the F-111B, boredom, astronaut, bad eyes and the bus route to downtown Washington, DC.

Shortly before graduating from Stanford, I received orders to Washington, D.C. and the office of the F-111B program manager's office located in old, WWII temporary buildings a stone's throw from the Washington Monument. After a pleasant drive across the country in our new 1965 Chrysler and a week or so at the farm in Tennessee, we found a tiny two-bedroom house to rent near the bus line into the big city, I bought two civilian suits (no uniforms) and reported to work in the muggy summer of 1965 with mixed emotions.

No one from the Navy's personnel headquarters had bothered to ask me where I might want to go upon completing the MBA program at Stanford. Had I been asked, the natural response would have been to request another fleet squadron, particularly in view of the escalating "war" in Vietnam. That said, I accepted my assignment determined to do the best job I could for the Navy.

My assignment as a senior lieutenant (at the nine-year mark) was to be the "configuration control officer" for the controversial and so-called TFX joint fighter, a combat aircraft that McNamara and his sharp-penciled advisors

True Faith and Allegiance

felt could serve the fighter needs of the Navy, Air Force and Marines. It was a giant, twin-engined monster of an airplane and no more a fighter than the B-52! The primary purpose of my office — headed by a Navy captain — was to kill the program for the Navy simply because there was no way the F-111B could have flown effectively from a carrier nor was it even remotely a fighter in the classic sense.

The first couple of months were tolerable; I met lots of good and dedicated civilians in the material side of the Navy, and was mildly motivated. Most of the folks worked 40-hours a week, never on weekends and seldom, as I recall, with any great sense of urgency. That said, this side of the Navy had a reputation for producing the best naval aircraft and weapons of any of the services including other nations'. It just was not for me. I got mundane (or no) assignments, little direction and on more than a few occasions found myself in the library just to pass the time. And, notwithstanding the pleasant life-style with my little family in the Washington suburbs, the late months of that year were ominous with many good Americans getting killed in Vietnam, including some of my friends.

Renee and Dad in Washington. Leather flight jacket going strong.

The saga of the TFX was bottomed-lined by whom to believe? The contractor had one set of performance parameters, the Air Force another and the Navy yet another. The gross weight was always the crunch point because carrier catapults could toss just so much into the air and the arresting gear could absorb just so much kinetic energy. And to add insult to injury, the Navy evaluation folks were deadly accurate in their ability to forecast weight gains. Even the most optimistic contractor performance figures were far worse than Navy predictions.

Into my dullish routine one morning came a retired Rear Admiral and classmate of my Dad; his name is not important. He was limping as he entered my windowless office space and sat at my austere wooden desk, his gripping handshake and charismatic smile in the fore. Sadly, his reason for the visit was to invite me to fly his new avionics display. I say sadly, because here was one of my heroes and role models who, in retirement, was hawking wares as a glorified salesman for a major defense contractor and who, by virtue of his enormous stature and reputation, was relegated to opening doors to the right Navy offices. The image remained with me for decades to come.

One day a few months into the "job," I got a memo asking if I was interested in becoming a pilot of the space shuttle, then early in its development. I wasn't really, but indicated I was, mainly to get some spice into my somewhat dull routine. Off I went to get a special physical and soon learned from a grim-faced doctor that "Your eyes do not meet the criteria for the space program nor to be a Naval Aviator." It was the part which tests for astigmatism wherein one must line up the lines just so. My world crumbled!

The doc was a good guy and suggested that I rest my eyes for a week or so and trek down to the nearby Patuxent River Naval Air Station for another opinion. Turned out my eyes were perfect with no problems. But, as best I can recall, I never heard from the space guys again, partly I guess, because Naval Aviation was going bonkers trying to get qualified pilots back into the fleet to make up for the rather high losses of Vietnam.

After but five months on the job, in late 1965, two events came in close succession: First, I made lieutenant commander and second, I was ordered to be an instructor pilot in the Phantom training squadron based in Key West to report no later than 3 January, 1966. And, as was the case in our previous two moves, Carolyn was totally supportive and was soon planning for the second move in six months.

On a scale of one to ten, my contributions to the F-111B Program Manager's Office were zero, but I learned a slice of the Navy that not too many of my compatriots got the chance to experience and met a few fine folks in the process. The lessons stuck with me.

EPILOGUE

- The **F-111B** never came close to being a fleet fighter on board carriers. Had it been shoved down the Navy's throat by the whiz kids in DOD, Naval Aviation would have been far less combat capable in the ensuing decades! Paradoxically, it did serve for many decades as an Air Force strategic bomber and electronic counter-measures platform.

MORE PHANTOMS

One fast-moving, shore-based year in the Phantom training squadron in Key West as an instructor pilot, tiny cinder-block house, hurricanes, air combat maneuvering, at least one DS and the looming war in Vietnam.

Frenchy Ducharme had a girl friend on Big Sugarloaf Key, about forty miles up the road from Key West. One day, he decided to do a little buzz job and show her what he already knew — that he was the greatest fighter pilot of them all. Somehow, someway, the high command got wind of the alleged incident and, flat-hatting being a real "no-no," I was assigned to do a JAG (legal) investigation. After due diligence to the cause of justice, I came up with the astounding conclusion that he was incredibly guilty! To add insult to injury, Miss Girl Friend was not even at home. Big deal — it didn't make any difference, for we were cranking up for war and the Navy needed every warm-bodied pilot it could find. In my case, I rejoined the ranks of Naval Aviation as a Phantom instructor pilot.

I spent twelve months — all of 1966 — in Key West and flew constantly! Our job was to instruct Naval Aviators in the intricacies of the F4 Phantom. Each student pilot or backseater (RIO) spent about six-months in the squadron and left with some 100 hours in the Phantom. I found that if you really wanted to get good at something, try instructing in it, because for sure you'll be exposed to the wildest assortment of questions imaginable and then some. I flew about 350 sorties and a few more hours in that one-year period. It seems I came home to our little two-BR, one-bath cinder-block house only to eat and sleep. I forgot all about space, shuttles and astronauts, partially due to the current fast-paced action and in part due to the fact no one ever called me back.

Like most instructor pilots, I started out in the familiarization stage — those first few hops that teach the basics of flying this particular airplane, like takeoffs, landings, stalls and loops. The new guys were always spring-loaded-to-the-excited mode, for the Phantom was still the glory airplane of the '60s. The first two hops were the best and went like this: Long brief, longer preflight, IP gets in front, new pilot in back and off we go. Demonstrate everything — supersonic, acrobatics, high angle of attack, all sorts of different landings and so forth. Then, without going back to the ready room, refuel, switch cockpits and go again.

How to fly a Phantom.

```
STEP 5: To enter the aircraft, approach it from the port side and leap lightly
on the access ladder without looking.

STEP 6: Pick yourself up off the deck and carefully extend the access ladder
and climb the steps. ( Note: Try to controle that tense felling in your stomach
and above all don't look down.This is the most important part of the flight
and must be done with precision.) Enter the cokpit in any manner you choose,
except that if at all possible you should try to avoid going in head first.

STEP 7: This is the disentangling step in which the pilot endeavors to sort
out and arrange oxygen hoses, radio leads, shoulder straps, hard hats, gloves,
knee pads, anchor chains, inflated life rafts, accy deucy boards, gum wrappers,
old issues of Playboy, and any other items he finds loose in the cokpit.

STEP 8: Next check stick and throttle positions. If the stick is in your
left hand, and the throttles are in your right hand, you're in the cokpit
backwards. Don!t panic; smile at the plane captain, wave to the bystanders
and slowly rotate your body 180 degrees. Now arrange all switches,buttons
and leavers in the cokpit in a pleasing and eye-catching manner and prepare
to start the engines(if they are installed in the aircraft.)

STEP 9: Upon starting the engines. Advance the throttles smartly to military
power and standby for the plane captains signals. When he begins waving at
you, resist the temptation to wave back. Rapidly rearrange the positions of
all switches, leavers and buttons untill the right combination is found,
wherepuon the plane captain will finally stop waving at you.

STEP 10: When the signal is given to taxi, advance the throttles to the
afterburner detent and roll smoothley over the chocks. Retard the throttles
to military power and try to aoid further use of the after-burners while
taxiing, as this irritates flight deck people.
```

What made it really interesting and sometimes challenging, was that the back seat was chuck full of radar, electronics gear, radios and circuit breakers, but totally devoid of normal pilot things like control stick, throttles, engine instruments and rudders or brakes. In addition, you had to be a contortionist to see out front. Even though I must have had fifty or so of these back-seat hops, I never had a serious problem. By and large, the new guys in front did what they were supposed to do. Every once in awhile though, the breathing rate would elevate, for the Phantom could at times be a user-unfriendly power house of an airplane.

We also trained the RIOs (radar intercept officers or backseaters). The only difference on these hops was, of course, that he stayed in the backseat. These guys had to hustle too, because they only had some one-quarter the flight time of their pilot contemporaries. But what you taught them, they remembered. The RIOs tended to scramble just a little harder than the pilots, so it wasn't long before the aviator savvy tended to equalize.

I don't mean to keep bringing up dumb things I've done, but it's one of those "there I was stories." Had a brand new RIO for his first hop and up we went into a demonstration text-book loop. We got near the vertical with about four Gs, in afterburner and speed bleeding down past 350 knots, when we felt a slight "thump." Well, if you're squeemish about thumps and bumps and funny noises, then you ought not to be flying a Phantom. But, we also smelled a little "something." Smart guy says we ought to abort and go in and land. No emergency, just a "give us priority and no wave off, please," to the tower.

Not to make excuses for my next performance, but our maintenance guys were having lots of problems and we pilots would do all we could to help them out. My part of this contributory effort was to stop the airplane in the warm-up area and while holding the brakes firmly, tap minimum after-burner on one engine and "WHAMMO!" A very big poof, lots of smoke, fire warning lights, tower yelling and my brand new GIBs (guy in the back seat) trying to be a trooper. I quickly unstrapped the ten or so impediments to leaving the airplane in record time, crawled back to my beleaguered back-seat friend who only had three of the ten undone, and helped him off the wing. I noticed then, that the machine was rolling very slowly backwards towards a full drainage ditch and tried to find something to stop it. I thought about my steel-toed boot, but opted to scramble back into the cockpit and activate the air brake, then ran for cover again as the fire crews arrived on scene. Lots of smoke but no fire.

As it turned out, that small "thump" turned out to be the ignition of raw fuel caused by a cracked fuel line. This line is about three inches in diameter, and pumps fuel to the afterburner at about 2,000 psi. So much for trying to help out the maintenance troops and, as so aptly put by a good friend of mine in the fix-it department, "Pete, next time please leave the trouble-shooting to us." He wasn't smiling. The only smart thing I did that day, was not to use my steel-toed boot to stop the airplane!

The Phantom was designed as an interceptor — not very maneuverable, but capable of awesomely high speeds. Doing an intercept at 1.6 IMN (about 1200 mph) was interesting, because the lead times were so far out. A 1.6 versus a 1.6 target meant that you fired your sparrow missile at about fifteen miles and then had to convert to a stern-aspect sidewinder missile shot. But, even with the stick full back in your lap, you could only get about 3-4 Gs at these higher mach numbers. As an aside, most all the intercept training was at night.

The low altitude variant, however, was much faster moving and more demanding and exciting. Because the radar had no "look down" capability, you had to position the airplane at an altitude at which the radar looked up — read as low as possible. A 500-foot intercept at 450 knots on a black over-water Key West night was usually thrilling. We could probably equip an entire squadron with the remains of those F4s that got too low. Compared to high speed and high altitude, the low altitude and high speed combination meant you could pull a very high G loading quite easily. It also took a 110% attention to flying the instruments and not looking out the window.

The good news about Key West weather was that it was generally superb. The bad news though, was that there were lots of shrimp in the nearby waters and hundreds of shrimpers plying their trade, each with a brightly twinkling light. On a clear night, the blending of the stars above and shrimpers below was often an invitation to the unwary for disaster; it was easy to get confused.

Soon after I arrived on board, we lost a jet with two guys in the water one night and I was detailed to go out and fly the same profile. We still weren't convinced that our losses were not caused by engine or airplane problems. Sure enough, it was eerie and it did confirm our gut feeling that "temporary disorientation" or vertigo could have been the cause. We did take the precaution of modifying this particular training flight, by moving its altitude up and reducing the required airspeeds for the newer pilots.

Our squadron, VF-101 (V for heavier than air and F for fighter), had as its logo the red silhouette of a skeleton-like figure with a long-handled and curve-bladed scythe. Appropriately, it was known as the "Grim Reapers." I suppose the name came from the squadron's birth in WWII, the origin of its rich heritage and combat prowess written in the hundreds of Japanese aircraft shot out of the sky by its pilots. So, once again, another patch for my well-worn leather flight jacket was added to join Homicide, the Executioners and a bunch of anteating Aardvarks.

Key West seemed to be a magnet for hurricanes and we had four near misses and one hit in our 1966 season. In each case, we would fly most of our machines up to Oceana near Norfolk and continue our training flights. It also seemed that each time there was a modicum of overactive imbibing at the O'Club.

I recall a happy occasion when one of the near misses was at its closest point of approach to Key West. Happy because we had been busy at the far-north Oceana Naval Air Station, trying to out BS our northern Phantom compatriots at the bar. It was not so happy at the little cinder-block house for my bride and two little

Laurie and Renee

ones, because the power was out, candles on and winds howling. It was yet another in a series of growing chapters about the rigors of being a Navy wife.

One monstrous hurricane was particularly awesome, was targeted for a direct hit on Key West and did in fact score a bullseye. Our families all camped out at our solid squadron spaces at the Naval Air Station. Flying one of the last jets to our Oceana safe haven, we swung south after takeoff and found ourselves above a vast area of low and counterclockwise winds swirling about at 100 mph below us. What a sight! This time we felt a bit contrite leaving the sinking ship and weren't quite so obnoxious at the Oceana O'Club.

The cinder block was a piece-of-work and we felt lucky to find it. I mean, it was tough! We borrowed money from the credit union to buy a Sears air conditioner, Sears curtains for the living room and a small Sears carpet for the linoleum floor. Quarters were not available, but even so, weren't much better and certainly not worth waiting for. Our two girls were weaned on Key West lobster in quart milk cartons and loved the occasional forays to the beach.

1106 Ashby 36-years later ... what stories it could tell!

Vietnam was really starting to affect the Navy and us. Sustained combat for our carriers started in early 1965. The Navy was pulling pilots in from all sources to go through the various training programs, including that of the Grim Reapers. Jet types in particular were grabbed from staffs, shore stations, and schools to fill the need. As a result, we were chuck full of pilots to train in the Phantom. But, for the first time in my career, I experienced something less than hyper-motivation to the task at hand.

First indication was our squadron executive officer, one of the original cadre of Phantom pilots on the east coast, who was scheduled to go to one of the fleet squadrons as XO and then fleet up to CO, as was the custom. He turned it down. Wow! I didn't understand. I'm not casting judgment from the sidelines and maybe I did not have the facts, but I know what I saw and it bothered me from a professional naval officer perspective.

The junior officers were also affected. In our squadron at Key West, we had about thirty instructor pilots, most of whom were extremely talented aviators and all of whom had experienced at least two full deployments in the F4. A lot of talent, to be sure. As with the more senior types, most were married with a growing family. But, in a three-month period, we lost six very-sharp lieutenants to civilian life, read airlines — (Hofstra/Braniff; Gore/Braniff; Mays/Braniff; Atkins/American; Toby/ Eastern; Seaman/TWA). This was not only a major exodus of operational talent when the Navy needed them the most, but a real loss of future leadership, for this particular group had their stuff together!

In retrospect I don't think it was hard to figure out what was going on or why. Jet aviators were bailing out like crazy, even in these early Vietnam years. Where were they going? Why, to the airlines, of course. Whereas Key West was a magnet for hurricanes, the airlines attracted young Naval Aviators like bees to honey. In fact the airlines make out in a time of mobilization and war simply because men and material move largely by air. Also, as the economy heats up, more people have jobs and money to spend and airlines usually ride this crest of relative prosperity. Ergo, the airlines need pilots and what better source than the highly-trained and disciplined carrier-conditioned Naval Aviator? The airlines were really sucking up the talent and the word got around fast.

Instead of eight-month deployments, sixty-days on station, lots of getting shot at by folks on the ground determined to shoot you out of the sky, tough weather and night flying, our lieutenant could join the comparatively undemanding world of the airlines — and be home with mama and the kids most of the time.

But for me, the name of the game was to get into a fleet squadron ASAP. We had been regularly briefed by our intelligence guys on all the growing action and were anxious to test ourselves and join the fray. For every guy that opted for the civilian world, there were a couple ready to go and do what we had been trained for. Politics at this juncture were a zero consideration and I don't recall anyone ever arguing the pros and cons of the national policy, morality or approach to the Vietnam war. There was clearly a war on, we were warriors, so let's go!

Training intensified and the pace for the pilots and maintenance troops became even more pronounced. More airplanes, more instructor pilots and more new guys stepping up to the plate called Phantom. Losses were picking up and hardly a week went by when we didn't get word about a buddy who was lost. Many shore-based

A rare night out!

pilots found themselves flying combat off a carrier in the South China Sea six-months after checking into our training squadron. While we did the best with what we had, it became apparent early-on that one prime ingredient was missing — air-combat maneuvering or ACM.

Whereas many would construe carrier landings as the epitome of Naval Aviation in terms of skill required and stress levels, ACM is the epitome of all aviation period. It is the most difficult to learn, the most demanding mentally and physiologically and the most fun you'll ever have outside your homestead. Problem was, we were sending new guys to the fray with only what they could glean from their own backgrounds or in their fleet squadrons. Compounding this lack of air-to-air training, was the fact that the Vietnamese had a pretty potent air force, some capable pilots and highly maneuverable airplanes.

By definition, ACM expressly implies high Gs, high angle-of-attack and slow-speed maneuvering. Whereas the Phantom was a great and classy interceptor, it was a lousy classic fighter. Slow it down, lay on a high angle of attack and you had your hands full, for it just was not designed for these machinations. As we started to teach the tactics gleaned from our gunfighter compatriots, the F8 Crusader (which had real guns as well as rear-aspect missiles), we started piling up ACM-related losses at a fast rate. Most of these accidents were of the stall-spin variety wherein the airplane would do what it wanted and not what you told it to do. The key was angle of attack. High angle of attacks were accompanied, as is true in most swept-wing airplanes, with all sorts of shakes and rattles and funny moves of the airplane. In addition, the Phantom wing tips would literally pump up and down a foot or so, just like an airliner, except at the staccato speed of a machine gun.

The instructors that taught in the ACM phase had precious little dog-fighting experience in general and practically none in the Phantom. Most were ex-Demon drivers who had been more interceptor pilots than "shoot-'em-down-with-guns" types. Furthermore, there was a pronounced lack of guidance or tactics coming from anywhere, so it was learn by doing. Compounding all this was the proclivity of the high command to shut down ACM when the community would have an accident. Oftentimes, the bar talk and ready-room rhetoric overtook any semblance of reality in the air. I was fortunate, however, to get in on the ground floor of this effort.

A typical ACM training hop went something like this: Brief for at least one-hour, fly the mission for forty minutes and debrief for an hour. All told, it would take a solid four hours to fly one forty-minute hop. It was not unusual to fly three of these in one day, Saturday, Sundays and holidays included. It was a good instructor who could take a new RIO in his back seat (they needed training too), be the lead instructor for up to four jets and keep detailed notes on exactly who did what and when. The hops always ended with a snappy 400-knot, reasonably-high-G break to a simulated carrier landing (always). This was partially to satisfy our own training standards, but also for the eternal kibitzers hanging out the ready room windows in the nearby hangar, who were quick to critique anything less than a Blue Angel performance.

My collateral job was kind of mundane, at least at the time. As a junior lieutenant commander, I was the NATOPS officer, which loosely translated, meant we were the drivers in standardizing and tweaking the standard operations of the Phantom community. It sounds grander than it really was, but nonetheless, it was a new effort by the aviation community to more tightly govern itself. It was indeed, a transition from the real "kick the tire, light the fire, brief on guard channel, I can fly anything" era to one of more complex and expensive airplanes and pilots that the Navy could ill afford to lose. The pilot's handbook evolved in the case of the Phantom from a simple one-half-inch booklet to three very-thick volumes over the next couple of decades. In retrospect, it was the greatest philosophical step forward made in Naval Aviation and resulted in a steady increase in our level of professionalism and safety.

After one demanding and busy year, I got a call from the people pushers in Washington saying in effect, it's time to earn your keep. So off we went, Carolyn, our two small ones along with a new puppy called Cricket to the Naval Air Station, Oceana, Virginia, the VF-74 Bedevilers and the first of three tours on Forrestal.

EPILOGUE

- The training squadron for Phantoms, the **VF-101 Grim Reapers** (skeleton with a scythe), continues its legacy of producing the best fighter crews in the world in the Phantom follow-on, the swing-wing F-14 Tomcat.

- **Cricket** beat the odds for a small dachshund and lived to the ripe old age of seventeen.

- The **pilots and RIOs** we trained for the fleet during that year, did a great and courageous job under mostly tough conditions flying from the carriers, including Vietnam.

- **Frenchy Ducharme**, bless his soul, went off to Vietnam waters and, flying off the carrier Roosevelt, was killed in an operational accident.

- **Bob Gilbert**, my friend the assistant maintenance officer, served with great distinction in many different commands, and is a microcosm of why Naval Aviation prospered under its aegis of combat readiness. Bob passed away not long ago with a legacy few can match.

- The **six lieutenants** who left the Grim Reapers for civilian life in 1966, are most likely senior airline captains and proud of the role they played in their active duty years in the Navy's fighter communities. Thanks guys!

- The **cinder-block house** hasn't changed. What stories it could tell!

COMBAT

One tumultuous year with the VF-74 "Bedevilers", five days of Vietnam combat, the Forrestal fire and sadness.

It was a gorgeous morning in the Gulf of Tonkin that summer of 1967, when we felt and heard a reverberating "thump" throughout the ship. Glancing up at the TV monitor in our ready room well forward in the ship under the bow catapults, we could see a rising fireball of smoke and flame — in stark black and white. The "clang, clang, clang" of the general quarters alarm was almost immediate. The aircraft carrier U.S.S. *Forrestal*, which was already alive and vibrant on this, her fifth-combat day, took on a new urgency — that of survival. It would hereafter be known throughout the world as the "Forrestal Fire."

Walking out to the starboard-bow catwalk area, a few of us watched in disbelief as our proud ship and airwing started going up in flames as bomb after bomb exploded on the flight deck aft. Looking down the flight deck at eye level, we could spot a few figures running towards the conflagration and then, as more bombs went off, there were none.

My heart was beating and tears welled up, for this could not be happening to us. During that first few minutes, many proud and dedicated sailors died with more to follow in the hours to come. My squadron, the VF-74 "Bedevilers," was to lose 42 men, most of whom were our night-maintenance personnel who had worked the 12-hour night shift on our twelve Phantoms.

They had the misfortune to have been berthed in a large compartment just below the after part of the flight deck and simply never had a chance. We lost a lot of fine Americans in several blinks of an eye.

Several months before, I had been given my choice of squadrons to go to and had simply told my Washington detailer to "get me any one deploying to Vietnam." It so happened the next deployer was an east coast ship and airwing, the Forrestal and Airwing 17, both Norfolk-based. Forrestal would be one of the first east coast carriers to sail to Vietnam, so we had the best and most of everything.

To begin with, VF-74 had almost new airplanes, not more than a couple-of-years old and all the parts we needed. We also had talent on top of talent. Not only were the maintenance folks top-notch and experienced, but 50% of our flight crews had had previous Phantom tours. As a still-junior lieutenant commander, I joined forces with seven others of the same rank. Top heavy, but a good group in that early year of Vietnam.

Our skipper at about the time I joined the squadron was Commander Hal Wellman, a warrior in the truest sense, a fine fighter pilot and exceptional leader. Our XO, with the same qualities, was Tom Wimberly. Our two-dozen pilots and RIOs and 220 enlisted maintenance personnel who maintained our twelve F4s were motivated, hard working and proud of doing the tough job for their country and Navy.

The pilots and RIOs of VF-74 ... What incredible talent and dedication! CO Hal Wellman front row third from right and XO Tommy C. Wimberly fifth from right. My RIO, Skip, on the wing just under the USS.

We spent the better part of six months at sea off Norfolk and in the Puerto Rico operating areas perfecting tactics and correcting mistakes. By "we," I mean the ship, the airwing, the squadron and the embarked staff with a rear admiral in charge of the ten or so ships in our task group. The more we sharpened our skills, the more intense the motivation and the better we felt about getting over there and joining the fray.

We did, of course, get a day-by-day and blow-by-blow account of the action in Vietnam. It wasn't a happy picture for we were losing a bunch of aircraft and people. The Oriskany had had a major fire with heavy loss of life a year before and more recently had lost eleven airplanes in one five-week combat line period. The war was wide open; there were few sanctions. The Rules of Engagement (ROE) were very liberal and figuratively read, "hit and hit hard and hit again." Navy carrier air was being used in deadly earnest.

Our little family plus Cricket had driven north in our Chrysler Newport and arranged to rent a small house in a nice section of Virginia Beach with one bathroom that worked most of the time, a large, unruly yard and gravel driveway leading to a one-car carport. Our landlords were my sister and brother-in-law, so we didn't complain when the john gave up.

Carolyn tending the home front in 1967.

Our shipboard training focused in three areas: ACM, alpha strikes and night work. ACM (dog fighting) was tough, as it always is aboard ship, simply because fuel usage is extremely high and it's difficult to work the standard cyclic-flight operations. Furthermore, the air-to-air "dog fight" practice we did do was flawed, because ACM at that time meant "slow down and work the vertical." With the high wing-loading of the Phantom, this is a contradiction in terms. Our A4 and A6 brethren would eat us alive when we did that. It took a couple more years for the F4 guys to learn to "keep the mach up" and embody the fighter maxim that "speed is life." Slow down in the Phantom and the only thing you can outfight is another Phantom. Complicating the ACM issues, was a high command (and a previous CO) that was increasingly concerned about losses due to training in ACM and which was lukewarm as to the need for realistic training in this area.

We practiced a bunch of alpha strikes, loosely defined as a gaggle of about 40-plus aircraft, the power of which was concentrated onto one target complex. It went like this: Eight Phantoms as flak suppressors, eight more as combat air patrol (CAP) for protection from other fighters, at least two KA3 twin-engine tankers, two EA6B electronic jammers, eight A6s with 22, 500-pound bombs each, fourteen A4s with 6, 500 pounders, two E2C radar controllers and a couple of search and rescue helos prepositioned should anyone go down. Launch of this group would be in total electronic silence, refuel overhead, join up and head for the beach at 15,000 feet. All the Phantoms carried two-to-four Sidewinder heat-seeking missiles and two forward-firing Sparrows in addition to the air-to-ground ordnance, which was usually 24, 5-inch high-velocity rockets carried in six pods.

By far and away, the toughest part of any attack mission is finding the target. As flak suppressors, our job was to light afterburners about 20 miles from the target, pull out ahead of the attack group, start dispensing chaff, roll in on the target and launch our rockets in a ripple mode at anything that fired on us (real easy to see once they start firing) or on the prebriefed anti-aircraft or missile sites. The idea was that some 200 rockets would be fired about the same time the attack guys were rolling in and that therefore, the eyeballs and heads of the gunners would be deep inside foxholes protecting their exteriors vice aiming and shooting at our guys. Sometimes there was a small sinking feeling in the lead flak suppressor when, at five miles and 500 knots, the target was not in sight. Anyway, it usually worked out and forty machines would converge on one target and blow it all to pieces.

Typical Navy fighter pilot at the ten-year mark.

The run-in altitude for these attack missions was interesting, because over the years, it started out low, went high, came down again and ended up medium. Initially, with our A4s, the maximum altitude was about 15 grand simply because the little machine couldn't go much higher, especially with bombs and one or two fuel tanks. In our case the latest tactics decreed we should go in high but not below 3,000 feet, because of small arms and 37MM fire. And, we could only make one run on the target. In other words, run-in, drop your load and "haul ass."

Surface-to-air missiles were a problem, but not overwhelmingly so. To begin with, our intelligence guys knew almost exactly where most of the SAMs were, so our ingress route would be planned accordingly. To counter these telephone-pole sized, radar-guided missiles, we had state-of-the-art electronic spoofers in a 100-pound black box behind the RIO, a box that enclosed some of the most sophisticated electronic wizardry our nation's technical folks could produce. They worked too. We also had radar detectors that would tell us when a missile, fire control or aircraft radar was locked on to us. When inbound, it was not atypical to have simultaneous warnings for a search radar, a SAM acquisition radar, multiple AAA sites and a SAM launch signal. It was like a Christmas tree, but embellished by all sorts of warbles, bleeps and beeps!

Bottom line is that by the time we set sail for the combat zone, we were ready. We had the best flying machines in the world, we were well trained, had a great ship, a squared-away staff and a talented and highly motivated team of aviators. Charge!

From Puerto Rico, it was thirty days at 18 knots getting from here to there. Included was a brief stop in Rio de Janeiro to assimilate the cultural aspects of this city down south, my second such visit.

This long voyage was characterized by practically no flying, but lots of briefings and ground training. My squadron, the VF-74 "Bedevilers," had the best ready room and officer berthing on the ship; all the way forward and high in the ship under the flight deck. We spent most of each day in lectures, fine-tuning our airplanes, pouring over photos in the intelligence complex and a few make-work exercises. The evening ready room movie was always followed by a mind-stimulating lecture on the intricacies of the Mark 12 bomb fuse, the sparrow missile or the asymptotic feature of our autopilot. The icing was on the cake.

The ship's library had a good many books on the history of this messed up area we were about to throw ourselves at. Two I remember well: *A Road Without End* by Bernard Fall and *The Fall of Dienbienphu*, the sad chronicle of the last stand of the French up North Vietnam way. Both described the misery and frustration of four decades of war. Because it was a region of immense natural wealth, it had been a target of colonial spheres of influence by first the French, then the Japanese, then the French again. Our interests were, of course, altruistic (stop communism) vice economic and we all understood this. But it was on this voyage, that I began to have silent glimmers of private doubts as to why we were there. This was, of course, far overshadowed with the spice, the excitement and challenge of combat. Once again, we were warriors, our country said go and we were ready.

Our first day on the line was spent in pouring-down rain, the only ones getting airborne being the helo and a couple of weather-reccee aircraft. The second day I flew my first "combat" hop chasing an RA5C photo "Vigilante" half-way around North Vietnam at the speed of heat and 5,000 feet. I never did figure out how we were supposed to protect them, as it was all we could do to not lose him in the terrain below. Day three, we did some alpha strikes against some nondescript target, more practice than for real as no one bothered to shoot at us. Our squadron, of course, was at the same time, flying a great deal of combat air patrol (CAP) north of the ships. We were busy with the euphoria of finally getting into action.

My superb RIO, Skip Holt, manning up on Forrestal's flight deck.

Our fifth day was the sad one. How sad it was! For that was the day our ship blew up and took 134 of our incredibly brave shipmates with her.

It all started with preparations for a large alpha strike against some tough targets, the first of three that day. I was to be one of the flak suppressors on the second and was really pumped up in anticipation of a "real" combat mission. Some of our F4s that first launch were loaded with 5-inch rockets and for some reason, one of the rockets went off while in the packed stern area full of fully loaded and armed aircraft. It went about 140-feet across the deck and hit another A4 in its belly fuel tank. Even though the rocket did not arm and explode, it did ignite the 300 or so gallons of JP5 fuel in the A4's external fuel tank.

Normally, this type of fuel-fed fire could have been handled in a heartbeat, but this time the cards were stacked against us. Because we were short of iron bombs, we were carrying the old M117 1,000 pound bomb — a Korean War vintage, very thin-skinned, general-purpose bomb. And because they were old and thin-skinned, they were very susceptible to heat. In just a very few minutes, just as the flight deck fire fighters were arriving to fight this then-localized fire, the first of several M117's exploded. Men rushing to the scene were literally scythed down, fire mains were cut, the fire spread and more bombs, rockets and missiles went high order. Flames and smoke towered into the clear sky. What a sad sight!

While I was safely in the ready room far forward, one of our pilots, Commander Tom Wimberly, was spotted aft in the midst of the exploding bombs and wrote the following:

Aircraft loaded with fuel were exploding: "ka-whomf" — a kind of nice sound of mayhem with soft edges. When the first bomb went — and they went high order, just as if they had been detonated by a fuse — it was a sharp, jarring dynamic force that came through the flight deck hard enough to jar your teeth. WHAM! I was calm until the first bomb exploded. Then my knees began to shake.

    The inferno below decks was as bad. The general quarters alarm had sounded almost immediately, calling all hands to their battle stations. Sleeping men just below the flight deck aft struggled into clothes so as to have the ship buttoned up and ready to fight within the five-minute time limit. Most of the loss of life was in these jam-packed berthing spaces (120 men to a compartment.) Those that moved at the first "clang" of the alarm lived. Those who tarried were less fortunate.

    Sadly, damage control and fire fighting as we know it today was a three on a scale of ten. In spite of awesome bravery by lots of folks, there were just too many who didn't have the knowledge of what needed to be done. The cream of the topside fire-fighting talent was gone with the first few exploding bombs, and a kind of void existed, at least for a few minutes. A couple of us donned oxygen breathing apparatus (OBAs) and headed into the dense smoke aft below the flight deck where we knew our maintenance troops were berthed. It was an incredible feeling, for you could not see your hand in front of your face, so dark and thick was the smoke. As an aside, we had never used an OBA and felt claustrophobic and had difficulty breathing. We spent many hours in those compartments trying to do something that would make a difference. It was a noble but futile effort that consisted mostly of dragging bodies out of the hell.

```
TO:   Lcdr R. J. KOCH, USN                              31 July 1967

FR:   Lcdr P. B. BOOTH, USN

      Noteworthy performance of duty of Lt T. S. TREANOR, USN

1.  Following the large explosions, Lt TREANOR was observed on the flight
deck aft actively directing and fighting the numerous fires. He took
charge of several fire fighting details and saw to the relief of his men,
their safety and that adequate materials were available to fight the fires.
On one occasion he was noted to be personally down-loading a live Side-
winder missile off an F-4 that was burning within 5 feet of himself. He
and his crew then jettisoned the missile over the port side. Lt TREANOR
remained at his post until all active fires were out on the flight deck.
At which time he directed his attention to combating the fires beneath
the flight deck. He did this by donning an OBA and proceeding to the O3
level, portside, frame 207 via an access ladder and bomb crater. Asses-
sing the damage inboard and in thick smoke he called for a hose and
directed water into the spaces.

2.  Lt TREANOR responded to no particular call other than his own sense
of duty. He aggressively filled a leadership void when it was sorely
needed and, in my opinion, materially contributed to the morale and
effectiveness of his men.

                                          Very respectfully,


                                          P. B. BOOTH
```

My squadron mate, Tom Treanor, was typical of hundreds of heroes on that sad day.

Thus the great ship Forrestal, tall plumes of black and acrid smoke pouring from her quarter, floated on a beautifully calm and glorious Gulf of Tonkin day, her combat days for the time, at an end.

Photos taken by author near VF-74 ready room, portside forward.

We limped back to the Phillipines from whence we had departed only days before, with ten huge holes in our flight deck; the acrid stench of spent fires and death permeated every pore of the great ship Forrestal. Incredibly, had it been necessary, the big carrier could have repaired itself on station enough to have continued reduced combat operations.

If a poll had been taken then as to who in the airwing wanted a fast return to combat ops, it would have been 97% in favor of so doing. Indeed, many of our A4 light-attack pilots were literally heloed to other carriers nearby and were in the thick of it again before we ever reached Cubi Point. My acquaintance, John McCain, later to be a U.S. Senator, was one of them. But the system back in Washington said nix to any other transfers and dictated that the airwing would remain intact for its long journey back to Norfolk and in-depth repairs.

That evening, at the Cubi Point O'Club, was kind of a blur — partly drink and with a good dose of sad emotion for the loss of so many shipmates. Somehow, four of us in VF-74, talked our skipper into letting us bum a hop back to the states rather than ride the ship back. So, early the next morning, with the barest of packed bags, a hurried farewell to our shipmates and still in our rumpled sea-going, wash-khaki uniform, we talked a station pilot into taking us to nearby Clark AFB and "pot luck" back to the states by bumming a ride on anything we could get. Getting off the venerable "Bugsmasher," we couldn't help but notice a big 707 transport with "United States of America" emblazoned on its side.

The very officious Marine major — an aide — said, "No way" to our request to ride back to Washington with him. The airplane, at the disposal of the Commandant of the Marine Corps following an inspection trip to his troops in country, was "not for those not in the official party." We stood there somewhat forlornly as the General and a more senior aide — a full colonel — walked up. Ignoring the red-faced major, we talked to the colonel, who whispered to the general, who came over, shook our hands and practically carried us onto the big silver and blue airplane! Can you believe it — before our squadron mates had breakfast on Forrestal, we were airborne, headed non-stop to Hawaii and then another non-stopper to Washington, D.C.! And what a flight it was.

The Commandant of course, wanted to know all about Forrestal and was a phenomenally interested and interesting person. We had prime steak done to order, excellent wine, blankets and some well-deserved snoozes. I kept pinching myself to make sure it was all true. It was.

On the Hawaii to Washington leg, I went up front and sat in the cockpit's right seat beside the aircraft commander, a full Air Force colonel. What a sight it was. Sun coming up in the east, this magnificent flying machine aviating in full autopilot at 500 knots in clear air and the colonel telling me all about his airplane.

The timing of all this was prophetic, for lots of Naval Aviators were bailing out to go fly for the rapidly expanding (due to the war) airline industry. I doubt if too many guys had not thought about it, at least in private and/or casually. No night cat shots, no getting shot at, no ten-month deployments, home with mama and a paycheck sizably larger than a lieutenants', were all tangible enticements. I had thought about it on occasion, albeit not seriously. But to my eternal gratification to that Marine colonel, an understanding Marine four-star and an Air Force transport colonel who let me sit in the right front seat of his airplane, this flight convinced me that sitting for 80-hours each month in such a position, year after year, would have been a giant mistake in my case, the more material aspects notwithstanding.

After three-hours with the colonel up front, we had covered the airplane systems (simple), flying qualities (like a brick with wings) and were soon talking about the Boy Scout endeavors of the colonel's two boys. I didn't even put the three hours in my logbook.

Arriving in Washington, still in our rumpled khakis, we thanked the general, his colonel and the major (he was just doing his job), and went directly to the Navy's Bureau of Naval Personnel with the objective of getting back into combat ASAP. Fat chance. The word was out not to even talk to us about transferring. So, I went to three places: The first was to the guy that handled Navy pilot exchanges with the Air Force. He offered me a slot with an F-100 outfit transitioning to F-111As which would "be in-country in eight-months." The second was to the riverine warfare representative, a group that drove boats up rivers and flew something I had never heard of called the OV-10 and who needed warm bodies now. The third was to an obscure office in downtown Washington (still in khakis), a front for recruiting pilots for an outfit called Air America — the CIA's clandestine air force in Vietnam.

Armed with these options — all in the space of five hours — I went back to my detailers, whom, I suppose, felt sorry for me, and offered me a slot in an already top-heavy squadron called the VF-102 Diamondbacks soon to deploy to Vietnam on the carrier America.

EPILOGUE

On the occasion of the 25th anniversary of the Forrestal fire at a ceremony in Pensacola, I wrote the following which was inscribed onto a bronze plaque:

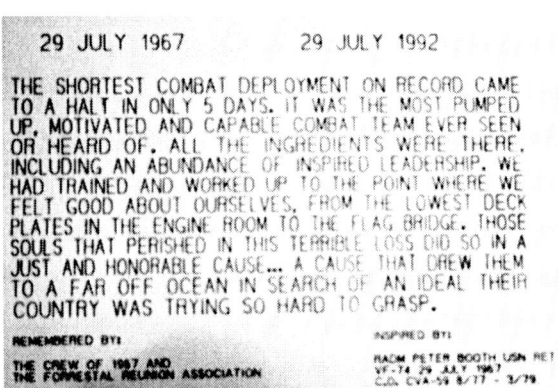

DIAMONDBACKS

The Diamondback snake was deadly; so too were its sea-based namesakes, twelve-sleek jets and 250 of our nation's best and brightest. This, a two-year snapshot of these everyday heroes during some tough times around and over Vietnam.

"Burner" Bill Beardsley was my wingman. The good news was that he was in a perfect combat spread — about a mile or so abeam. The bad news was that it was dark and we were over the dead center of Vietnam at 10,000 feet looking for targets of opportunity in the countryside below. But the really bad news was that Burner had his external lights on bright and flashing, including the strobes! It was just another uneventful mission over Vietnam in that summer of 1968.

We had gone through an identical training and build-up regimen as we had with VF-74 and the Forrestal the preceding year. What an unbelievable team we had — a great and talented squadron, an equally combat-ready, 85-airplane airwing, the most awesome ship with the best leadership I've ever seen, and even a fine admiral's staff. The blackness of the Vietnam hole had yet to sink in on the American people, and amongst our ilk, there was only the occasional whisper of discontent. We were warriors, we were trained to do the military will of our nation's leaders and we were the epitome of combat readiness.

True Faith and Allegiance

Roger Mehle, a WWII fighter pilot and local rear admiral, came down to wish us well as we flew out to the U.S.S *America* underway off Norfolk and eventual combat early in 1968. We had a good feeling about ourselves and stood just a little taller when the admiral told us to "give 'em hell."

Our squadron, the VF-102 Diamondbacks, had beautiful, brand-new F4J Phantoms right out of the St. Louis factory. The systems all worked, and importantly, it had a new-type doppler radar that allowed us to look down and still pick up airborne targets. I was maintenance officer and what a nice deal it was to have shiny-new airplanes that wouldn't break when you looked at them. I mean real quality and job-one from the folks at McDonnell up in St. Louis.

On our training workups, we spent lots of time at sea on the super-carrier America, flew more at night than in the day, dropped hundreds of bombs and rockets, practiced several-dozen, 30-airplane Alpha strikes and filled in with the perpetual combat air patrol.

The airwing was by far and away the most sophisticated wing in the Navy — E2C early warning machines which could detect incoming aircraft an order-of-magnitude better than its predecessor, A7E light-attack aircraft that could fly faster than 300 knots with a normal bomb load (12, 500-pound bombs) and hit with awesome accuracy and the latest version of the super-sophisticated EA6B electronic jammer. Plus, we had all the latest in black-box wizardry to thwart the growing missile arsenal of the North Vietnamese.

Our Phantoms were really slick airplanes. They were about a thousand-pounds heavier than our early models back in 1961, but crammed with the latest state-of-the-art gadgetry including automatic throttles (euphemistically called "approach power compensator system," don't you love it!), leading-edge droops in the stabilator to help the airplane rotate quicker on cat shots, electronics on top of electronics, drooped ailerons to fly slower on approach, a revolutionary radar and alas, the capability to land hands off on the carrier!

I've been scared a few times coming back to land on board ship, but none gets the heart rate up more than a fully-automatic (mode I) night-carrier landing to a trap totally untouched by either hand. It went like this: While hundreds of miles from the ship, you engaged the autopilot and "coupled" the airplane to an airborne E2C or ship system. That system then flew the airplane like a drone. All you had to do was drop the gear, flaps and hook and hit a few buttons. It's the wierdest flying I've ever done. There you are, in an absolute black hole at 1,200 feet and ten-miles astern of the ship with the stick pumping furiously, the rudders pulsating and both throttles jumping to and fro! What makes most guys not like the system, is that for the average carrier pilot, it flies a better carrier pass than he can. This was true at least most of the time and this little caveat is what got the heart rate on the occasional high end. More later.

Our euphoria for the war was at a high warble for we were bombing everything in sight including some targets with minimal military value. When we were not bombing or doing "night reccee" over the beach, we were providing air cover for the ship in the Gulf of Tonkin in the direction of Haiphong. These

VF-102 pilots and RIOs on flight deck of USS America. Skipper Ted Fellowes and XO John Florence front and center surrounded by two dozen of the best of the best - unseen are our 220 maintenance troops. Heroes all!

CAP hops were a study in contrast, for we would sit in air-conditioned comfort at 20,000 feet, 25-or-so miles from Haiphong harbor, get refueled a couple of times to keep our fuel nearly full (combat package) and watch all the foreign ships heading in to unload their war-making wares into North Vietnam. You didn't have to be a Ph.D. to realize that the next night we'd be trying to ferret out these same supplies wending their way southward by bicycle and WBLC (water-borne logistic craft — really sampams).

One day on our first line period, we lost our skipper, Commander Gene Wilbur and his RIO, Lieutenant Bernie Rupinski. His wingman, Lieutenant Emory Brown, saw the MIG close behind Gene and called for his leader to "break hard right," but got no response. Emory fired a sparrow missile at the homeward-bound enemy, but to no avail. Bernie, we think, went down with the airplane and Gene became a long-term POW. Sad day, for both fliers were respected and liked within the squadron.

That first line period we flew mostly at night. In fact, our normal flight operations were from 1800-0600, for 40-straight days. We really got comfortable around the boat at night, which is a statement few naval aviators get a chance to make. Usually returning to the ship at night generates at least an order of magnitude increase in resting pulse rate (defined as 70 to 140).

A typical-night hop for us had one machine loaded with a bunch of magnesium flares in pods (18 total) and the other with 6, 500-pound bombs. No matter what our mission, we always carried a minimum of two heat-seeking sidewinders and two radar-guided sparrow missiles. We would launch, take on 3000 pounds of fuel from one of our friendly airborne tankers, go feet dry over the beach and "look for targets of opportunity." When the weather was good, we could usually make out bends in the rivers or a bridge on our radar.

Out would go a covey of flares at about 5,000 feet and #2 would lay some bombs at whatever WBLCs or bridge he could see. Invariably, there would be a visual snake or two of colorful 37mm tracer fire. Usually, the only thing that could get us into trouble was leaving our external lights on!

Later on in that deployment, I recall a similar mission in which the weather was bad and we essentially dropped our loads in some obscure river, because we couldn't see anything and it was a "no-no" to bring live ordnance back aboard. It was my second over-the-beach flight that night, I was tired, wanted to hit the sack, but as was de riguer, had to debrief with the intelligence guys. I told him, "We didn't hit anything."

"You had to hit something," says the staff guy. I stood firm. A staff commander came in and we went through the same exercise. Though I didn't acquiesce, I'll opine that the report went in "Destroyed 17 WBLCs last seen exploding and burning." The PR aspects of the war were becoming a driving force, or so it seemed to some us guys on the deck plates.

We had a light-attack skipper who seemed to always get his name in the daily public relations drivel that went out from the ship. "Jack E. Russ, 39, Orange Park, Florida," made the news quite often and we all thought it kind of funny. Jack though was a good guy and, like all of us, just doing his thing the best he knew how.

Just prior to trap. Note tail hook down, sidewinder and sparrow missiles and empty 600-gallon center-line tank.

One day my Dad came out to see "his boys" and his oldest son. Dad was a three-star admiral and head of the Atlantic Fleet carriers and airplanes and was on an inspection trip to see his two carriers in action off Vietnam. I was kind of sensitive about my Dad because of his position and mine (lowly LCDR). Earlier in our training in the Puerto Rico area, I had been detailed to fly him in one of our F4s from Oceana to the ship — a 1,200 mile trip. We had been a little late getting off and, in order to make our scheduled recovery time at the ship, had done the last 200 miles supersonic. We made a fast letdown, smoked into the break at 400 knots, frantically cleared the fog from the windscreen rolling into the groove (I'd forgotten to put the heat up) and barely snagged the last arresting wire. Dad thought it was all great and I was pretty proud of him too.

True Faith and Allegiance

At any rate, we had a nice visit, dinner, movie, et al. and at 0100 I launched into a black Gulf of Tonkin night to do my thing. Dad awoke at whatever hour admirals wake up and asked if I had slept good? I loved it!

One night my good friend and fellow-maintenance officer in our sister squadron, VF-33, Lieutenant Commander Zeke Burns, was shot down (we were airborne nearby) by a SAM (surface to air missile) and he and his pilot shelled out. They were about 30-miles inland so a SAR rescue helo was dispatched to attempt a pickup. There then ensued one of naval aviation's incredible stories of survival, guts and determination on the part of a lot of folks that night, because the area that Zeke landed in was infested with Vietnamese troops. Using a handheld radio, they vectored in the pilot of the rescue helo, Lieutenant Clyde Lassen. Braving gunfire from all directions, Zeke and his pilot were picked up and deposited on a destroyer with but five-minutes of fuel left in the rescue helo. Clyde's Medal of Honor citation is an awesome litany of five guys in a rickety old helo on an overland trip, low on fuel and hundreds of folks on the ground trying to kill them. It was just another chapter in the heroism repeated thousands of times each day in this eight-year war. As those who knew him would expect, Zeke was in the air the next day!

Our new skipper was a seasoned fighter pilot named Ted Fellowes. Ted was probably the most engaging and likeable person I've known. He also had made two combat tours flying the F8 Crusader and his brother (a classmate of mine), had been shot down and was presumed to be a POW. My recollection — right or wrong —was that Ted's prime objective was to get all of us and our airplanes back to Oceana in "one piece."

The Diamondbacks were blessed with seven, spring-loaded-to-the-go-position lieutenant commanders in addition to the CO and XO, both full commanders. Day by day and night by night we did our best in the air and about the ship. Hard work, good spirits, teamwork and honest leadership were common traits. We were pros and good at our chosen profession and proud of it. But, we had glimmers of disappointment in the way the war was being fought. We wanted to go north; we wanted to hit the ships in Haiphong harbor; we wanted to go into the Laos sanctuaries just 100-miles to the west. The bosses would have none of it and even if they had wanted to, it would have made no difference, for unbeknownst to us, the war was being minutely manipulated out of a big white house at 1600 Pennsylvania Avenue in Washington, D.C. by an unknown covey of gratuitous advisors and a political president in way over his head.

The politics of the war in our case in that summer of 1968, dictated that we were prohibited from attacking the enemy's underbelly up north. Earlier and later in the war, the action in the north in and around Hanoi was far more intense than we were to experience simply because the northern targets were more lucrative and therefore more heavily defended with gobs of Soviet-supplied AAA and SAMs. But, even in our case, the available targets were subject to micro manipulations from inside the Washington beltway. The list of allowable targets was heavily skewed to the restrictive side of the ledger.

Diamondbacks

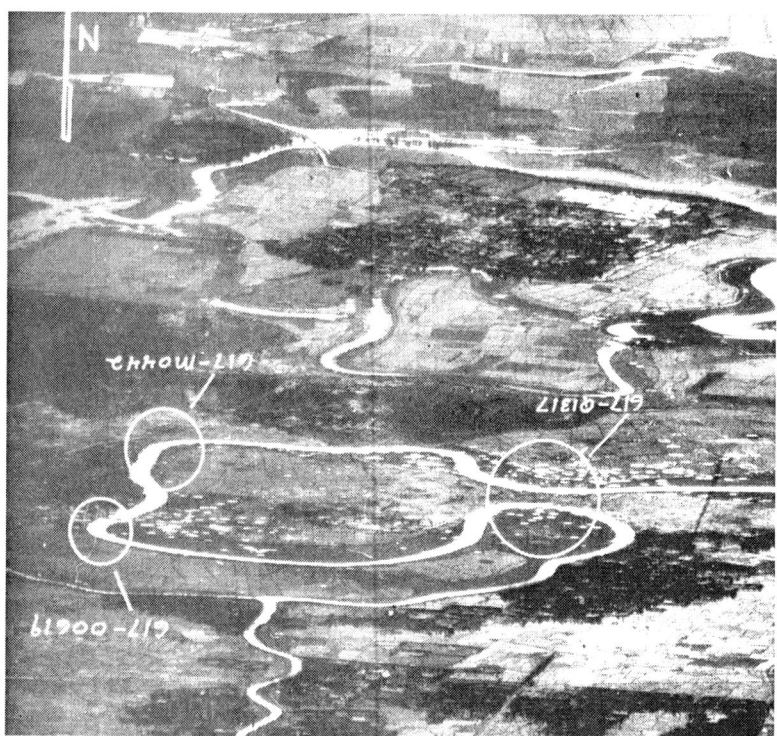

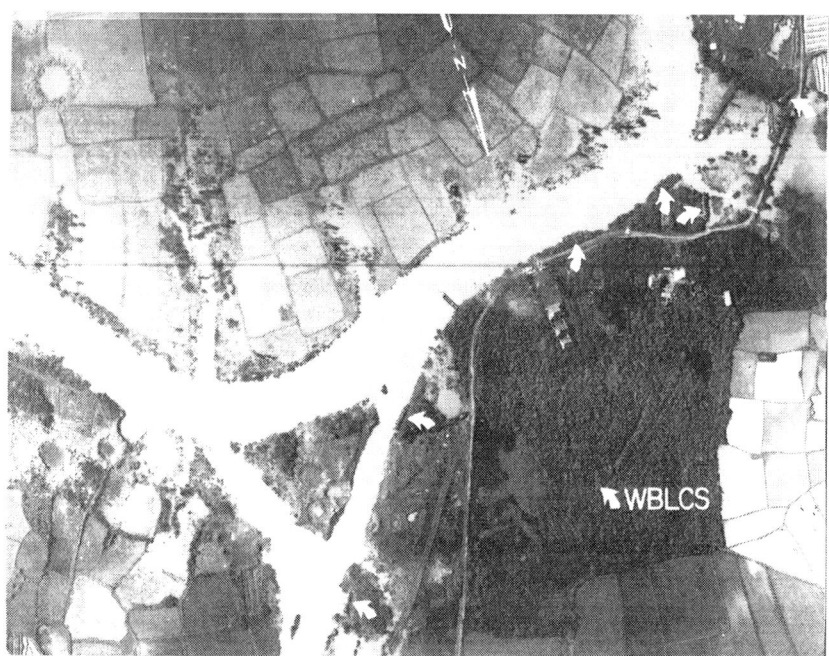

Vietnam targets. Top is oblique view looking north and bottom a closeup of WBLCs — waterborne logistics craft — plus lots of bomb craters.

Not long after our second line period, I awoke in my room in a delightful Kowloon hotel to the sight of the USS *America*, 85 airplanes and 5,500 guys anchoring in the harbor below. Beside me was a good-looking lady named Carolyn whom I had met a few years before in Memphis, Tennessee. She was also the mother of our two daughters. I had flown a machine at the end of our second line period around midnight into the Phillipines and met her there for a fun seven-day respite, thanks to a considerate skipper and parents of mine that chipped in $500 for the trip. We didn't talk about the war, ships or airplanes. Needless to add, everyone was kind of envious, because four months into an eight-month deployment starts to wear thin.

Back in the saddle of a far-off war, I had a real scare one night after a 0200 catapult shot with a full load of flares. It was one of those hurry-up evolutions and the ordnance was loaded after we manned up. Well, for some reason, four flares in one pod weren't locked in and on launching from number-one cat on the bow on a particularly dark night, I noticed an eerie glow in the rear-view mirrors. What happened was that the flares had stayed put in accordance with some law of inertia when the catapult took us from 0 to 160 knots in 2.3 seconds, and of course, ignited like they were supposed to. From 5,000 feet overhead, it looked as if the entire forward part of the ship was on fire! The carrier Oriskany had had a terrible flare-fed fire a couple of years before, so we all knew the extreme danger of one flare on a flight deck full of bombs, rockets and fuel. And, the haunted personal memories of the Forrestal fire one-year prior, added to my brain's confusion. The America's problem was compounded by the combination of 30 knots of wind over the deck and deployed flare parachutes dragging the flares aft. This heart-stopping story had a happy ending because a couple of average young-American sailors grabbed the parachutes and literally hurled the burning infernos over the side and into the sea, where even underwater, they continued to burn. More heroes!

We had about 150 aviators aboard America and 5,300 others, all, I suppose, in a support role. Cooks, fuelers, engineers, clerks, ordnance handlers, airplane fixers, dentists, et al. made the ship go. When you look back on our country in that summer of 1968, it was starting to be a turbulent mosaic of drugs, draft dodgers, massive discontent, racial problems and so on. But on the great ship America, even though it wasn't all peaches and cream, it worked. Our guys did their job twelve-hours a day, seven-days a week, far from home and loved ones, in austere living conditions and for an hourly rate of pay far less than the minimum federal standards. Many did it two and three times in a row before going back home or to shore duty. What great people they were, this team of 5,500, from all parts of the country, young and old, various ethnic and religious and economic backgrounds and how grateful am I for their enormous sacrifice and contributions!

One thing good about being on a carrier, is that the mail comes most everyday. In our case, we had a small, twin-engined airplane for mail and logistics and its nickname, appropriately, was "Miss America." And, when Miss America was in the groove to land, the boatswain mate on watch would dutifully play the, "Here she comes, Miss America" theme song, and several thousand troops would smile and be thankful for little things.

We had two carrier COs during that period who taught me a lot about enthusiastic and positive leadership. One morning, a booming voice in no need of introduction, came on the loudspeaker system with an upbeat "Good morning America! I want you to know we have just won five of six "Es" for excellence." Indeed the America was a super ship with an even greater crew. That's why she won all those Es for being the best! The pervasive voice was that of Captain Fox Turner, a spring-loaded leader who set the standards, was fair, who cared for the troops and the troops knew it. Quid pro quo — something for something.

Don Engen was America's previous CO and while our ship's airplane was Miss America, the ship just plain America, Don was Mr. America. Tall, confident, an extraordinary aviator and unimpressed by his own importance, Don was to me the ultimate leader. He did much towards keeping the collective bubble pumped up!

Dirty, sweaty, getting shot at, land, debrief and 45-minutes later be seated in the officer's wardroom all cleaned up and laughing and scratching at "our" table. "Our" table consisted of VF-102's stable of lieutenant commanders, plus a few others. Our table's leader was Gordo Murray, an easy-going, friendly, original-no-sweat artist who fancied himself the world's greatest aviator. He flew with Gar Magnus, a bear of a backseater whose nickname came from the once-a-mission cigar he lit up in the back seat, no matter the type of hop. Served by smiling stewards, we almost dined rather than ate and always had a steady stream of laughs, usually led by Gordo. When Gordo laughed, it took a hardened soul not to join in.

As astronauts enroute to the moon would one day watch our shrinking globe, so too would the enormously-busy enclave of a carrier viewed from high above evoke wonder. The activity quotient within never slowed, but went on around the clock. Indeed, there were as many troops up and about and working at 0200 as at two in the afternoon. Sleep, eat, watch an occasional movie, fly, brief, debrief, hawk the intelligence center for the latest photos of "targets," tour the maintenance spaces and chat with your troops, fly again, write a letter and so on. Excepting the thump and vibration of the four big catapults and thunder of the jets, the ship was quiet — no bells to tell the time and no yacking over the ship's announcing system (excepting a daily update late in the afternoon by the Captain).

The regimen for the troops was much the same — 12-hours on and 12-off ad infinitum. Work, eat, sleep, write letters home and more work. Humping 40 pounds of chain, heavy fueling hoses, tending boilers far below, loading ordnance and little time to reflect on their more fortunate shore-based brethren in hometown USA.

Author, Bob Gilbert, Jack McHugh and Danny Michaels on flight deck of America.

The aviators, of course, were the pointy end of America's spear and highly visible, particularly in landing. Each squadron placed a high priority on quality carrier landings and maintained the inevitable "greenie board" in the most prominent spot in the ready room. Green was good, yellow was marginal and red was bad. Landing grades were decided by the landing signal officers (LSOs) from their vantage point far aft on the flight deck. No matter the rank of the pilot, the words of the LSO were sacrosanct and not even the big carrier's honcho atop the bridge would venture to counteract.

Landing a big, fast-flying (145 knots) Phantom aboard a carrier, is mostly an exercise in discipline — the pilot must put the airplane where he knows it ought to be. The guy that gets an occasional "yellow" or even "red," is most likely one who just does not work the airplane to the "nth" degree, but relaxes a bit. Testimony to this sense of excellence and folks on the ship, is that most squadrons will display a "greenie board" that is mostly green. There is one exception: the automatic carrier landing. Many of the airplanes aboard America had the capability to land totally hands off including the Phantom.

Most pilots did not like to do this, but every five or six landings at night were Mode I, fully automatic. Though the heart rate of most pilots coming aboard a carrier on a black night is about double the resting pulse rate, I guarantee that the automatic approaches add another 10%. The problem is that most aviators like the notion of being master of their own destinies rather than the recipient of trillions of speeding electrons. A Mode I landing gets the auspicious remembrance on the greenie board of a blank space.

One personal flashback regarding carrier landings: On one sixty-day line period, my carrier landing grades put me number three in the air wing out of some 100 pilots. I mention this because only eight short years prior when flying the Demon aboard the Hancock, I came within a hair's breath of losing my wings due to a rash of unsatisfactory landings at night far out in the stormy South China Sea. And the reason I insert this mini-tale is that from that moment on in the winter of 1960, I worked at most every landing ashore with the same mindset as an actual carrier landing — day and night. If my airspeed or lineup or glide slope were not perfect, I tried to make up for it on the next landing. Consistently excellent carrier landings are the result of minute attention to detail and a mental attitude that accepts nothing less than perfect.

One day near the end of the deployment, the time came for all us pilots to get our periodic standardization check to determine if we were flying like the book told us to. It was the ultimate in dumbness, because we had been flying together intensely for over a year and there was very little about any pilot's abilities or idiosyncrasies that was sacrosanct. Nonetheless, Gar was to check all the pilots.

Well, Burner Bill, my wingman, had a habit when he was on a CAP hop (no bombs or rockets) to roll inverted and hold one negative G for the maximum allotted time of ten seconds. He would never tell Mike Joslin, his regular RIO, and old Mike just figured everyone did this. (Burner said it helped clear his head and the bilges of the Phantom). So, here comes senior RIO and NATOPS checker, Gar Magnus. Now Gar, once airborne, always loosened his straps, got out his sand ash tray, took off his oxygen mask and lit up a big stogie. So, we're up on CAP, thirty miles off Haiphong on a gorgeous morning with the sun just starting to peek at us, the centerline tanks about empty, when Burner, as was his wont, gently pulls up his nose, rolls inverted, holds it for ten seconds and puts exactly one negative G on the airplane. Gar, ashtray, cigar and foul words were all over the back seat. They pulled up close alongside and I could tell Gar was really torqued off. I thought at first they had a bee in the cockpit, so frantic were the backseat machinations. When we landed, old Burner got a "down" from Gar which of course, made zero difference, for Burner was out again that night trying to make big holes in the North Vietnam transportation links.

We lost another pilot soon after this — Chuck Parrish. If Don Engen was Mr. America, Chuck was Mr. Junior America — smart, a good stick, a motivated and smiling junior-officer leader, he took a direct hit from a 37 MM in a bomb run and just went in with the airplane. His RIO, Bob Fant, barely made it out and was captured to become a many-year POW. It was doubly sad because Chuck was Captain Don Engen's son-in-law.

Our final line period at an end, we had a memorable party in the ready room behind closed doors, a scene replicated in six other ready rooms throughout the big war ship. Then it was docking at Cubi Point in the Phillipines and a departure for most of the wing back to the states in a chartered DC-8. What a trip!

To begin with, we hadn't been airborne an hour when, near the northern part of the Phillipines, the giant people-hauler starts to orbit. After some 15 minutes, the pilot came on the air, announced he was lost and "was there anyone who could fly an airplane aboard?" Then, landing in Tokyo for fuel, he came up again and asked over the PA system if he "should let his new co-pilot make the landing?" to which 150 aviators chorused in unison, "no way." When the co-pilot greased it on, there was a huge round of cheers and applause from the back end of the airplane, the ultimate in aviation accolade.

If you want to see a bunch of combat-hardened and raucous aviators go deathly quiet, put them in the back end of a big airliner with a bunch of very bright and noisy thunderstorms in the night sky. So it was the last couple-of-hundred miles into Norfolk and home. Give any of us on that airplane the choice of a night combat mission or bouncing around in the packed back end of that DC-8 in thunderstorms and it would be unanimous!

Homecoming back in the idyllic world of our Summerset Lane home was sweet.

EPILOGUE

- **My Dad** has passed away, but one of my most prized possessions is a candid picture taken by a young Navy photographer of my Dad and me on the flight deck of the America after a 1,200 mile flight in a Phantom.

- **Don Engen** went on to become a three-star admiral and the head of the Federal Aviation Administration only to be killed in a glider accident in Colorado.

- **Bob Fant** married his Oceana sweetheart after his POW stint, taught survival at the Navy's training camp up in Maine and is an enormously positive person.

- **Burner Bill Beardsly** became a Blue Angel, a captain for Delta Airlines, flew the Bud Light micro jet in airshows and still goes negative one G for ten seconds.

- **Mike Joslin**, Burner's backseater, was killed in a training accident not long after this tale.

- **Gar Magnus** is a college professor and still smokes big cigars.

- **Gordo Murray** used to be the world's greatest fighter pilot and still is.

- **Ted Fellowes** commanded an aircraft carrier, made flag rank, retired from the Navy and is now a practicing attorney in Virginia.

- **Fox Turner** became a three-star admiral and the head of all Naval Aviation.

- **Roger Mehle** retired in the Virginia Beach area and has passed away.

- **Zeke Burns** became the first Naval Flight Officer (non-pilot) to command a fighter squadron, commanded a large supply ship, retired from the Navy, became a merchant marine chief mate on big tankers and is still as tough and feisty as ever.

- **Clyde Lassen**, the Medal of Honor winner, lived in the Pensacola area, sold real estate and before retiring, commanded the helo squadron that trained all the Navy and Marine Corps pilots. Sadly he passed away not long ago, a hero's hero.

- **Emory Brown** went on to Navy test pilot school, commanded a Phantom squadron and now flies DC-10s for Federal Express.

- The U.S.S. **America** continued doing her thing for many years, a proud instrument of national policy.

- The **5,500** men who so-ably crewed the magnificent war-ship America have scattered, their collective excellence and sacrifices sometimes forgotten by too many.

- **I'm** still waking up beside the same good-looking Memphis lady as I did so long ago in Kowloon.

True Faith and Allegiance

Peter B. Booth

19 January, 2004

Dear Joan, Jennifer, Kim, April and Nathan:

How sad I was to have learned of Skip's passing yesterday afternoon. It must have been only hours after Carolyn and I left. I wish Skip could have been awake because I would like to have conveyed to him my thanks, appreciation and respect for the three or so years we had together so long ago during the mid-sixties. Here's roughly what I would have said to him:

Skip was a warrior through and through. In our many missions in the F4 Phantom together in good weather and black nights at sea, I never heard Skip grump or complain. He was always ready to go, never needed any prodding and was a solid 50% of any success we enjoyed when airborne. And, too, though I can't be specific, I'm sure he kept me, as his pilot, on the straight and narrow on many occasions and out of the water at least a couple of times. Whether it was over Vietnam, during the Forrestal fire, a 0200 launch in lousy weather or just a routine cross country, Skip was always the consummate professional. I wish now we had stayed in touch more over the years

The bottom line is that Skip relished taking on the tough jobs. He never even remotely shirked or made excuses; he just got better each flight. To his fine family he left behind, there can be no greater legacy for his short life than what he gave to you all and what he so willingly gave to his country and Navy. Our nation is better off for having had men like Skip available for the tough missions that lasted months on end and for families like yours that stood behind their father.

With great respect to a fine man, father and real hero.

Sadly, but proudly,

Rear Admiral, U. S. Navy (retired)
Pensacola, Florida

615 BAYSHORE DRIVE, #408   PENSACOLA, FL 32507-3565
850-456-2400   FAX 850-456-4445   e-mail: pbooth@bellsouth.net

Skip Holt - my RIO in VF–74 and VF–102 - recently passed away. His service was symbolic of so many who did so much for their Navy and Nation.

DETACHMENT OCEANA

From 12 to 54 jets, shore duty, carrier qualifications, tiny home to palace, more great sailors and a CO far away.

As the lieutenant commander in charge of the Phantom carrier qualification at sea aboard the U.S.S. *Kennedy*, I found myself standing at a modified parade rest on the bridge trying to explain to the captain why we ought not to continue the quals. As the captain glared at me, the diminutive executive officer, a full commander with an absurd mustache, barked at me like I was a plebe at the Naval Academy and practically yelling, hollered, "What's wrong Booth, your guys can't hack one wire?"

Speechless, and trying my best to control my tired emotions, I respectfully replied, "That's right, sir!" I knew I won that round as the captain acquiesced and we quit flying for the night, but was not sure the word would not be twisted up the line. Here's the situation: As the OinC of a twelve-Phantom detachment of the main VF-101 squadron down in Key West, I had taken the opportunity to lead this particular evolution. After many day and night practice flights in the local Norfolk area, the new pilots and RIOs, headed for the ship with the objective of getting ten day-carrier arrested landings and six at night. This particular night was particularly onerous because there was

Our Detachment Oceana detachment. Check two guys in starboard intake and high atop the rudder. Everyone got a copy. Somewhere, one adventuresome soul has an unfolded "Playboy" centerfold. 95% were super sailors!

a solid overcast at a thousand feet with the wind howling. Initially, our guys had done reasonably well, but the weather kept delaying the action. Then we were told that in order for the arresting gear troops to get a break, the ship went down to two wires and then one. It was at this time that I trekked to the bridge to argue respectfully that the conditions, though barely legal, were not conducive to safe operations and that my guys too, were tired and stretched out.

I don't recall the specifics, but upon return to our home base with the VF-102 Diamondbacks in early 1969, I ended up as Commander Don Primeau's assistant officer-in-charge of this squadron-sized mini command. It was a good deal because there would be no move from our comfortable new-home digs on quiet Summerset Lane in the largely Navy community of King's Grant. Furthermore, it kept me in the cockpit and deep into the Phantom arena. Shortly after I checked in, I did get some rumblings that the Navy needed my type as a student at the Naval War College up in Rhode Island, but Don did some finagling and I stayed put. At about the same time, though no one bothered to query me, I got word through Don that I was being considered for the Blue Angel lead which was, at that time, a lieutenant commander OinC job. Truth be known, I was kind of happy to be settled and come home to Carolyn and the kids at night.

VF-101 det O changes officer's in charge from Primeau to Booth with stylish wives flying close wing position.

The job of our detachment was to take the pilots and RIOs who had completed about five months of training in Key West and train them in conventional weapons delivery and carrier qualifications. When they finished with us, they then went direct to their fleet squadrons, and in many cases, straight to forward-deployed squadrons on the combat line or in the Mediterranean. It was mostly a Monday-through-Friday operation, though much of the carrier practice was done at night. We had twelve, non-radar (lead-nosed) F4J Phantoms, 200 maintenance and support troops and about twenty instructor pilots and RIOs.

One of the more challenging training hops was a combination bombing and in-flight refueling mission down south of the base. Because night air is fundamentally different from day air and the guys were new to the missions, we invariably had some fun times.

True Faith and Allegiance

After launching with five jets, the first task was to find the tanker orbiting at 15,000 feet in the dark skies about one-hundred miles to the south. Naval Aviators learn early in their undergraduate training how to properly execute a rendezvous by keeping at roughly the same altitude, getting a good 45-degree angle and sliding smoothly into position. Trouble is, that after winning their wings of gold, all this theory goes out the window. This was particularly true in the Phantom, because if you got sucked and ended up in trail position, all you needed to do was to tap the afterburner and zoom into a nice parade position. Of course, the tendency is to overshoot as the rate of closure is hard to discern from the astern aspect. Anyway, at night, the join-ups were usually exciting and like most of Naval Aviation's lessons, simply had to be practiced.

Then there was the tanking, usually from a tiny A4 jet with a buddy store refueling package, which once again, can be beat to death in the classroom, but can only be learned by doing. In that most every flight off the carrier will involve some tanking, this evolution, though not overly difficult, must be done with absolute precision and attention to detail.

Finally came the bombing. The target was an old, derelict, partially-sunk destroyer in Pamlico Sound in the area around Cape Hatteras. The objective was for the instructor to drop two flares to illuminate the target and the four jets would make six or so runs at the target and drop their Mk. 76 practice bombs (about twenty pounds and two-feet long) in a 45-degree dive starting from 10,000 feet. At precisely 5,000 feet and 450 knots, the pilot would press the bomb button on the F4 stick grip, transition to the instruments, pull four Gs and then do it again. It's not worth describing all the permutations and combinations of this night-training evolution except to admit that the multiple bombing attempts generally left the old ship with no new holes.

Carrier qualifications in the F4 were 50% of our mission and the leaders of this phase were a covey of fleet-experienced landing signal officers (LSOs). Symbolic, was Lieutenant Drex Bradshaw, a pilot of exceptional skill and aggressiveness and a superb LSO. His job was to groom the cadre of new pilots (and RIOs) for the ship. After about 100 practice landings, mostly at night, at the nearby practice field, Drex would pronounce them ready for the ship. His standards reflected those of the carrier-based Navy — absolute and with no compromises. If he said the guy was ready, he was ready.

At the ship, the new pilots would be paired with the new RIOs, get a few day landings and then go for the night work. Catapult shots were always on instruments, even in the daytime so as to be ready for the totally-black night work. Because the jets were light (about 6,000 pounds of gas), SOP was to hold the stick full back until the nose rotated to 12-degrees nose-up on the attitude gyro. Once again, there is no way to teach this in the classroom; it's learn by doing.

Each session at sea with a dozen or so pilots always had its measure of screw ups and near disasters and clearly it was not an evolution for the faint of heart. That said, the majority gritted their teeth and went out and did the tough job and came out winners.

New guys go day and night in the Phantom for carrier qualifications aboard Forrestal. Super landing signal officers 3rd thru 5th from left front: Tom Inderlied, Billy Boatright, Doyle Borchers. Drex Bradshaw in far back.

I wish now that I could have taped some of Drex's debriefs with the crews. If a guy was having problems (not unusual), he would work with him in the ready room for as long as it took to get his point across. Anyway, this final phase for the new guys before they went to their fleet squadron, was usually successful, thanks in large part to dedicated guys like Drex and his LSO compatriots.

Vietnam would still have another four years to run and the Navy was hard at it in the Gulf of Tonkin as two-to-three carriers were on station around the clock and no days off. And the losses continued. Many of our newly-minted pilots and RIOs would go direct to a deployed squadron on the combat line to replace those lost.

We had moved from a small house we rented from my sister about a mile from the Atlantic Ocean with a one-car carport, portable dishwasher and one bathroom that worked most of the time. The new house was a standard, two-story, very-typical, four-bedroom home which we bought for around

Carolyn and I at new home on Summerset Lane.

$34,000 with monthly payments of $333. Nice home on a quiet street. Our neighbors were mostly Navy folks, half of whose husbands were off on the high seas somewhere in the world. The elementary school for our two girls was a short walk away. Good living! Carolyn, like most all the wives, minded the home front, kept the lawn mowed, fixed the car and hosted all sorts of squadron socials.

One day, we got word to ready six jets for an across-the-ocean flight to the Kennedy, then with the Sixth Fleet in the Mediterranean Sea. I selected myself to lead the flight. Good so far. The bad news was that the jets were old F4Bs from the Marines which were in incredibly poor shape with numerous systems, including the radar, not working. Long story short, we put lots of maintenance effort into them and got them reasonably full-system capable.

The plan was to launch from Oceana and fly direct to Bermuda with a pathfinder twin-jet A3 bomber leading the way as the only navigation in the Phantom was a Tacan that gave us range and bearing to a distant station out to about 200 miles. We would then go direct to the Azores the next day after refueling from two Marine KC-130 tankers, lumbering, four-engine transport airplanes with a maximum speed in level flight of about 180 knots. In that this leg was around 2,000 miles, we absolutely needed the tanking. From the Azores, we would take a 900-mile jaunt to the Navy base in Rota, Spain and then on to Italy where the Kennedy squadron's would take delivery of the jets.

The first 600-mile leg was easy. We parked the airplanes with the plan to depart very early the next morning. I advised all our stalwart aviators of two imperatives: First was not to ride the motor scooters as I didn't want anyone killed before we got the airplanes delivered and further, "get plenty of sleep."

I guess I should have been more commanding or assertive, because it was hang-over city the next morning. Fortunately, all the airplanes were in good shape and we briefed with the Marines and our A3 navigation lead. The first tanking was to be with the 130s about 500 miles east of Bermuda at 20,000 feet. Because the tankers were so slow and we did not want to lower our flaps, we planned to tank while headed in a gentle descent at 190 knots. Technically, this was interesting, for we had three external fuel tanks which, by the time we reached the rendezvous, were about empty.

Hot-shot fighter pilot on the Bermuda tarmac – You write the caption.

A small technical sidelight that only aviators will comprehend, involved the actual join-up on the tankers flying at such a slow speed. At 190 knots, a heavy F4 is close to stalling and each time the stick is moved laterally, causes the nose to wander off in the opposite direction (adverse yaw, guys). Anyway after some yacking on the radio, we managed to find the tankers and settled in for our ten-thousand pounds of gas.

As each jet started filling with fuel, it would require more and more power just to stay in position. In technical terms, we were way on the backside of the power-required curve with momentous amounts of adverse yaw. Towards the final couple-of-thousand pounds, one engine would have to be in minimum afterburner just to stay in position! Anyway, all went reasonably well and the six airplanes were delivered in good shape.

Another of our evolutions was a canned low-level flight for the replacement pilots and RIOs. They would plan the flight at 500 feet which proceeded roughly due west up and over the Appalachian Mountains, into the next valley, then wind their way back to the bedraggled destroyer in the bombing range south of Oceana, pop up and deliver one, teeny, Mk. 76 practice bomb with deadly accuracy. The icing on the cake was the return one-hundred miles to home base with the emphasis on look-out doctrine. In that several Phantoms would launch within a few minutes, the flight called for a maximum of one turn when attacking one of our own and a minimum altitude of 5,000 feet. I always thought it to be the most absolutely fun hop in the entire syllabus.

One nice day, I landed back at Oceana with a happy student RIO who had done well and got the word that one of our airplanes was missing. We immediately instituted the search and rescue assets and found the remains of the airplane in shallow water just north of Kitty Hawk. There were no survivors.

The pilot was a superb Naval Officer and Naval Aviator, Lieutenant Doug McCarty who's family was nearby. While the parents of the backseater were being notified in central North Carolina by a nearby recruiting officer, Carolyn and I made the long drive to inform Doug's wife. How incredibly sad! We never did come close to finding out what had happened as none of our guys had even seen his airplane.

```
But, I also knew the Doug that was your son; kind, gentle and
strong in character.  He held himself tall and was quick to
smile.  As a man and an individual he was genuinely liked by
all.  Doug deserved the confidence and respect this squadron had
in him.  After meeting and talking with you both yesterday, I can
readily see why Doug was the man he was.  You are wonderful people
and have a beautiful family.  There is no finer legacy that
parents can leave the world we live in, than to provide that
world with men like Doug.
```

Excerpt from letter I wrote to Doug's parents.

The loss of the crew hardly made the news simply because so many good guys were being lost, killed or taken prisoner in Vietnam or in operational losses. I recall the trek to Gasdon, North Carolina to attend the funeral of the backseater. Dressed in my high-neck whites, I became immersed with good folks and sad parents and friends who, in the end, were so proud of their son and what he stood for. Same for Doug's service at Oceana. Missing-man flyovers at this master jet base were not uncommon in that era.

Our main problem — as it had been for decades — was in getting spare parts for our airplanes. With twelve F4s on board we would generally have need for fifty parts ranging from radios to actuators to nuts and bolts. Even on the front-line deployed outfits, the need for parts was the prime constraint to putting airplanes in the air. The standard and time-honored method to alleviate the problem on the deckplates, was to take one airplane and cannibalize it for parts.

Detachment Oceana

I can't recall the specifics, but late one Friday afternoon, I took a machine with an empty back seat and two cargo blivets under the wings and arrived at the Marine's Cherry Point ramp just south of Oceana. With an official list of needed parts for our airplanes, the Marines not only got most of what we needed, but loaded it into my airplane. Not really legal, this was simply illustrative of what lots of maintenance chiefs and leaders did to get max airplanes in the air!

After a year or so, I made full commander and the main squadron was ordered to quit Key West and return to Oceana. My skipper for the first year was one of my typically great COs who let us do our job without nitpicking and only occasional course corrections, Commander Roger Boh. He was relieved by Commander Dan McCormick, my former squadron mate in my first Phantom squadron back in San Diego and the Kitty Hawk. Both of these gents I might add, were specially selected to lead this large, shore-based training squadron following an exceptional job as a regular fleet commanding officer.

Their change of command was in Key West and we volunteered from up north to do a "flyby" at the conclusion of the ceremony which was, in typical Navy fashion, replete with guest speaker (the local rear admiral), high-necked whites and shiny swords. Dan says, "No lower than 500 feet and no faster than 350 knots."

At the appointed time in the ceremony, our four jets from Oceana swooped low over the august crowd at slightly less than the briefed altitude and a tad faster than the allowed speed. Because the admiral came slightly unglued, Dan wasn't visibly happy to see us after landing. In private though, my guess is he thought it right on the mark. (Real speed and altitude are left to the reader's imagination).

Dan was a wonderful CO, but about this time the job started losing its luster. Problem was that each week we would get a couple more airplanes for which we were not manned to maintain. And more and more of the training missions were being assumed by the detachment. Eventually we ended up with 54 Phantoms of several variants and mods, without the troops to maintain them. I am proud to state that during this tough period we kept a weather eye out for the welfare and working conditions of our sailors and officers and heeded the temptation to work excessive hours on the job, which was, of course, shore duty for our hard-working guys.

I say guys, but we got two WAVE officers on board in the administrative area, Ensigns Sue Cantlin and Josephene Shelton. Both were excellent officers and respected by our rather large (by this time) "detachment." They both wanted rides in the Phantom, so we sent them off to the obligatory training in swimming, ejection seats and the like.

By this time, over the years, I had taken maybe forty or so non-flight crew up for rides in the airplane both ashore and aboard ship and my approach was a bit different from what was considered the norm. Rather than impress the new person with max G or rapid acrobatics, I would always approach each evolution with care. Remember, the guy is in a totally strange environment, is

wearing an oxygen mask and tight-fitting hard hat, can't see anything ahead and before takeoff, is sweating profusely. This environment is hyper-conducive to getting sick! And, I can state with zero bravado, I want it known that no one ever got sick in my back seat.

Anyway, back to Ensign Shelton. After getting airborne, I would usually do some gentle turns and climbs and glides and progress to a demonstration of G loads in level turns where your body multiplies its weight several-fold. Sustained four times the force of gravity were done in military power around 10,000 feet. Then, we pulled five Gs. I could peek in the rear-view mirror and see she was still fine. "Want more Gs, Josephene?" said her pilot.

In a clear and unstrained voice, she said, "Bring it on, skipper!" And once again, we would roll into a level turn and hold five Gs for a full 360 degree turn. Now the Phantom with a centerline fuel tank was limited to 6.5 Gs once the tank was empty, so I cranked on a bit of AB and held max G for two circles in order to show her how the real pilots did it. By the end of first 360, she said words to the effect that ". . . this sure was fun!"

Unbeknownst to my trusty backseater on her first hop in the Phantom, her pilot was starting to get tunnel vision and by the end of the second 360,

Detachment Oceana

was ready to stop such foolishness. After landing, she bounded out of the aft cockpit with a broad smile and a firm handshake. Another win for Naval Aviation!

One day in 1970 I got word that I was to be assigned to Fighter Squadron Eleven — the Red Rippers — first as executive officer and then fleet up to CO given that I didn't do anything too dumb. Good news, bad news. I was glad to stay at the same base and homefront, but disappointed that the new squadron was to be on the Forrestal headed for yet another Sixth Fleet deployment in the Med vice Vietnam.

```
1. NOTE FROM CDR BOOTH:

    1. As of 1 April we are no longer a Det. CDR MICHAELS, whom many of you
have met, will be X.O. CDR MCCORMICK will spend some of his time up here as
C.O. and CDR MCCARTELL (ex VF-114 C.O.) will releive as C.O. 10 June.
    2. My compliments to LT FARRELL who landed 151 with one wheel gone. A
really fine job. We will have a personnel inspection this Friday at 0900,
present some awards and welcome the C.O. to Oceana. Look sharp - its been
awhile since we've had one. Afterwards there will be a free all hands picnic
at the picnic grounds complete with beer trucks, barbecue and sports. All
of you are invited. I think it will be fun. Uniform is blues for inspection
and ??? for the picnic.
    3. I am off to VF-11 in the Med as X.O.. I would like to say thanks to
all you fine men, senior and junior, long hair and short, young and old and
black shoes and airdales. Each one of you affirms my beleif in the greatness
of America, because you all are America. Each and every one of you is great.
Continue to do your best on the job and off and try to have fun doing it.
```

Final plan of the day note from me (Don't sweat the typos!) and eight truly great young Americans doing the tough job for their Navy and country.

EPILOGUE

- **Don Primeau** moved up the ranks serving his country and Navy with exceptional distinction, retiring as a rear admiral.

- **Dan McCormick** continued to harass me over the ensuing years, but remained in my mind as one of those naturally-gifted leaders who led by personal example and served as skipper of the carrier America and as a flag officer.

- The **talented Lieutenants** who formed the nucleus of our detachment went on to varied careers in the service of their country and Navy. Just doing their tough jobs, they most likely never realized their massive contributions.

- The hundreds of **enlisted maintenance men** who tended to the growing stable of Phantoms in this shore-based operation went on up the ranks in the Navy or back to hometown USA, their legacy one of learning, contributing and service.

- **Lieutenant Doug McCarty** was symbolic of so many who died in the service of their country in hot war and cold, leaving behind loved ones and friends who understood the meaning of service.

- Though VF-101 detachment Oceana was shore duty, for most it was an interlude between tough shipboard tours. Throughout, the **Navy Wives and Families** stood tall, resolute and proud and kept the home fires burning brightly.

---

16 December 1969

Mr. and Mrs. Fred Hickowski
1023 Morton Ave.
Moundsville, West Virginia, 26041

Dear Mr. and Mrs. Hickowski,

It was with great pleasure that I recently authorized your son's promotion to the rate of Aviation Structural Mechanic (S) Third Class.

You may be justifiably proud of this accomplishment for his promotion was the result of his meeting high standards of knowledge and proficiency in competition with thousands of Navy personnel throughout the world. These high standards help keep our Navy the world's best, able at all times to carry out its mission. To your son and to me, this occasion is noteworthy. For him, it means an increase in responsibility and authority in his already vital duties. For me, advancements like your son's assure Fighter Squadron ONE HUNDRED ONE Detachment Oceana of high-caliber petty officers. Thus we are better able to contribute to the national security in these critical days of international tension.

Sincerely yours,

P. B. BOOTH
Lieutenant Commander
U. S. Navy
Officer in Charge

Typical letter sent to parents or wives on special occasions. No big deal, but most welcome back in hometown USA and to the sailor.

> Woodville, Miss.
> Jan 20, 1920
>
> Lieutenant Commander
> P. B. Booth
> U S Navy Officer in Charge
>
> Dear Sir;
>
> Many thanks for the letter I received concerning my son. (Charles A Goodrick)
>
> I don't hear from Charles as I wish but I always pray he is safe, I do ask God to take care of you all.
>
> I am always glad to read a letter explaining Charles Job. I hope he obeys the rules of his officers in charge.
>
> May God always watch over you all.
>
> Respectfully
> Ollie M. Goodrick

Typical response from grateful parent.

THE RED RIPPERS

Three years with a bunch of pig-headed, baloney-slinging, two-balled, he-men bastards.

Flying left seat in the big, pulsating, SH-3 Sea King helicopter hovering at 40-feet over the broad expanse of a placid Mediterranean Sea, there appeared out of the corner of my eye, an F4 Phantom jet, close aboard to port and below us! Furthermore, it was from the VF-11 Red Rippers of which I was the resident commanding officer. Flying very low is a sometimes requirement in the fighter community, but certainly not in such close proximity to a helo dipping its submarine-seeking sonar into the water.

So, upon return to the Red Ripper ready room aboard the U.S.S. *Forrestal*, I checked the flight schedule and indeed, we had four machines airborne at the time. Who could the pilot have been? To anyone who knew him, it could only have been Lieutenant Bill Pfeiffer. Bill, an ex-IRS auditor, loved to fly, was good at it and could tell more good 1/10th-true sea stories than the rest of our 36 aviators put together. He skirted lots of trouble, but was a slippery one, and nothing ever stuck. When confronted by his C.O. about the dastardly deed he had allegedly committed (scaring one of our wing helo pilots), he said with a wink of the eye and grin from ear to ear, "You know how it is, Skipper!" I did and he beat the rap again.

"How it is," is the balance one weaves in any combat fighter

Lieutenant Bill Pfeifer just before start engines.

squadron between instilling aggressiveness and the will to win versus not doing dumb things and losing yourself and the airplane. Our job was not to be safe — our job was to "shoot down the enemy and win and anything else was rubbish." A fairly new philosophy, known as "train the way you fight," had emerged in the aftermath of Vietnam which was a euphemistic way of saying, "No guts, no air medal" or, "OK, we're going to lose a few in training." It was the skipper's job to keep the aggressive spirit in high warble, but still stay within the conceptual rules box of Naval Aviation.

Our squadron had a rich legacy too, and was (and is) the Navy's oldest fighter squadron, having been formed in 1927. I had a particular affinity for it, as my Dad had been CO back in the early days of WWII aboard the old Ranger. With a call sign of, "Ripper," its logo was copied from the boar's head on a Gordon's gin bottle, that being a rather fashionable pastime in those days of prohibition. It had a backwards red lightning bolt going through two equally red balls, above which was the snout and head of an ugly wild boar underlined by rolls of bologna. In Ripper parlance it meant, "A bunch of pig-headed, bologna-slinging, two-balled, he-man bastards." What a deal! What brass! What class!

PR shot over Sicily's Mt. Etna

The Red Rippers

The good news was that I was the skipper of a front-line, U.S. Navy, carrier-based Phantom squadron in that fall of 1972. The bad news to me, was that we were in the Mediterranean Sea, while our brothers-in-arms were slugging it out in the waning months of the Vietnam war. Not that we were necessarily pro-Vietnam; far from it. But, we were warriors, our job was to do the dirty work if our country called, and besides, it was a lot more challenging than playing NATO war games in the bureaucratic Med. I suppose many folks throughout our country just never realized, that during those eight years of Vietnam, we guys in the sea-going Navy still had an obligation and commitment to NATO's southern flank.

Helos were a blast! I had befriended the skipper of our anti-submarine helo outfit, Wil King, and he would let me fly with him as co-pilot on occasion in the daytime. As long as I was not flying a Phantom that night, I'd grab at the opportunity. Besides being good at their primary mission of ASW, the big helos delivered mail, hauled passengers amongst the various ships of the battle group, woke up sleeping merchantmen coming too close, picked up men overboard, and, on one occasion, rescued hundreds of Tunisians from ravaging flood waters.

Wil had asked me if I wanted to go with him on this latter mission, as all his pilots had been flying a great deal and were tired. The Forrestal had nudged in close to Tunis so as to afford Wil's helos more time in rescue operations. For hours we flew in and about flooded areas, picked up people and took them to high ground and safety. Almost all had never seen a helo, much less crowded into one. Because the ground was soft from so much rain, Wil would hold his big helo barely airborne so as not to bury the wheels in the mud. It took some skillful piloting!

On one foray about 70 miles from Tunis, we came upon hundreds of bedraggled, forlorn and wet Tunisians, including lots of kids. Wil says, "load 'em up." And load they did. By our count, there were four crew and thirty-seven scared passengers on board, most except Wil, with eyes wide-open. All got candy, compliments of Wil and his troops who had the foresight (and dollars) to buy out the ship's store in anticipation of making some little ones happy. What a guy! What an outfit!

Our previous cruise was also on Forrestal in the Med. We had gone through months of intense ship and air wing training before both deployments, just as if we were going into combat. Night-carrier landings, air combat maneuvering, rockets and bombs, detailed study of our adversary, the Soviets, and big attack strikes were the order of the day and night. We stayed busy and were forever away from our home base of Oceana near Norfolk. When the ship was on one of its infrequent in-port periods, we would be off to Key West for hot pad duty.

Hot pad was a piece of work. Because Senor Fidel Castro, aka "the thorn of the United States," was but 75 miles to the south of sovereign U.S. waters, we maintained a strategic base in Key West. The tip of the spear of this presence was a 365-day-per-year, four-to-six Navy or Marine Corps fighter contingent, all on five-minute alert. Should Fidel decide to mess with anything the U.S. felt he ought not to mess with, we would be the hot guns to stick it up his rear end.

Very seldom were we ever scrambled for real, but we would have one- or-two-practices daily and always unannounced. It was just like the movies and went like this:

The Phantoms were fully loaded with assorted missiles and rockets and about 100 feet from the hot pad ready shack where us pilots and RIOs hung out — spring-loaded-to-the-go position. When the klaxon sounded (it would wake the dead and is one small reason that I have some hearing loss today), we would race to the airplanes, leap in, pull the seat pins, hit the start button, start strapping in, bring one throttle around the horn, continue strapping in, lower the canopy, start the other engine, pull the chocks, give it a lot of go power, talk to the guys who scrambled us on the radio, do the take-off check list and — from a card game in the alert shack to wheels lifting off runway seven at Key West, would be consistently less than five minutes. It sounds a bit slap dash, but this was our profession, we were good at it and it was an extremely professional evolution. Old Fidel knew well, that if he messed with the bull, he'd get the horn.

Everyone, it seemed, had nicknames, one being that of our maintenance officer, Lieutenant Commander Dave Anderson or "Shag." It originated during one of our air combat maneuvering (ACM) flights which we would do at the drop of a hat. Off would come the rockets and fuel tanks and up would go two-to-four F4s and really have at it. The heat-seeking missile, the AIM 9 Sidewinder, was a deadly accurate weapon, but needed to be fired in that era, within a stern aspect to the target of about 30 degrees and a mile-or- so away. When the attacking pilot was in the envelope, he would call "Fox 2," signifying that indeed he was the victor and the target was dead. One day, high above the Key West waters, Dave and I were hard at it. Dave called a "Fox 2" at about 90-degrees off and three miles, well outside the missile's capability. It was there and then that the acronym "Shag" was coined, meaning roughly, "Super (or whatever suits you), Hot, Aerial, Guided."

Key West hot pad duty with "Shag" Anderson.

Another typical shore-based excursion was a one-week foray with eight machines to Tyndall AFB in Florida to work ACM with the Air Force. Our adversaries were F-106s from the Wisconsin Air National Guard. Well, one would reasonably surmise that the pride of Naval Aviation could handle an Air Guard outfit with one engine off the line. Not so. These guys were not only good, they were exceptional. So, I asked their skipper if I could ride in the two-seater 106 to see how they did it. My pilot was a mustachioed major (insurance guy) who flew that big beautiful jet better than anyone I've ever been in the air with. I mean, he made it dance and flew it to the absolute stark edges of the 106 performance envelope. He was good, no doubt, but he also had the advantage of having flown nothing else for the past twelve years. From this episode, I gleaned a better appreciation for the Air Force in general and the Wisconsin Air Guard in particular.

These were supposed to be rough times in the Navy from a people perspective and I suppose "they" were right. Down on the deck plates though, I really didn't see it. Our country was deeply caught up in a Vietnam scenario read, "How do we get out of this morass with a glimmer of honor?" Lots of folks getting shot up and killed for a cause that many American people could not comprehend. That said though, the 250 troops that made up the Red Rippers were simply a microcosm of America and reflected to varying degrees, the ills of the country — long hair, drugs, independence and so on.

Typical, were two that consistently stood out: Senior Chief Bob Skeeto was the maintenance chief and took care of our stable of twelve jets working 14-hours a day and, though he did not smile all the time, his infectious enthusiasm could be felt all the way to the corrosion control folks doing the dog work down on the hangar deck.

Petty Officer Broomfield was our "equal opportunity" adviser. Back then, racial problems during the extremely high operational tempo of the Navy — reflecting the nation at large — were not uncommon. To his credit, he worked in and amongst the troops and command and did a wonderful job of making our team color blind and performance oriented.

But, our guys were also <u>90% great</u>, 5% OK and 5% no good. The great ones were a daily dose of inspiration in those troubled times of 1972. Hard workers, professional, high spirited and proud. And I was proud of them. These guys got paid a pittance, were away from their homes and loved ones for eight-plus months at a shot, worked 12-hour shifts 7-days a week when at sea or on ops, lived in cramped, tiny spaces and, by and large, felt good about themselves and what they were doing.

Super CAG and leader, Moose Meyers

The "no goodniks" we kicked out as fast as a sometimes overly-permissive and paperwork-laden people system would allow, and with the worst discharge we could muster.

A portion of our squadron on the flight deck of Forrestal.

"Z grams" were one major manifestation of those turbulent times; a way in which the Navy's head guy (the CNO), Admiral Elmo Zumwalt, communicated direct to his 560,000 troops. There were Z grams on everything, including haircuts, liberty and uniforms. Out of the blue would come a naval message addressed to "The Navy," stating that, "The bottom of the sideburns should be no lower than the tragus." Not only did this totally exclude the guys who were trying to run the complex job of the operational Navy, no one had the slightest notion what the tragus was. Can you believe it?

Z grams and tragus' notwithstanding, we had more good fun than most ordinary folk have in a lifetime. Hard and demanding work in the air was the norm. Fun on the beach was *de rigueur*.

Our squadron mascot was a small, cute and smelly male piglet named "Ensign Double Nuts." We felt that our mascot, kept on a farm near our home base of Oceana, would grow into a reasonable facsimile of a wild boar and hence, be a worthy embodiment of our illustrious heritage. Our parachute riggers even made him a "vest" with the bold insignia of the Red Rippers on each side and shoulder boards befitting his rank and status.

The Red Rippers

Our junior ensign, Butts Butler, was assigned a collateral duty as the "Ensign Double Nuts Control Officer" and would appear with our noble creature on appropriate occasion, the more august the better. On one such foray to our shore-based topside spaces adjacent to the Commodore's office, Butts failed in his duties, the little pig got loose, squealed into the Commodore's conference room in full afterburner, scared the hell out of several senior officers and pee'd all over the new carpet. The CO didn't take any heat, nor did Butts. But as XO, I sure caught it, the chain of command being quite effective in this case.

Ensign Double Nuts all tuckered out. Note classy vest and head gear.

Pretty soon old Double Nuts grew up and was the star attraction at an all-hands party and picnic before our first cruise on Forrestal. He was lovingly prepared the night before his grand entrance by our farmer friend, whom we fortified with a bottle of Jack Daniels. The wives and girl friends cried, the kids wondered where Double Nuts was, and we Red Rippers licked our chops on the best Virginia barbecue we'd ever had!

Some time later, while deployed aboard Forrestal, we had received a Z gram on tee shirts which directed that all officers and chiefs must wear vee-necked tee shirts vice the regular crew-cut style. You'd think this would be simple seeing as the Navy's head guy wanted it to happen. Not so. Our guys could think of ten reasons why this simple directive could not be complied with, including non-availability aboard ship, wrong sizes and so forth. One day, in an all-officers meeting in our shipboard ready room, the XO and myself decided that policy was policy, let's execute it and forever put this momentous issue behind us. To assist those with more excuses than execution, we demonstrated the art of converting a crew-neck tee shirt to vee neck with the aid of some large shears borrowed from our parachute riggers. At the exact time of the first cut, someone called "attention on deck" and in walked the Forrestal's Captain, Jim Linder, who was, no doubt, intrigued by the specter of the squadron's CO holding a pair of monster scissors to the throat of our XO, Jim Taylor. The XO and I could not believe what we saw, for the Captain was wearing — you guessed it — a crew-neck, non-reg tee shirt. End of story, end of the "vee-neck-tee-shirt debacle" and back to the status quo.

One serene day, on our first deployment while the Ripper XO, I was conning the big carrier alongside an oiler in the Med. It was ridiculously easy — all I had to do was keep the ship in position fore and aft by changing the revolutions of our four huge screws ever so slightly and keep our distance abeam at about 160 feet, all while steaming at a gentlemanly 12 knots. Piece of cake! After 30 minutes the next guy got his chance and I went down to the flight deck to kibitz with some of our maintenance troops. Soon, I noticed the oiler and the FID (first in defense) getting real close and followed by "emergency breakaway." We didn't hit hard, but we did hit, the result a holed smoke stack on the oiler. It was by definition, a collision at sea which, along with allowing the bottom of the ship to touch the top of the seabed, has the 100% probability of ruining a captain's day. The cause? A carrier steering system that, on occasion, had a mind of its own.

Booth and Ramsey clan at change of command.

In typical Navy fashion honed by generations of practice, I relieved our CO, Austin Lindsey while ashore at Oceana. It was more auspicious than normal in that it coincided with the every-five-year reunion of the Red Rippers, billed as the Navy's oldest fighter squadron having been established some forty-five years prior. Those assuming command traditionally (and hopefully) keep their remarks short. Directed to the flight crews and troops, here's what I said (unedited from my scratchy handwriting):

- *When I joined this squadron one year ago, the goal of Cdr. Lindsey was to turn over to me a squadron that was combat ready.*
- *He has succeeded. We are combat ready with as fine a group of sailors, flying types and machines as could be found anywhere.*

- *The policies of the past year will continue unchanged.*
- *Our pilots and RIOs will continue the emphasis on sound, professional ACM.*
- *We will continue our policy of no radar, no fly.*
- *We will continue the command emphasis in the systematic, standardized and correct maintenance of our machines.*
- *Our officers and chiefs will continue to lead by personal example and to set the pace for our troops.*
- *And lastly, I will continue firm in my belief that the U.S. Navy sailor of today — and particularly the Red Ripper sailor — is absolutely great.*
- *I propose three cheers for Cdr. Lindsey from the Red Rippers.*
- *Chaplain Elder will now give the benediction. Will the guests please rise.*

Two Red Ripper COs (author and Dad) separated by thirty years.

Touring Barcelona.

In the winter of 1973, we spent a lot of time in and about Greece, which included another Zumwalt initiative, dependent's flights. He figured that because the Navy was operating at a tempo even higher than WWII, that if the ships could not be home more, he would fly the families to the ships. During one long 26-day, in-port period over Christmas, my bride, Carolyn and our two girls came over, and what a time. We had the world's scrawniest Christmas tree, but to us it was a ten footer!

An interesting sidelight to this long, no-flying period, was when we finally got underway in typically cold, overcast and windy winter Mediterranean weather. Most fighter aviators have an intense desire to fly anytime and anywhere. But, a fact of carrier flying is that if you lay off for awhile, the motivation factor can wane. And so it was with the world-famous Red Rippers. After living the good life with mama and the kids or home for the holidays on leave and no night-catapult shots, it took some pumping to inflate the motivation bubble. Soon however, we were back in battery.

This was the Sixth Fleet deployment that our sister squadron aboard Forrestal became the Gray Ghosts of Marine Fighter Squadron 251. Though routine now, in those times back in the early '70s, having Marines in the air wing was somewhat unusual. As only a handful of their pilots and RIOs had carrier experience, the start prior to cruise was rocky. But the learning curve was steep, their maintenance superb and motivation typically high-order USMC. Though one could argue who was the best, the Rippers or the Gray Ghosts, the instant replay would have called it a dead heat. Though competitive by practically any measure, on the deck plates, both outfits worked as a team, were mutually supportive and totally ready to do the combat job should the balloon go up.

Because the Navy had notions of home-porting lots of ships in Greek waters, we spent too much time swinging at the hook near Athens. Each time we did this though, we'd fly a half-dozen machines to nearby Souda Bay on the island of Crete. Besides being one of the most absolutely beautiful spots on earth, Crete was home to some of the best operating any of us had experienced. Off would come the bulky-and-draggy external fuel tanks and up we went to sharpen our fighter skills. Old Shag really ate this up and on selected occasion, would expand his "Fox 2" envelope.

One day, the resident Greek fighter squadron flying old F-84s (soon to get U.S. Phantoms), invited us to dinner at their officers' club. Of course, all the Red Rippers knew that the name of the game was to behave, be gentlemen and have fun, in that order.

We arrived at the appointed hour and entered a large, bare room with an expansive U-shaped table. The Greeks, like most all aviators, could speak English, but not their wives. I sat between Lieutenant Colonel Stavros Ferflionis, the CO, and his smiling wife, who were most polite and reserved. The party went on for about an hour as course after course of sumptuous Greek cuisine appeared before us accompanied by equally excellent and copious measures of local wine. But still, it was quiet and Bill, Butts, Shag et al. were uncharacteristically minding their Ps and Qs. I just knew the guys could not wait to get out of there.

A small band set up as the main courses were being cleared and, on the first note from the bazooki band, my exceedingly reserved and proper host, Stavros, leapt upon the table, pulled me up with him, and it was all downhill from then on! What a party and what fun. Dishes flew, wine flowed, feats of airmanship expanded beyond all logic and the Greeks and Americans were bonded in the firm fellowship of drink and fighter talk.

Ned Lee marries Lucy! Note duty officer and my RIO, Mike Fitch, the "greenie board" above his head, CO's cigar and boar's head fronting lectern.

It was on one of those short deployments that I came back from my second 30-minute ACM hop, all sweaty, tired and ready for a cold one, when I spied a large P3 Orion with a bunch of guys standing around. Shuffling over, I found that they were off for a night mission, asked if I could go along for the ride and off we went. It was my first flight ever in a P3, a big four-engined, prop-jet powered, Soviet-submarine-hunting patrol plane. This mission was headed up by a young lieutenant, who, along with his 15-man crew, was to work the southeastern chunk of the Med in search of an elusive Soviet quarry.

True Faith and Allegiance

Three things happened soon after takeoff at about 1700. First was that one of the big propellers was feathered (stopped), which caused me a five-ten increase in pulse rate, but which was SOP for these guys. Secondly, was the delicious steak dinner (cooked to order!) served to me in a very comfortable chair beside a large picture window back aft. And finally was the answer to my question as to "when we would land," and the laconic response — "0500." Wow! That one 12-hour flight would equate to the same flight time we would log on 15 ACM flights. It was phenomenally interesting though, and gave me a glimmer of an insight into a part of the Naval Aviation scene that few tactical air types like me ever see.

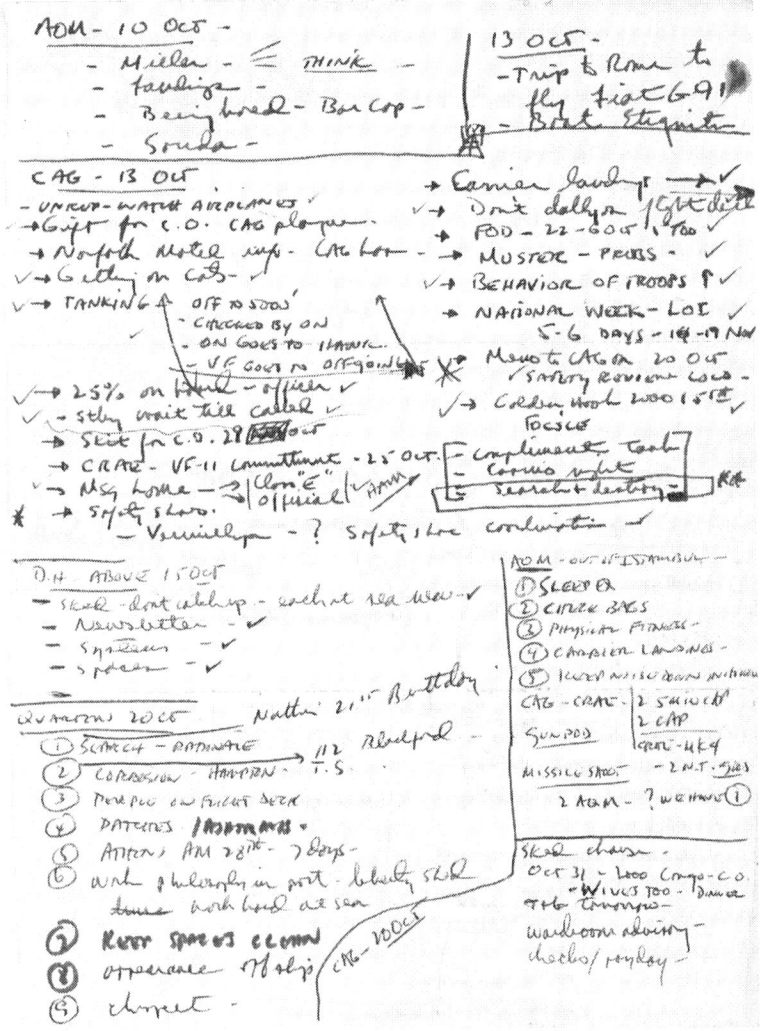

Random notes of cag meetings, talks to troops, all officer meetings, etc. Lots going on!

Jerry Tuttle was a friend and Commanding Officer of an A7 light attack squadron, VA-81. At a meeting late one evening after flight ops, the air wing

The Red Rippers

commander (CAG) had assembled his eight COs and I was waxing eloquent concerns over the lack of airborne fuel for the F4s. (Fuel is to the Phantom as the annual budget is to the Congress — you always need 25% more than you get). Well, I had it figured this time and indicated that if the A6 tanker guys couldn't hack it, "we could configure some of Jerry's A7s with fuel-dispensing buddy stores and extra fuel tanks." Jerry came instantly unglued, leapt to feet and clearly stated, "No way!"

CAG played along, told him to sit down and asked him, "Why not?" I thought Jerry was going to croak, so torqued was he at the sacrilege of using his bombers as fuel givers to the Phantoms.

Jerry says, "We need practice in bombing and shooting our gun." Fortunately, I had had the foresight to arm myself with the fact that each pilot in his squadron had dropped 154 small practice bombs in the preceding 30 days with an accuracy of about 26 feet. I mean these guys were so good they didn't need smart bombs!

Jerry acquiesced under the cold stare of the CAG who said, "Lets go with it." So, in typical Tuttle style, he and his guys did the tanking job with gusto and within a week were the heroes of the entire wing and the recipient of many a kind word of endearment from the F4 troops. What a guy.

The A7 was a remarkable airplane — long legs, large ordnance load, an accurate bombing system and an inertial navigation system. It even had a great HUD, heads up display. The Phantom, despite its awesome performance, was more of a stick and rudder machine with an old-fashioned bomb sight, short legs, rudimentary navigation and two guys vice one.

One day, Jerry let me fly one of his single-seat A7s while we were at Souda Bay. I had studied the book, done a blindfold-cockpit check and knew the emergency procedures. It really wasn't quite kosher, but Jerry's style was the 1972 equivalent in the aviator world of "Damn the conventional wisdom, full speed ahead!" We had a great flight in our two airplanes and my horizons were broadened one more notch.

Operationally, we spent our time at sea doing a bunch of NATO exercises and a few real world scenarios. One of the latter was to escort large, slow, electronic spy planes like the EC-130 whose job it was to monitor the goings on inside Libya. Even back then, old Qhadafi was more than a thorn, he was a real burr under the saddle of the U.S. Suffice to say, we were ready should he try to stick it to us. We would be loaded for bear with missiles and execute a weave over the 130s flying at 190 knots (close to our stall speed). In later years he would venture out to challenge our right to this chunk of international airspace and come out a double loser.

German Generals. Lots of good will on these VIP daytime hops with the Sixth Fleet.

We worked extensively with the Air Forces of other countries whenever we had the chance. Turks, Greeks, Brits, French, Spanish, Germans and Italians were always anxious to come visit us at sea and execute mock attacks on our battle group. At least once a day it seemed, we would host a visiting senior dignitary, take them for a back-seat hop off the ship, do some mild air work, refuel in the air and do a touch-and-go or two before grabbing the arresting wire. To any aviator anywhere, flying off a carrier is the ultimate in aviation. There is simply no equal. Our Navy and country made many friends this way, and left a legacy that paid off big time in terms of good will and respect for our capabilities.

Night carrier landings were always exciting because we never got enough to get comfortable. Two or three night traps per month was enough to double most resting heart rates. If the weather was good, you could see the outline of the lights of the landing area from your inbound perch three-miles astern and 1200 feet, but only if you put your seat up until your hardhat touched the top of the canopy so as to be able to see over the long nose of the Phantom. The key to any carrier landing was absolute and precise control of airspeed (angle of attack), rate of descent (glide slope), and lineup. All were critical and made even more so when the ship's officer of the deck decided to change course with yourself in the groove, the seas caused the stern to go up and down, it was raining, there was a low overcast or some combination of the above. From three miles on in to the trap can best be characterized as an adventure — it was never routine. Most guys worked hard, did these well and felt better for having hurdled the barrier once again. And, go out and do it the next night.

John Manning - A great fighter pilot and citizen soldier.

When the time came to turn over the squadron to our able XO, Jim Taylor, we wanted to 1) have a good guest speaker and 2) enjoy a memorable change of command reception. So we invited a Greek Air Force General whom we had taken for a ride some months prior, to grace our podium on Forrestal's flight deck. And, we sent old Butts to our next port of call, Corfu, Greece, with the charter to ". . . arrange a unique change-of-command reception for not more than $400." The dollar constraint was because Jim and I had to pay for such expected socials out of our own pockets.

From this resulted a great change of command speech by Forrestal's Captain, Jim Linder, as our friend, the Greek General, somehow became unavailable on the appointed day.

The reception, however, went down in the record books as an absolute piece of work, for Butts had rented a large Greek ferry boat, complete with copious food, drink and genuine bazooki band. The guest list included our admiral, his senior staff, all of our officers and other assorted air wing and ship officers. Loading up in Corfu, I was presented with my going away gift, a pair of chrome-plated F4 tail hooks ("Priceless," I told Carolyn), and the party got underway, literally. Well, the ferry's captain was imbibing with relish, kept circling the anchored Forrestal, all the while blowing his whistle, and periodically took some concoction up to the bridge for his helmsman. Though no damage was done, the ferry touched the dock on return with about six knots of forward speed and came to an abrupt stop. Few on board noticed.

What a party! What a squadron! Glasses raised, the final toast, of course, was a rousing rendition of, "Here's to the Red Rippers, a bunch of pig-headed, baloney-slinging, two-balled, he-men bastards."

Once each port call, the squadron COs and XOs would get together. Incredible talent. r to l: Ken Dickerson (VA-83); Jerry Tuttle (VA-81); Bill Quirk (CAG); Hal Berson (E2C); Mike Hall (A6s); Wil King (Helos).

EPILOGUE

• **Bill Pfeiffer** continued a distinguished career in the Navy training reserves and after retirement, flew as an airline pilot. One day, he just dropped dead leaving a legacy of service to his country and a legion of folks who missed his spirit and smile.

- **Jerry Tuttle** went on to three-star admiral where his focus on non-conformist combat capability would be felt for decades. My guess is that when he writes his memoirs, he'll omit the part about providing fuel for the thirsty phantoms back in the early seventies.

- **Jim Linder** continued his service to his country as a flag officer and to this day does not know why he was called in at the last minute to be the guest speaker at the Red Ripper change of command and still wears a non-reg tee shirt.

- **Bob Skeeto** eventually retired to the Pensacola area, went to work for a civilian contractor doing the same as he did in the Navy and still looks back with pride to his days as a Red Ripper.

- **Broom Broomfield** left a legacy of common sense and major contribution to his Navy and nation. Sadly, I lost track of him. Thanks Broom!

- **Dave Anderson** went on to command of VF-74 on board Forrestal when I was CO, made captain and later, flew for the airlines.

- **Jim Taylor,** my XO, continued his distinguished career and tough service to his country in ever-increasing positions of responsibility and served as a flag officer in charge of the Navy's reserve naval air forces.

- **"Butts" Butler** left the Navy for the civilian aviation business world, proud of his days and nights as a carrier-based Naval Aviator.

- **Greek General** was never heard from again, but most would agree that the flight he had with the Red Rippers from the Forrestal was a highlight of his flying career.

- The **Red Rippers** completed their 75th reunion at the Naval Air Station Oceana in 2002 where Rippers from many generations gathered to trade sea stories. I wish my Dad could have been with us as he had been the Ripper CO back in 1942 aboard the old Ranger. Happily, the toast is the same as it was back in those ancient days. The troops stood tall, the pilots and RIOs were ready to go and the wives and kids smiled all the way!

Note from the Skipper

As I sat in the Ready Room waiting for my second flight of the day, I reflect once again on the people within this squadron that make it possible. Our men are absolutely tops. It makes no difference to any of us whether he be tall or short, Protestant or Catholic, black or white or any of the multitudes of categories that Americans tend to put other Americans into. Our people work hard, do a fine job and - I hope - have more fun than not, doing it. We have airplanes to fix, people to take care of, food to fix, spaces to keep clean and all the tasks associated with a small town. The pay is lousy, the working conditions worse, the berthing could certainly be better, but when I pass one of our people and he says "Hi" with a toothy grin, that's my reward. Keep the home fires burning.

P. B. BOOTH
Commander, U. S. Navy

One part of family newsletter while deployed in 1972. If I were to rewrite the above today, the words would not change. Typical maintenance petty officer being publicly congratulated.

AIDES AND THE PENTAGON

> *The Pentagon — a five-sided wind tunnel from whence emanates the spending of over 20% of our national budget. Perhaps more so than any assemblage in the past fifty years, it has markedly influenced the course of recent history, its bottom line, in spite of a course and speed of zero, being the successful avoidance of a nuclear war. This two-year glimpse into its inner workings, circa mid-'70s, is from the admittedly narrow perspective of a displaced Navy fighter pilot.*

After eight-straight years of flying Phantoms, I found myself about a mile from the Pentagon in some obscure, sterile and treeless parking lot. It was a typical Washington, D.C. summer: hot, hazy and humid. On the long walk to the Navy part of the "bigger than an aircraft carrier" Pentagon, replete in my civilian coat and tie mufti, I began to understand why guys did not like duty in the Pentagon.

As a recent F4 Phantom squadron skipper, I was assigned to "506F3" on the Navy headquarters staff. 506 consisted of a group of highly experienced and spring-loaded-to-the-go-position aviators — all commanders and captains. These guys represented the spectrum of Naval Aviation from helos, to fighters, to attack, to logistics support, to patrol planes and a wide array of weapons. They orchestrated the requirements for each aircraft, all munitions and indeed, were instrumental in mapping the future of Naval Aviation. My job was to coordinate all research and development connected with aviation, so it cut across all aspects of the Naval Aviation game plan.

I had never been in the Pentagon, even to visit, so was somewhat unprepared for the culture shock that awaited me. To begin with, 1973 was not only the year that the Vietnam quagmire ended, it was the heyday of the mini-skirt. I mean it was incredible! You have to understand that fighter pilots are inbred with a swivel head so as not to miss any potential targets or get themselves shot out of the sky. Wandering the halls of the Pentagon kept this tactical expertise constantly energized.

Parking was unreal. A half-mile away was the norm — unless one car pooled. So, I teamed up with a fellow commander, Mike McCaffery, a neighbor of mine in our little subdivision about twenty minutes from the big building. We were awarded a fair section to park in, only a couple of blocks away. It worked out pretty good because Mike and I both had similar working hours, from about 0700 to 1800. Because Mike was in the heady world of strategy, working with the other services and policy issues, a lot of his staff work rubbed off on me. Both of us, of course, knew the solution to most of the Navy's ills, if only someone would listen to us.

The third aspect of the transition from fleet to Pentagon, came when I saw "my office" and desk. Wow! Austere was inadequate. Run down, noisy, no privacy and the first one in to our 20-man den made the coffee. Two harassed secretaries rounded out the perks. The alcove I was assigned was home to two captains, one Marine and two commanders, was 15-feet square, had a small wooden "conference" table, at least seventeen, large, standard-Navy safes (first one in opened them) and one, heavy, wire-meshed covered window looking out over a dirty roof to the barred windows of an adjacent office some ten-feet away.

A Marine lieutenant colonel, J.P. Monroe, sat beside me and what a character. A flamboyant fighter pilot with a loud and commanding presence, JP greeted me with the phone to his ear and kept saying words to the effect of, "Yes sir, admiral, right on, admiral." This continued for several days, so I finally asked him how come he, a lowly Marine lieutenant colonel, knew so many admirals. His matter-of-fact reply: "All you Navy squids are admirals to me." Old JP was a real piece of work!

Actually, the job was pretty exciting. The aviation side of the Navy staff clearly drove the Naval Aviation game plan. Dollars, bullets, flying hours, deployments, new weapons and so on, were all influenced by guys like myself who were fresh from the fleet and knew what was needed to improve our sea-going combat capability. On my second day, the three-star admiral who headed Naval Aviation asked my opinion on something. What it was and my response is not important; the fact that he asked at all was. The 506 group had talent at every desk — guys who were smart, had been around the block

Aides and the Pentagon

a few times and all of whom were combat and carrier-duty hardened. Naval Aviation had ridden the high road since WWII and most of the reasons were in the succession of guys like the 506ers who kept blooming up through the deck plates.

After six years in Virginia Beach, we jerked the girls from friends and schools, moved to Washington and found a little house to rent in Sleepy Hollow Woods, with no inkling of what the future would hold for all of us. Culturally, it was OK with museums and the like nearby, but the move was tough on the girls. I might add, that some of my ilk assigned to Washington duty at this stage of their careers, opted to drive home on the weekends in order to keep the homefront on an even keel.

Most of our time in 506 was spent in planning for the future, which is a euphemism for budget building. Despite what one hears about extravagant waste and excessive spending in the Pentagon, the fact is there is intense competition for scarce dollars — between the fighter and patrol-plane types, the submariners and the carrier guys and always between the services. Though few ever liked the final budget plan sent to the Congress each year, all would agree it was very closely scrubbed, with very few, if any, "nice to haves." On the Navy staff, the closer the program came to improving the combat capability of the forces at sea, the better chance it had in the battle of the budget. Unfortunately, however, our Congress sometimes had differing criteria and motivations and routinely foisted upon the services, budget busters that no one excepting themselves and a grateful constituency wanted and which generally resulted in a lesser bang for the buck.

The close quarters of our 506 group acted as a catalyst for sharing ideas. We would spend any free time arguing tactics, mods to airplanes, the need for better night vision, improved reliability and even women aboard ship. It was not a sterile environment; it went on ten-to-twelve hours per day and often on weekends. We did not always get our way, but those in the drivers' seats in the corner offices sure listened. To me this was the best perk of all. There were constant attempts to improve the process by inviting the wisdom and collective talent extant on the Navy's top staff.

Charlie Fritz was one of my "cell mates." An attack pilot of some intra-Navy fame, he had more medals than most of us put together, drank martinis out of a mayonnaise jar and considered himself the Navy's premiere light-attack pilot. He tolerated fighter pilots like JP and me. Anyway, at Charlie's prodding, we decided to have a BYOB party and cookout at our modest home for all of 506. Great party and fun. I vaguely recall, when I got just a bit "woozy" and horizontal on my bed, Charlie leaning over me and, in a loud, penetrating voice, proclaiming that, "I always knew fighter pilots couldn't hack it." Carolyn just smiled.

George Matt, a much-decorated and talented A6-bomber pilot and I were cruising the corridors one day enroute to a meeting, when Vice Admiral Bill Houser, the head of Naval Aviation, grabbed us and said, "Come with me."

True Faith and Allegiance

Falling in loose trail, we ended up in the Pentagon movie theater and witnessed a most incredible two-hour documentary, "Threshold," the story of one Blue Angel season flying the F4 Phantom. It was awesome photography, gorgeous music and had a strong message that said, "If you want to be the best, come fly with us." "Us", of course, was generic for Naval Aviation. As much as George and I enjoyed the Pentagon duty, the love and attraction of aviation at its best, made us pine for duty back on the deck plates and cockpits.

One day, in the spirit of participative management and in anticipation of an upcoming every-six-months gathering of the senior Naval Aviation hierarchy, us guys in the pits were asked to submit agenda items for discussion and possible resolution at this august gathering of the eagles. "Hot damn," said I, "here's a chance to get the supply system squared away." So, I submitted words to the effect that, "From my recent fleet perspective, the supply side of the Navy was doing an incredibly poor job in supplying parts for our airplanes. Too many aircraft were down for parts, it took too long to get what was needed and the cannibalization rate (taking from one airplane to the other), was exorbitant." Lots of 506 heads nodded with empathy. I mean that input of mine had not been into the front office more than five minutes before an extremely irate and very senior Supply Corps captain appeared at my humble desk and demanded to know "What I was talking about?" He was torqued to the absolute nth degree and demanded I retract my input! I did not.

CDR P. B. Booth, USN
OP-506F3, X55295
17 December 1973

SUBJECT

Weapons Systems Readiness

DISCUSSION

The readiness of aircraft weapons system has been at a level of considerable concern to top Navy leaders for many years. Despite the continuous effort of every major staff and OPNAV, we have not experienced significant improvement. The primary contributors to a less than desireable combat readiness posture of our fleet squadrons could be summarized below:

- Shortage of personnel and personnel instability. Manning at 80% to 90% per year are not atypical.

- Supply support remains at a critically low level and is crisis oriented. The problem is not so much one of dollars as it is with management of the system.

- Emphasis on reliability and maintainability is lacking. We have been too preoccupied with state-of-the-art performance to the detriment of R&M. The present emphasis on life cycle costing coupled with rising personnel costs reenforces the necessity to acquire weapons systems that will work and can be maintained on-board ship.

RECOMMENDATIONS

1. **Personnel**. Recognizing that every unit cannot be manned at full allowance, concrete efforts must be instituted to markedly improve personnel stability within squadrons.

2. **Supply**. NORS figures have been misleading for years because of high canabilization rates. There is needed a high level and in-depth examination of supply support at the squadron level. This should be accomplished by non-supply personnel familiar with aircraft maintenance.

3. **Reliability and Maintainability**. Recent emphasis on operational test and evaluation will assist in obtaining more reliable weapons systems. However, those offices responsible for the acquisition of weapons systems must become as concerned with reliability and maintainability as with costs and capability. Emphasis in this area must test with top management. A strong resistance should be exerted from the top to preclude deployment of a system for which the R&M contractural goals have not been met or proven.

Aides and the Pentagon

Early on, I was asked by the aviation three-star to draft some ideas for a pitch he was to give to an industry group re the future of Naval Aviation at the turn of the century, twenty-five years in the future. This was another opportunity to input the message of reliability. Two excerpts from the draft are below:

> The goals of Naval Aviation as I see them are three fold -
>
> (1) Maintain a progressive capability to counter the threat.
>
> (2) Reduce the number of types of airplanes, weapons support equipment and spares.
>
> (3) Whatever we have - we must make it work.
>
> Now, these may not appear to be earthshaking goals. But if you remembered my earlier point as regards the increasing threat, the increasing weapons system complexity and resultant cost increases - all rising at an exponential rate - then the message is clear. The technological breakthrough we need from you people and the vast community you represent is in <u>weapons systems cost</u> and in the ability of that <u>weapon system to work when the sailor or pilot turns it on</u>. I am convinced that you all can stay one step in front of the threat- you have done it in the past and you will be able to do it in the future. I am not so sure we can tackle the cost and reliability problem.
>
> I need not remind you all that it does no good to design a highly automated system that requires one man to operate if that system requires 10 men to maintain it and a floating Sears and Roebuck warehouse to service it.
>
> As I see it then - from a naval aviation viewpoint - 25 years hence, our expected and attainable goal of meeting the threat with our high mix of big carriers and sophisticated, highly capable aircraft and the low mix with V/STOL and SCS can be met. I am firmly convinced that the concentrated efforts of the technological community must as well be looking seriously into the awesome task of how to get the required capability with a <u>dramatic</u> reduction in costs of ownership and at the same time an equally <u>dramatic</u> and quantum jump in our ability to make our weapons systems consistently work as designed on a small ship or airplane as well as in the laboratory.
>
> Gentlemen, it has been my pleasure to have had your time and attention.

The Pentagon was absolutely fascinating from a physical perspective: five stories, three basements, 31 miles of corridor, a huge gym complex, at least ten restaurants, a complete shopping mall, three small hospitals, headquarters for the Army, Navy, Air Force and the Department of Defense and the working home to some 25,000 people. My every-two-week haircut in the mall barber shop would take five minutes, plus or minus one. There were lots of beautiful original combat art works, displays such as a Congressional Medal of Honor Hall and numerous models of ships and airplanes. In the basement, were some of the most super-secret enclaves in the country.

Incredible as it may seem, uniforms for military personnel were worn only on Wednesday, in the case of the Navy. This, presumably, started at the behest of President Eisenhower at his inauguration in 1952, "So as to reduce the visibility of the military in the Washington area." Hard to believe!

The Pentagon has to be the absolute ultimate in entrenched bureaucracy. Ten levels can say no, but no one can say yes. Everyone has a boss. Even the head Navy guy, the CNO, answers to the Secretary of the Navy, who answers to the grossly inflated defense department staff, who in turn must answer to the president. The large Joint Chiefs of Staff jumps into the fray at all levels. And over all of this are 535 members of the Congress and their 5,000 (or so) staff members. And each one of these thousands of folks can ask questions of, demand answers from or call on the carpet, the troops and military folk such as those in the Naval Aviation staff trenches. It's a formidable process!

When I checked in with Vice Admiral Bill Houser, the Navy's head aviator, he said the key ingredient for getting things done in the Pentagon was persistence. "Don't give up," he said. He's dead right!

Decision making in the Pentagon is one of its most fascinating aspects. While the military officers in each of the services generate the program they want (consistent within a broad framework established by the Department of Defense and with a common Navy denominator of winning the war at sea), the Secretary of the Navy sprinkles the program with a touch of carefully-ground politics. The bloated and oft-times out-of-touch and inexperienced Department of Defense staff gives it massive doses of political and their own special-interest flavor. When the Navy's program finally gets to the hallowed floors of the Congress, it filters down to its ultimate watery and politically balanced finality, with more "nice to haves" than are necessary or reasonable.

It sometimes grates on folks like myself, whose job it was to fight the wars and man the ships, to have a congressional staffer or senior civilian who has never seen a sailor or combat or tough times on the deck plates, carve up a program put together with the best minds the Navy can muster.

Even down at the lower levels of our three-star-led aviation staff, we were constantly bombarded with requests for studies, answers to questions or requests for appearances by a myriad of the civilian hierarchy. In fact, as the civilian staffs of the Congress and the DOD expanded beyond all reasonableness, a very large portion of the workday was spent in question answering. The pace was indeed frantic a good deal of the time. Asked about my job by a friend in San Diego, I described it "As akin to a guy with a one-ton truck who had two tons of canaries to transport and who therefore had to keep 50% of them airborne at any one time."

Because of the enormous sensitivity to special interests, those in the business of acquiring weapons or aircraft in the Pentagon, which most of the Pentagon did in one way or another, the rules of contractor favors and ethical standards of conduct were tightly regulated. Even a contractor-bought lunch was a "no-no." In order to preclude any semblance of impropriety, we were warned not to accept anything from a contractor whose job it was to sell to the military.

One evening however, I compromised this trust. Here's how it went: One of my 506 friends asked Carolyn and me to "cocktails" in a hotel hospitality suite prior to the large and widely attended annual Navy Ball. The "cocktails" were hosted by a contractor with a many-decade record of producing Navy aircraft. So, off we went. After a glass of wine and a couple of carrot sticks, we excused ourselves as the festivities were about to start down below in the hotel. "No way," says our host, "stay for just a bit longer." In a few minutes, several large dining tables were wheeled in, and the 30 or so in attendance sat down to an absolutely ornate and five-star dining extravaganza. Was I ever suckered! This was, in retrospect and in my judgment, clearly outside the bounds of reasonable ethical standards. I think the contractor knew it, too.

Despite its occasional meanderings, the Pentagon is, in fact, run and staffed by 96% ethical, smart and public-service-minded folks. But all, no matter military or civilian, senior or junior, entrenched or new guy, have their own agenda whether it be from the perspective of an F4 front-seat, the biggest employer in St. Louis or the congressional staffer representing the 1st Congressional district of Florida. Its products of course, have been a nuclear confrontation avoided, a mostly credible combat mix and a sprinkling of political largess into America's body politic.

After a year or so in 506, I found I had passed the hurdle of what's called a "bonus command" or follow on to a squadron CO slot. This would have been as a carrier air wing commander or as CO of the F4 training squadron and would cut short what is normally a three-year tour for a commander in Washington. As far as I was concerned, this was good. It meant that I was doing OK professionally (moving up), could probably get back to Virginia Beach and the house we owned and most importantly, return to the real Navy of sailors, machines and action.

Almost at the same time, however, I was summoned to the office of the number-two guy in Naval Aviation, Rear Admiral Jack Christianson. If you could write a movie script for a "senior naval aviator," you would describe Jack. He was the squarest peg in a round hole I'd ever seen! The exact opposite of a staffer, he was the real Naval Aviator — charismatic, flamboyant, natural leader and extremely operationally savvy. He was the precise antithesis of the "Pentagon Cowboy," defined as one who has spent a disproportionate chunk of his professional military life in the Pentagon corridors vice out on the deck plates and in the cockpits.

My boss, the Navy's top admiral at his stand-up desk on the Pentagon's fourth-deck E ring. Note painting of USS Enterprise which Admiral Holloway commanded.

The admiral said that it was time that I quit flying and did something that would "broaden my horizons and what did I think?" I kind of thought that whatever I did do must be pretty good to compensate for giving up a bonus command that involved flying and said so. The next day I got a call to go see Admiral Jim Holloway, the Navy's number-two man and soon to be the next CNO. He needed an aide. Someone suggested I remove my mustache, as ". . . the Admiral didn't like them."

I found my way to the front-office complex and, replete with mustache and a twinge of indecisiveness on my part, met the Admiral. With no preamble, he said that "My flying days were over" and that I was to be his aide when he stepped into the CEO slot for the Navy. I mumbled something half-way intelligent and left to turnover my 506F3 duties to Commander Dick Dunleavy, a friend and A6 Intruder Naval Flight Officer. Carolyn was pleased because it meant staying another year in our nice little rented house, good schools for the girls and a reasonably pleasant shore-based quality of life.

An aide is defined as a "horse holder," so called because in years past, the generals needed someone to hold their horse whenever generals did whatever generals do when not horsebound. When horses went away, the Army guys called them "aides de camp." Hence, the call sign, aides. Personal aides were generally lieutenants, except those for four-stars, who rated a full commander.

So, here I was, a full-fledged aide. It was kind of ironic, for there were three jobs in the Navy I had not wanted — aero engineering in PG school, aircraft handling officer on a carrier and to be an aide. I wasn't too enthralled, but like a good trooper, would put forth my best to do the Admiral an above and beyond job.

The job description for being an aide is kind of nebulous. There are no books. My background was heavily oriented to the rather narrow niche of Navy fighter aviation. I had been the beneficiary of two MBA graduate years at Stanford, but had not attended any other non-flying schools or staff jobs in my seventeen years. As it turned out, it was close to the most interesting year of my life.

Admiral James L. Holloway III, U. S. Navy, was a carrier pilot, had been an early commanding officer of the nuclear aircraft carrier Enterprise, was a championship wrestler at the Naval Academy, was an early-on shoo-in to make full admiral and had an absolutely squared-away wife named Dabney.

Required mug shot that goes in your record.

One of the first trips on the Admiral's busy agenda was to the annual Tailhook Convention in Las Vegas, a pilgrimage devoted to the adulation of all carrier aviators by themselves. Always there was a prestigious guest of honor and my boss got the nod. At his behest, I worked up a dynamite speech for him to give, the essence of which was "How great you all are." It was clearly a roof-raising testimonial which would buttress the high esteem all carrier aviators had for themselves. I was proud of the job I had done for my new boss.

As the CNO, Admiral Holloway could take Dabney with him when he flew in his airplane, an old, twin-jet carrier bomber, modestly converted to VIP use. So, while Dabney needle worked, the Admiral busied himself with the contents of two suitcase-sized "work bags." With no meetings or phone calls, he would accomplish a lot on those flights.

Anyway, about over the Mississippi River headed for Las Vegas, he pulls out the speech and proceeds to color it with red ink and big bold "Xs" through my painstakingly crafted paragraphs. He smiled all the while.

At the appointed hour, the Admiral mounted the podium in front of 2,000 expectant aviators to the tumultuous tune of a standing ovation. Here's what happened: The CNO said, "I asked my aide to write a speech for me and here's what I think of it." He tore it up — literally. The place went wild. He then said, "I got rid of that speech, now I have to get rid of the aide that wrote it." I mean that Las Vegas banquet hall went absolutely ballistic! They loved him — he could do no wrong! Cowering low in my seat, such was my introduction to the vagaries of being an aide.

The Admiral's first real job was to reestablish a chain of command that had taken some heavy hits in recent years. To this end, he continuously preached the involvement of the fleet commanders, the COs and the Chief Petty Officers. The reaction down on the deck plates was predictable and refreshing. Once again, the leadership in the middle of the field were players and not observers.

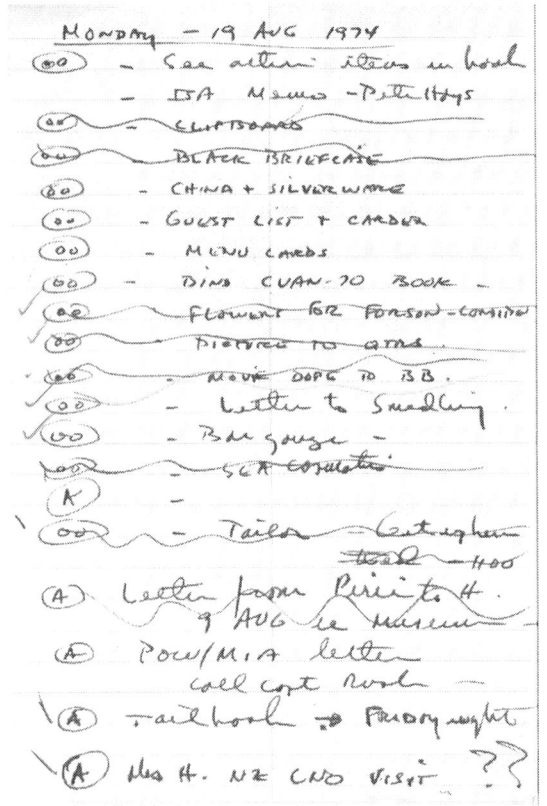

One day's worth of action items early in my tenure.

The post-Vietnam Navy was at a crossroads. The Navy's focus for eight long years, of course, had been on the incredible people and ship-draining hole of Vietnam. Our troops were tired and our ships in poor shape from years of deferred maintenance due to an awesomely high operating tempo. At the same time, the Cold War, with its omnipresent umbrella of nuclear destruction, wasn't about to go away. As a result, my Admiral devoted a great deal of his brainpower and any free time, to rethinking naval strategy and, equally as important, how to present this to the Congress, AKA, the people of the United States.

After a couple of months on the job, I noticed the Admiral looking kind of tired, so the next time I was at the official quarters, I asked Dabney about it. Her pragmatic response was, "Well I guess so, he's been getting up at 0500 every morning working on his upcoming congressional testimony." And indeed he had been. Getting the Navy's message across in coherent form to the ilk of the Senate Armed Services Committee, House Appropriation Committee and so on, was a tall order. In typical Holloway ethic, though, he attacked this with gusto and was the best advocate and articulator of Navy strategy, policy and its raison d'etre the Navy's ever had on that hill called Congress.

Aides and the Pentagon

While I had some fun, the Admiral had lots, often at the expense of his aide. Meeting with the Commander in Chief of the Atlantic Fleet in Norfolk, we were enroute in a converted carrier helo, too old for use in the fleet. From his big seat back aft, the boss motioned for me, pointed to a small tug towing the daily refuse barge out to sea and said with a broad grin, "Your next command." What a guy!

Admiral Holloway had been one of the first aviators to have been selected for nuclear aircraft carrier command and had attended the grueling academics of the world of Admiral Rickover, ". . . the father of our nuclear Navy." About halfway through this one-year endurance contest, Rickover called Holloway in and asked, "Captain Holloway, how is it that you have three Fs and a D?"

The Captain's rapid response: "Admiral, I guess I spent too much time in one subject."

Later, when Rickover, by far and away the Navy's senior admiral, was a guest at the quarters or at his most-every-Saturday-morning visit to the CNO's office, it was my job to ". . . keep him occupied." It was tough, for Admiral Rickover was not one for small talk. Suffice to say I was no better at this task than in writing "Tailhook" speeches.

And broadening it was. Sitting in on meetings, all sorts of official "dos," dealing with other services (he was ex-officio a member of the Joint Chief of Staff) and being a sometimes springboard for ideas of his. If asked, I would venture an opinion, but, in general, kept my mouth shut, for my boss got enough gratuitous advice in one day to last an ordinary mortal a lifetime. I wasn't about to add to it.

Our Navy of course, stayed close to the Navies of other nations. Our strategy had never been a "go-it-alone" one, but rather intertwined with that of other nations through numerous treaties and alliances. The CNO therefore, spent a good deal of time with other Navies and their CNOs.

One such visit, to his Italian counterpart in Rome, comes to mind. The setting was late in the Italian day — about 1930. We had been in the air and busy since early that morning with a late night the evening before. And we were tired. So, here we sat, the Italian CNO, my CNO and me in a very large, three-story high, ornate room which was quiet as a tomb. An aide brought coffee. The Italian CNO droned on and on in a soft monotone. The eyelids of my CNO began to droop and I'll be damned if he wasn't falling sound asleep, head nodding to and fro. What to do? I coughed loudly and with a start, my leader awoke. This repeated itself several times, but if it hadn't worked, I had it planned to spill my coffee, figuring that the resultant hoopla would break the monotony and wake my boss. For balance, I should note that my Admiral stoutly maintained he was simply ". . . concentrating on the Italian's thoughts and was not dozing." Dabney, the equalizer as usual, only smiled.

It was on this trip that we went to Naples where the Admiral was to meet with the head of the Southern Flank of NATO, a four-star Turkish General. We were to arrive by an old Navy H-46 helo, the only adornment for the CNO having been to provide a white sheet over the canvas bench seats. Arrayed in full-dress whites replete with high choker collar, swords, gloves, medals and formal aiguellettes for me, we landed in front of the headquarters with flags flying, bands playing, more brass than I had ever seen and a seat upon which the Admiral was sitting, that collapsed. His tail went down to the floor boards, feet toward the overhead, sword pointed to the vertical, and the worried face of his host peered into the helo. Dabney tried not to laugh, the Admiral sputtered, the pilot was aghast and I did my best to haul my boss to an upright position more befitting the head of the most powerful Navy in the world.

```
                TAB A
        CHIEF OF NAVAL OPERATIONS
              TRIP SCHEDULE
                SAN DIEGO
              29-31 JAN 75

WEDNESDAY, 29 JANUARY

0650   Depart Quarters for NAF Andrews with Mrs. Holloway,
       CNO car and driver. Uniform: Service Dress Blue.
0730   Depart NAF Andrews by A3/LUNO 144857, Pilot: CDR
       Newcombe, ETE: 6+00, less 3 hours. Breakfast on plane.
1030   Arrive L.A. International, Butler Aviation (Phone 213-646-
       8787). Met by CDR Bill Graves (CHINFO). LCDR Dewey
       accompany.
1115   T.V. press interview.
1200   Luncheon with L.A. Times editorial board.
1300   Depart for L.A. International Airport.
1330   Depart BY A3 for NAS North Island.
1400   Arrive North Island. Met by VADMs Salzer and Baldwin and
       RADM Gilkison. Proceed to Sea Cabin.
1445   Depart Sea Cabin for COMSURFPAC.
1500   Call on COMSURFPAC
1525   Tour PHIBASE.
1600   Press conference at Phib Base.
1645   Depart for Sea Cabin.
1700   Arrive Sea Cabin.
1800   Reception hosted by COM 11 at O' Club NAS North Island.
       Uniform: Service Dress Blue. RON Sea Cabin.

THURSDAY, 30 JANUARY

0755   Depart Sea Cabin. Uniform: Service Dress Blue.
0800   Meet with VADM Baldwin (CNAP).
0825   Present awards to CAPT Crayton.
0840   Depart NORIS for NTC.
0900   Meet with local area C.O.s.
```

CNO visits to the fleet were fast moving and jam packed with meetings, talks, visits and business socials. Aide worked strawman plan.

The CNO would get literally hundreds of requests to speak or visit groups throughout the world. One of the aide's jobs was to screen these and make a recommendation to the executive assistant and then to the Admiral. One of these was a request from Representative Bob Sikes for the CNO to speak to a group of 1,500 civilian workers at a function in his district of Pensacola, Florida. I recommended "No," because I felt the CNO had bigger and better things to do with his time. I soon learned however, that when Bob Sikes asked the CNO for something, he generally got it. So, off we went to Pensacola.

Sikes was the first politician I had seen at close quarters and what an absolute piece of work! In the Congress for some twenty-seven years, he was a powerful friend of the Navy. After a long and eloquent introduction of the CNO that took longer than the Admiral's speech, he and Bob returned to the hotel. Sitting in the front seat, I soon learned why the CNO had been asked down by the venerable Sikes. The gist of the Congressman's comments went something like: "Admiral (long pause), I have down here in Escambia County, 4,000 acres of prime land on deep water and I would like you to seriously consider moving the U. S. Naval Academy from Annapolis to Pensacola." I dared not look at my Admiral's face, for if I had done so and smiled, I would have been off to Keflavik, Iceland for a tour of duty as the assistant officer-in-charge of the galley. At any rate, the Admiral handled it well and it was just another routine day in the life of a CNO, a senior Congressman and an aide.

One morning back in his Pentagon office, at his usual 0700 arrival, my boss limped in to the office, said his arm hurt, was overweight, had a cold and finally, that, "I'm a living testimonial to the biodegradable nature of the human body" and to "please get me some Rose Hips."

Well, I understood biodegradable, but no one knew the Rose Hips connection. So, I called Carolyn, who said words to the effect of, "Dummy, they're Vitamin Cs."

It was during this early period that Admiral Holloway addressed the issue of why Navy personnel in Washington did not wear uniforms as a matter of course. In short, he wanted our Washington contingent to wear the Blue Service uniform year-round, including the oppressively hot summers. His point, well taken, was that the entire civilian business hierarchy wore suits and ties all year, so why not the Navy?

So, the system produced a lightweight version of the blue service uniform and us Pentagon types began to wear them everyday. Well, complaints surfaced galore — would not hold a crease, too hot, too expensive and so on. The CNO, who had an upcoming visit and speech to the New Orleans Navy League, said he would settle it "once and for all" by wearing his blues to the 100-degree temperature and high humidity of the Mardi Gras city.

Off we went in our converted ice-cold bomber to be met with an equally-cool car four-feet from the airplane's hatch, drove to within four feet of the New Orleans Hilton hotel, with a repeat scenario the next day on the return trip to Washington. His pronouncement the next day when ensconced in his big and cool office, was to proclaim how "cool the new uniform is" and, "I can't understand all the fuss." It's all in the eyes of the beholder. Wisdom prevailed and year-round blues did not.

Admiral Holloway was really good at explaining to ordinary folk why we needed a strong Navy — a Navy second to none in the world. Arguments such as, ". . . a strong conventional force is the best deterrent to the use of nuclear weapons; . . . we are an island nation, our economy is global, our interests are global, and our Navy needs to be forward deployed and globally oriented; . . . the striking power of the Navy is not just carriers, frigates or subs, but rather the convergence of this power into the battle group; . . . the accessibility of land bases is increasingly on the wane, but our Navy can and does sail with total impunity, all international waters of the world; . . . ergo, the U. S. Navy." It was an understandable message to those on board and made a lot of sense to the people through their Washington contingents. The Navy was emerging from Vietnam tall and confident in the saddle.

Guest list for a dinner in honour of Commander and Mrs. Peter B. Booth hosted by Admiral and Mrs. James L. Holloway III on Friday, 16 May 1975 at 1930 aboard the CNO Barge, Pier 2, Washington Navy Yard. CIVILIAN INFORMAL/CASUAL.

HOSTS: Admiral and Mrs. James L. Holloway III

GUESTS OF HONOUR: Commander and Mrs. Peter B. Booth

GUESTS: Captain and Mrs. John S. Leffen

Captain Edward H. Martin, USN

Commander and Mrs. Diego E. Hernandez

Commander and Mrs. Daniel J. Michaels

Commander and Mrs. Paul W. Parcells

Captain and Mrs. William E. Ramsey

Commander and Mrs. Richard R. Tarbuck

It was getting time to move on. Move on in my case meant going to a large multi-purpose supply ship as CO. This was a good deal, for it was a command and any command can be rewarding, both professionally and personally. I say "can be," because any sea-going command had its pitfalls and at least a few of my contemporaries had bitten the dust enroute up this particular career ladder. There were aviators commanding all sorts of large logistics and amphibious ships and most of these had as their immediate superior, non-aviators. Some of these folks reacted with a sledge hammer to minor digressions of the aviator ilk, when they strayed from the straight and narrow. Right or wrong, it was my perception that the leadership in these communities were overly aggressive in addressing what they considered errors in judgment or approach and, as a result, a sort of defensive crouch on the part of some aviator COs had developed. I wanted to know what it was that caused the downfalls by asking a bunch of guys who had been through the process, to "Tell me the three best things you did while commanding your ship — and the three worst."

In the big bomber one quiet evening en route back to Washington, Dabney busy with her needle work, I ventured the question to the CNO, who responded for some twenty minutes on all the good things he had done as CO of a seaplane tender and then silence.

After a respectful pause, I said, "How about the three worst, Admiral?"

"Didn't have any worst," said the boss, leaning back in his big seat.

Dabney just smiled and said something like, "Jimmy, how about the hurricane off Guam you hit?"

So, bit by bit, I got the rest of the story.

What a guy!

EPILOGUE

- The **Pentagon** continues on a course and speed of zero, not much having changed except the length of the skirts.

- **Washington** continues to be the only place in the country one can run five miles in any direction and not leave the scene of the crime.

- **"JP" Monroe** went on to command a Marine fighter squadron and air wing, worked in the Washington office of McDonnell-Douglas and is now a retired spokesman for Marine Aviation.

- **Admiral Rickover** went on to retire, his irascible demeanor transcended by a fleet that is now mostly nuclear and which has never experienced a significant accident.

- **Jack Christianson** retired from the Navy, worked for Grumman Aircraft and is still vocally aggressive and constantly out in front.

- **Bill Houser** retired as a vice admiral and has worked in several non-defense-related companies.

- **George Matt** retired as a captain and now works in the Norfolk area.

- **"Threshold"** never made it commercially, despite its beauty, but is today my favorite aviation documentary.

- **Admiral Holloway** did three more years as the CNO, left the Navy in better shape than when he took over and has served on many non-remuneration citizen study groups at the highest levels of our government. He still denies he was asleep during his meeting with the Italian CNO and, though indeed biodegradable, looks better than he did thirty-years prior.

- **Mike McCaffery** went on to make flag and continue his major and unselfish contributions to this country.

- **Dick Dunleavy** commanded an aircraft carrier, rose to vice admiral and the head of Naval Aviation, but fell victim to an early '90s Tailhook convention clearly out of control and was retired as a rear admiral.

- **506** continues as the premiere think tank for the future of Naval Aviation.

- **Charlie Fritz** is reputed to still bad-mouth fighter pilots.

- **Bob Sikes** finally retired from the Congress, his sizable military legacy in Florida's First Congressional District continuing intact, notwithstanding the "loss" of the Naval Academy to Annapolis. Sadly, he passed away in 1994.

- The **old A3 executive** transport is in the boneyard, replaced by bigger and better.

KING TUT, LOGS AND SYLVANIA

King Tut crosses the Atlantic, large supply ship lost in the North Sea, daily diary and Rickover.

KING TUT CROSSES THE ATLANTIC

King Tut lived in the land of Egypt circa 1450 BC. The discovery of his treasures and remains in his Egyptian tomb are one of the real finds of the 20th century. The subsequent triumphant tour of the United States is known by many. But, how King Tut got from there to here is not.

The dilemma faced by the U.S. and Egyptian governments, given that both countries wanted the treasures to tour America, was how to get them our way. Because the artifacts were priceless (literally), there was no insurance available and it was a geographical given that they had to go by sea or air. Air was considered too risky. Ergo, the U.S Navy to the fore.

The vessels chosen were the U.S.S. *Milwaukee*, an AOE, and the U.S.S. *Sylvania*, an AFS on duty in the Mediterranean due to return to the states after a Med deployment. So the story starts with on-loading Tut et al. onto the Milwaukee in Alexandria, Egypt and after a short Med crossing, going skin-to-skin with the Sylvania in Naples harbor.

The Sylvania was the second of six versatile all-purpose (excepting ammunition and fuel) replenishment ships. She carried everything from jet engines to electronics to toilet paper (can you imagine the fleet running out of toilet paper!), to Canadian bacon. It was literally a floating supply center.

Sylvania had a crew of about 350, could do 20-knots cruising and 21-knots flat-out with three boilers and one big screw. We would normally service each ship in the 6th Fleet at least once a month along with numerous forays into the Atlantic and North Sea. A fascinating operation to say the least.

Back to Naples harbor: With copious safety nets rigged, numerous civilian security guards, State Department reps ad infinitum, we commenced loading the 100-or-so separate boxes that contained King Tut and his treasures into our number-two hold just forward of the bridge. All went well and we set sail for a brief port stop in Rota, Spain enroute to Norfolk and home.

I must say that in our exuberance to return to home base, the good steaming weather, the spotlessly-clean ship and no underway replenishments in the middle of the night, it was an upbeat and positive crew. We knew we had done a fine job on the deployment and the attitude of the crew reflected a good feeling about themselves and the ship.

Our euphoria was short lived, however, because smack in the middle of our great-circle route home and in the dead center of the Atlantic Ocean, was a late-season major hurricane named "Emmy."

The storm was forecast to continue curving to the east and south, so the fleet weather center folks in Norfolk suggested we deviate to the north to give it a wide berth to our south. We concurred in this plan.

However (isn't there always a however!), the forecast proved wrong, the hurricane continued its northward track and we concurred once again in a further deviation to the north under the premise that Emmy would indeed curve to the east.

As the wind and seas started to pick up, the 15,000-ton Sylvania started to gently creak and groan. The XO (a submariner), the operations officer (surface warfare), and myself (an aviator) huddled over past-October hurricane tracks and thumbed through our friendly maritime bible, Bowditch.

It soon became apparent that if we continued on our PIM (point of intended movement), that we would rendezvous with Keflivik, Iceland, or South Greenland in a couple of days, So we made the decision to alter course from about 330 degrees to 150 degrees (a 180!) and keep our 20 knots. This time we did not get a recommendation from our Norfolk friends.

Because the winds in a hurricane in the northern hemisphere are counter-clockwise, the dangerous semi-circle was to the east which was where we were. So, we were somewhat conservative in our quest to get south of the hurricane center and then head west to our beckoning home-port of Norfolk.

The next night, about mid-night, and still at 20 knots, we were due east of the hurricane center (which finally started moving as forecast all along, to the east — Ugh) and headed south. The ship was riding well, but it was moving a good bit along with some more pronounced creaking and groaning. And — the wind was howling!

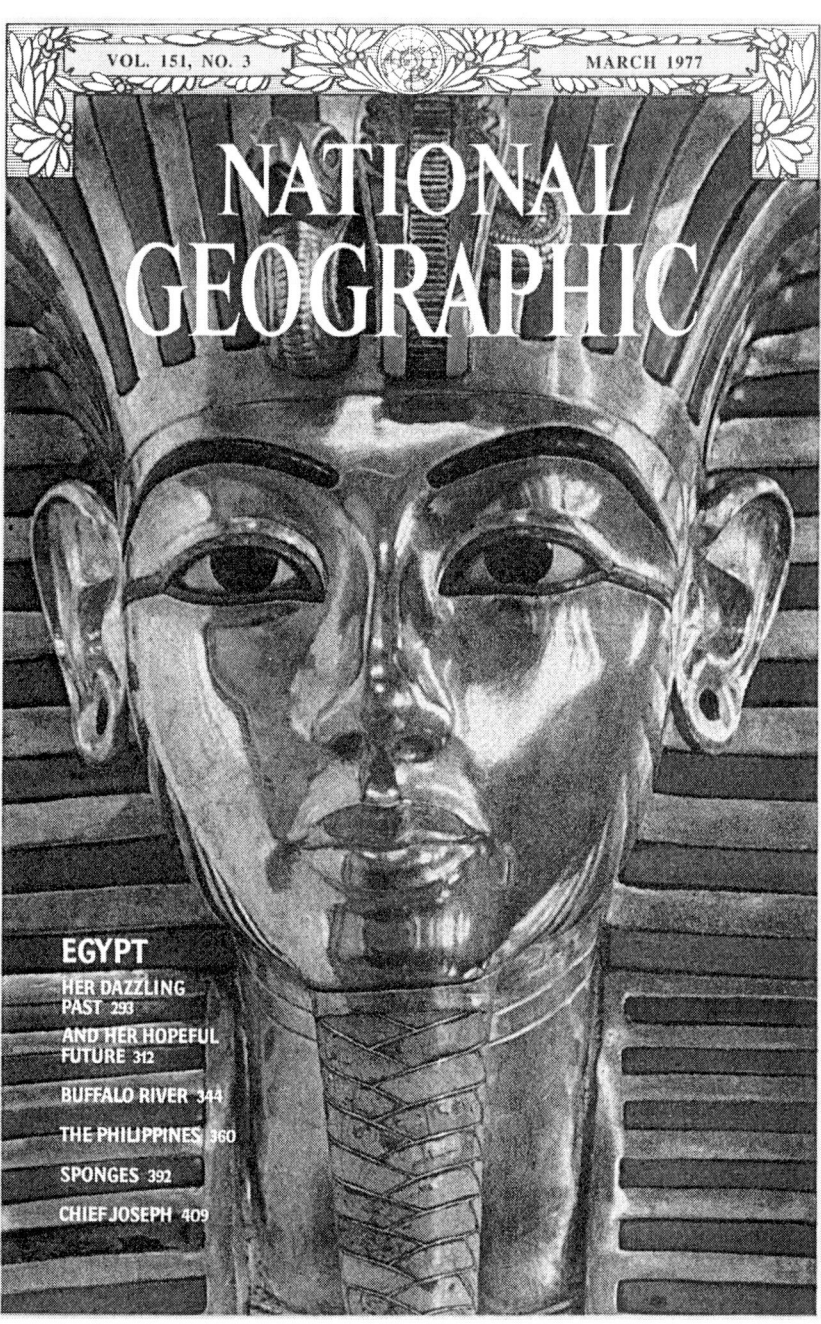

Back to King Tut: Throughout the voyage, we had taken the precaution of having a watch around the clock outside the roped-off area in the number-two hold. In the middle of this dark and stormy night, the Exec and Master Chief requested permission to secure the watch because there was a distinct edge of nervousness on the part of the youngsters we had down there. In fact, there was real concern amongst at least some of the crew, that King Tut really did not appreciate the TLC we were giving him and in fact was rebelling!

I went down to the hold at about 0200 (with the Exec and the Master Chief — both big fellows) and it was eerie and definitely scary. Dark, creepy, groaning, the ship heaving and the wind really whistling and heavy rain bouncing on the overhead hatch cover!

The next morning revealed sizeable seas of about 15 feet, a 45-knot wind on our starboard bow, soggy clouds and in and out of heavy rain. We were inching our way to the south five degrees at a time with the hurricane center about 150 miles to our west.

We got the crew together on the messdeck and showed them what the game plan was (which we had been doing all along) and as forcefully as I could muster, told them that King Tut was really enjoying being at sea and that he had absolutely nothing to do with our present state of affairs.

King Tut and the Sylvania, of course, cleared Emmy to the south and kept our 20 knots to home base and a great Norfolk welcome. No one expressed concern over the late arrival. We all knew it was due to the vagaries of a strong hurricane and had nothing to do with our valiant King Tut.

UNEDITED LOG OF THE COMMANDING OFFICER, USS SYLVANIA (AFS-2)

- 15-23 August, 1975: Got together with XO, Commander Tim Marvin, and stressed that I wanted an open and honest relationship with XO and that I intended to work the chain of command. Gave him my first impressions to wit:

> Strong department heads and officers
> Competent group of Chiefs
> Crew 90% good
> Ship filthy and crew not sharp in appearance

Spent most of week just reading, wandering about and talking to anyone who would talk to me. Stayed on ship in shipyard — up at 0600 and to bed at 2400. Mast problem is unreal. Thought previous masts had been too lenient. Started out tough in first ten cases. I want those bad guys in crew to get what's coming to them. We have too many fine people in crew for a few to tarnish the reputation of others. Had two suicide attempts, two administrative discharges and one man that tried to swim the two-mile wide James River!

Chief Engineer is great and really digging in. What with most equipment torn up and lots of new guys, he has a big job. See no reason why we can't be best in the fleet by next year.

- 25-30 August, 1975: Met with officers, chiefs and E-6s this week and got some good feedback. Main points stressed were adherence to the chain of command and reasonable U.S. Navy standards. Overhaul is progressing, but there are glimmers of an extension. Have come down hard with contractor on meeting contractual commitments. Captain's mast again. All were up for at least the 3rd time. Hit hard. Chief Engineer really hard at it and working 18-hour days. PEB upcoming which will be a first for Sylvania. Ship appearance up markedly, but still unsat. XO, I am delighted with. Works 0630 to 2200. He and I are getting it off right. Big job ahead and lots of programs and tasks to push. We must do well on: Load out and fill; PEB; Reftra; Insurv; Deploy to 6th Fleet on time; Complete overhaul on time. I am absolutely excited about job. Without a doubt, it is the most demanding and exciting job a man could have!

Exhorting the troops at an early personnal inspection in the shipyard flanked by command master chief and senior chief.

- 2-9 September, 1975: Talked to crew on APL. I think it went well although talked too long. It was a good balance of humor and seriousness. My main objective was to show them that I cared for them, but yet I fully intended to be tough when it came to supporting our traditional standards. Feedback indicates it went well. Main point was we needed to complete on time or, "take contractor with us." They say all on track. Not sure Supships knows what's going on. 24-hours later contractor asking for major extension. My first credibility crisis. I suspect skullduggery on part of contractor due to fact if we were to leave on time, there would be a 5-week hiatus before next ship comes in and contractor would take it in the ear. This place is a lousy environment. Morale is low, troops are far from home, the ship is filthy and we have a long ways to go.

- 9-15 September, 1975: This was a very disappointing week in that it is obvious contractor is dragging his heels big time and has no intention of finishing on time. And to top it off, the TYCOM authorized sizeable evaporator work against my objections. It was a CYA, because they messed it up to begin with. I am torn between whether to yell louder or wait and see. If I yell louder, there is the chance the ship's reputation would be hurt. I think the best thing to do is to wrap up the overhaul as fast as we can and indicate in our completion report the complete lack of any management on the part of the contractor and a contract that is essentially worthless. The fact is, that it is in the best interest of the contractor to let things slide.

Congrats on a job well done.

- 16-20 September, 1975: This has been a good week. I feel I have the confidence of the crew, they know I won't BS them and that I am the union leader. UAs are down from twenty a month ago to six or seven. We had no mast this week and have reenlisted three first termers. The ship is looking ten-times better as are the troops. The PEB comes aboard next week as will the Commodore for the first time. I rest easy in the satisfaction that our guys

King Tut, Logs and Sylvania

have absolutely busted tail. What more could a CO ask? Though we are way behind, the contractor president, all VPs and our ship's superintendent were all off fishing. Rotten to the core! Worked a good bit on affirmative action plan. It will be a doozy.

Front row: Cdr Jay Nace, supply officer; Lcdr Jim Harris, operations officer; Lt Phil Moaney, first lieutenant.

- 20-27 September, 1975: What a week! We failed PEB. Dark day. The first time I have ever failed since being in Navy (well, almost). Our guys tried hard and did their best. We have nothing to be ashamed of. Contractor attitude and productivity finally satisfactory. Don't know why. Our Master Chief died of a heart attack on Monday. Just dropped dead. He was a sailor's sailor and is a big loss. Everyone chipped in. Phil Moaney did a great job as CACO. I think we are at a low-point morale-wise, although OK. The A/C does not work, no fresh water, heads don't work and its been raining all week. This plus the loss of the Master Chief and the PEB failure, has caused my enthusiasm to be damped a bit. Call from Commodore repeating dissatisfaction of the high command regarding failure, didn't help. I end this tough week still convinced that we can be number one. We need to get out of yard, back to our home berth, get cleaned up and press on.

- 29 September- 4 October, 1975: I am encouraged by attitude of all. This goes for entire ship. My people are doing great. I have never seen such hard work and productivity.

- 6-11 October, 1975: This week was highlighted by apparently high interest in getting out of overhaul in reasonable time. Got one contractor VP mad at me and suppose I am persona non grata on 2nd deck of office. Expletive. Indicators are all go. UA running about 3 and had another reenlistment. Had 7 cases at mast and for once, they were all relatively minor. Mast felt good for first time. Had a personnel inspection complete with cake cutting by youngest member of crew and a few words on Navy's 200th birthday. Really went well including our first "hip, hip, hooray" for us guys. Started officer interviews. Went well. These young guys are really sharp. All in all a pretty good week. Will feel ten-feet tall when we finally get out of this crummy environment and cleaned up.

- 13-18 October, 1975: It has been a good week. Lots of activity all over ship and I can tell spirit is picking up. Reenlisted another first termer and have another on Monday. Mast cases are less complicated and fewer. New guys seem sharp. Old ones leaving seem pleased with the way things are going. I'm impressed.

- 20-25 October, 1975: This has been the most productive week since I've been aboard. I have never in my life seen more thinking, more initiative or harder working people. Hours very long, but I am satisfied that departments are handling liberty well and allowing more people off. The work is getting done. Affirmative action plan taking shape slowly. Its an attitude more than anything else — an attitude that gets leaders interested in their men and men interested in their ship and the people around them. We are getting quite a few new people in. They all seem enthusiastic. I'll talk to them again three months after reporting aboard and try to get a feel for their perceptions and attitudes as compared to first coming aboard. In two months, I think that I have done a lot to generate enthusiasm and develop a personal touch with crew. I feel things are going awfully well. But, we have a long ways to go.

- 27 October-5 November, 1975: Much activity and work. Lots of engineering problems, all technical. Auto-combustion system messed up continually. This is particularly frustrating, as all components were recently overhauled and ought to be perfect. Lots of new men on board. I am impressed with their general sparkle, enthusiasm and hope.

- 5-15 November, 1975: We finally got out on sea trials and what an absolutely exhilarating and exciting experience. Beautiful weather and 70-degree days with unlimited visibility. Real problems with the combustion controls. Back at ship yard we are trying to finish up the continuing serious problems with winches, conveyors and ACC. Post sea-trials conference was a shambles as no one had the answers from the supships and contractor. Very frustrating.

- 16 November,1975 - 14 February, 1976: My log dormant simply because I was too lazy. Should keep this up as one day it will be interesting. Yard overhaul finally complete. Wrote tough recap of ridiculous contracting and contractor. Had one week of ISE in early January in lousiest, coldest weather I have ever seen, including two-straight days in heavy pea-soup fog. Came up channel at 15 knots with an 8-degree crab due to 40 knots of wind on our beam. Have spent last 3 weeks in Gitmo. Up and at it early in the morning and in after dark. Lots of drills and hard work, but crew has responded nicely. Recap follows: Morale and attitude of crew not as good as I would like. Retention: After a good start, we have not had a first termer in six weeks. Material condition: This is biggest problem. Ship is sparkling now, but gets dirty awfully fast. There are just too many things wrong that don't get fixed. Can't see the light at the end of the tunnel. Only those things wrong that approach a crisis stage get fixed. TVs, ice machines, PMS and etc. all play second fiddle and stay down. Mast: Not a big problem, but we have a few losers. Just hit them hard and try to kick them out. UA: Way down; only 1 or 2 at a time. There are periods when I wonder whether all the worry and gut work is worth it. Got a letter a month back saying I screened for carrier command. Was not elated, although I suppose I would have been disappointed had I not made it. The key to my success thus far has been super enthusiasm and hard work. If I lose the will for either, then I become ineffective. In this job you have to stay pumped up all the time, or those around you will sense it.

Jim Harris, operations officer and super Naval Officer.

- 26 February - 23 March, 1976: Reftra at Gitmo was a success by any measure. The days became awfully long and the guys really turned to. We ended up with an 88 overall, which is well above the average. Sent message in on XO saying what a great job he had done and what a major contributor. On return from Cuba, had gorgeous weather until abeam Jacksonville. By 200 miles from Hatteras, the wind had increased to 50 knots and ship was rolling up to 30 degrees. On one occasion at about 2300, a drain plugged which caused the gyro alarms to go off. Rough seas and thunderstorms contributed to uncomfortable feeling in the ship. Made it fine. I still have gut feeling that we, from a leadership perspective, are overly interested in getting the job done and people come second. Perhaps not true, but nonetheless, a feeling. We took two-days off this week which, I think, will show troops that yes they have done a good job and yes, we the leadership recognize this.

- 24 March - 2 April, 1976: UA rate, which had been zero has come up slowly to 6. Two are gay and two will desert. Not a one of them are a loss to the ship or Navy. I wish they would return so we could court martial them and kick them out. Have received about 40-new guys in past month. Good first impressions. At the end of each week, I usually reflect on how the week went. I am continually amazed with how hard our guys work and the positive attitudes they seem to maintain. I like the way we run things which is through the chain of command. It's easy to say, but it works. My enthusiasm quotient has been sky high. I sometimes feel bad because I don't have meetings all the time and spend half the day on the phone solving problems. The message is to let your head guys know what you want and give them the rein to do it. It works 9 times out of 10, for usually they will solve the problem and feel better for it. The ideas and initiative these guys display is phenomenal. Our department heads, like the crew, have been an inspiration to me.

- 3 April - 26 April, 1976: This has been a formative month. We have been inspected to death. Major ones were PEB, ASI, Admat and Safety. Supply loadout continuing well. The PEB was outstanding. I was told before that the heat was on from the high command because seven service force ships in a row had failed. We made it. And what a boost to ship morale. And we did it without running our guys into the ground and with a low UA rate. All in all we have done a pretty fair job in facing all the problems of a ship in the yards, sea trials, reftra, lots of new guys and a hundred inspections. The next phase starts when we leave for the Med next week. We must maintain the expectations of the new guys, keep the ship clean and neat, and get the job done. I have no doubts we can be the best ship in the Navy upon return from the next deployment. We are ready for the 6th Fleet.

- 27 April - 20 May, 1976: The crossing was great. Got lots of cleaning and painting. Joined with a carrier group returning from the Med in mid-ocean and went alongside Rigel. Helmsman got 3-degrees off course and was going in wrong direction! Day and night before Rota was poor weather with a 29.60 barometer and 50-knots of wind. Our final navigation was DR and fathometer. Underway from Rota to Med, had to cut across outbound Gibraltar traffic. Had two big ships loom out of haze at 3 miles on our port bow. Never seen so much traffic. Worked about 17 ships throughout eastern Med and all went quite well. We worked hard and showed a great deal of flexibility. Troops doing fine. Nothing ever routine. This is an interesting and ever-changing business.

Still too many pieces of equipment not working and we don't seem to have a handle on what's not up.

- 20 May - 4 July, 1976: In Naples on Sunday loading out for our next ops — mainly fresh fruits and vegetables. Supply effectiveness very high. Great effort and initiative on part of Jay Nace. Deck 4.0 in all respects under leadership of Phil Moaney. He is an amazing officer. Reenlistments sky high. Spirits are high and positive.

- 5 July - 25 August, 1976: Outchopped four days ago and have been under the influence of a great Bermuda high. I have never seen the weather at sea so beautiful. I am continually amazed at the hard work, conduct, appearance and initiative of these guys. I can honestly say that this ship and her people have their stuff together and that this is the best ship in the Navy. Objectives continue to be combat readiness, get the job done and take care of our troops. Have serviced about 50 ships all over Med and transited Messina twice and Gibraltar four times. Lisbon was interesting because of tough currents and pilots and tugs that don't show up. Never a dull moment. Wish sometimes, I could climb to FL 350 and escape some of it. It was a fine cruise. Our guys did 4.0 in every category and we can return with our heads held high.

- 25 August - 15 September, 1976: Trip back was eventful due to Hurricane Emmy. Letter received from OP-05 directing me to interview for Rickover's nuclear program. Not pleased. Preparing for North Sea trip in October as well as an insurv and engineering inspections. AFSs are busy ships!

A DAY IN THE LIFE OF SYLVANIA'S CAPTAIN

The job description of a ship's captain in the U.S. Navy is hard to describe: the task is multi-dimensional; it never stops; it's seldom routine. His responsibility is total, his authority unquestioned and the accountability quotient is 100% plus.

Three priorities take center stage: combat readiness; the safe navigation of the ship; and the maintenance of good order and discipline — read standards. To be sure, there are many other competing priorities like appearance, reenlistments, preventative maintenance, training, budgets, equal opportunity and the like. But, as VADM Kin McKee was to remind me when I later served as his chief of staff, "The average CO takes care of the top priorities — the best CO meets all of them."

A typical day moored alongside in our home port of Norfolk was reasonably close to that of my shore-based compatriots; that is normal working hours and Monday through Friday. And like ashore COs, the duty officers would know how to contact me if needed, which was the exception.

Underway though, the complexion changed dramatically to one of 24-hour days and seven-day weeks. For example, early in our training cycle after completing the shipyard overhaul, we spent many weeks at sea in the Norfolk area or with the training group at Guantanamo Bay in Cuba. Drills went on most of the day and night — general quarters, engineering, man overboard, shooting our four, twin 3-inch guns (another story for we could not hit a large barn at 2,000 yards) radar navigation, damage control and so on.

Smiling gunners topside atop one of four three-inch gun mounts.

At some contrast to this high activity level though, were long transits, such as Norfolk to Rota, Spain via a series of rhumb lines forming a great-circle route wherein we steamed at a steady eighteen-or-so knots from one invisible waypoint to the next. We still managed our daily dose of drills and stayed on the go titivating, deep cleaning and maintaining the big ship. On most such voyages I would turn in around 2300 and generally sleep the night until 0600. During the day I would wander the ship from top to bottom and forward to aft, fly one of our H-46 helos, have a cup of coffee with the chiefs, tour one of the engine room spaces all the way to the bilges, geehaw with the supply guys (our main battery) have lunch on the mess decks, mentally note problem areas and tend to the inevitable paper work that made its way to my level.

A short digression here to address the creature comforts of the captain: In my case, the captain's inport accommodations were nice — not luxurious — just functional and comfortable. One deck below the bridge on the starboard side, one entered a spacious living, dining and office area with several large portholes looking forward and to starboard. Off that was a bedroom and bath, once again, quite comfortable. As the captain had his own mess and two cook/attendants, I would try to invite some of the officers or chiefs on occasion for lunch or dinner. Underway, like most captains, I would sleep at night in a separate sea cabin just abaft the bridge, so as to be more accessible to the officer of the deck. Starkly austere, this small room had a bed, head, sound-powered phone to the bridge, small desk and a large, protruding compass repeater.

The contrast between independent steaming and the majority of our underway periods was dramatic because the latter was packed with a series of 24-hour adventures. The most obvious was when we were doing our mission of fleet resupply wherein the norm were ships from small frigates to aircraft carriers on both sides with up to six high-line transfer stations going at once and two helos frantically lifting one-thousand pound pallets of everything from lobsters to toilet paper. All captains were, of course, on their respective bridges and alert to good station keeping and wandering merchants threatening to occupy our piece of ocean. Spice to the mix were high seas, zilch visibility and strong winds. Days and nights would morph into one!

Sylvania supplies the Sixth Fleet ... frigate to starboard and amphibious ship to port. Multiple lines and two helos.

A note here on civilian shipping: with about 8,000 major ships at sea at any one time on the oceans of the world, the greatest concern on the part of many captains was avoiding collision which occurred literally hundreds of times per year (including a few on the part of the Navy). Each time a merchant had a closest point of approach of less than around two miles, my defensive driving antenna was fully alert to the distrust position. I've seen and heard of too many absolutely dumb actions of supposedly professional mariners on the high seas. By dumb I mean a reasonable person would suppose there is no one on the opposite bridge and the ship is on automatic pilot. While most in the sea-going profession are licensed and competent, my assessment was that there were far too many that were clearly incompetent or inattentive.

Thus it was that early-on in my time as Sylvania's commanding officer, I developed a philosophy that a ship's captain was paid his big bucks to exercise proper judgment — the ability to make reasonably correct decisions — to take the right courses of action most of the time. Because Sylvania was a national asset owned by the American people, had a necessary mission and 450 young men in her crew, safety at sea was a consistently top priority. Not only would a collision or grounding ruin a captain's day, it could result in a loss of life and the Navy out one needed combat support ship.

So — bottom line is that like most responsible captains, I spent a good deal of my brain power and attention directed to the safe navigation of the ship. Some areas were particularly challenging such as the Straits of Gibraltar (six transits), Straits of Messina (between Italy and Sicily — eight transits) and the English Channel (two transits). In all cases, traffic lanes notwithstanding, I sometimes felt that the mate on watch on a lumbering merchant at 0200 was asleep: wrong-way traffic, cross traffic, and meandering traffic, seemed the norm. Our tools on Sylvania's bridge were old-fashioned maneuvering boards, eyeballs connected to a brain and grease pencils on the radar screen. During particularly busy evolutions, I would ask our experienced Jim Harris and Phil Moaney (both department heads and therefore not on the watch bill) to man the bridge and buttress the judgment factor.

Entering port was another one of those evolutions requiring the nicest sense of seamanship and attention to detail. As a Navy ship, we were blessed with a full-time navigation team as well as a small electronics center below the bridge for radar navigation. Still, dealing with foreign pilots who spoke fragmentary English and did not know your ship, was sometimes exciting and a bit unnerving. And once again, it took the total attention of the captain for even slight miscalculations could prove catastrophic.

In general, I would be on the bridge (or close by) when in piloting waters, working with other ships or in heavy shipping lanes — or a combination of all three. Thus a captain's day in my case was scenario dependent and varied from the relative luxury of independent steaming in the middle of the Atlantic or tied securely to a Norfolk pier, to a forty-eight hour endurance contest steaming north through the English Channel in rotten weather to an eventual berth in Rotterdam.

THE REAL STORY

The first I had heard of Sylvania was at a small dinner party given by the then CO, Captain Jim Linder. The reason I was invited, a squadron CO, is that his Supply Officer, Bob Moore and I had been at Stanford together in the MBA program. For four hours, Jim and Bob regaled themselves with stories of things nautical like anchors, replenishments at sea, conveyors, freeze holds and commodores. It was the most totally-boring social event I had experienced since the mandatory dancing lessons with my roommate at the Naval Academy twenty-three years before.

My next exposure to Sylvania was some four years later, only this time I was to be the CO. Walking up the gangway in a trashy Hampton shipyard, I was desultorily greeted by a bored, cigarette-smoking, first class petty officer. The ship was high and dry in the drydock, dirty and in a state of massive disarray and confusion. The troops seemed down.

My Dad and Sylvania's XO, Tim Marvin, at change of command in Newport News shipyard.

By change of command standards, ours was the ultimate in low key. Twenty guests, no bands, a boring speech and zero pizzazz. I thought we needed out of this soul-smothering world of shipyards fast.

Prior to reporting to Sylvania, I had attended the third class of the Senior Officers Ship Material and Readiness Course (SOSMARC — don't you love it?) at a picturesque desert site sixty miles to the west of Idaho Falls, Idaho. Two admirals and thirty captains, all destined to command ships or groups, attended an intensive, four-month academic course initiated by Admiral Rickover at his nuclear engineering site in the desert. We lived in WWII barracks, cooked our own food (eight guys to one refrigerator), had no TV (too distracting), had to get permission to buy a barbecue grill out of our own money and had eight-solid hours of engineering work each day with lots of night study.

We all got leaner and smarter and gained a much better appreciation for the propulsion plants of our ships. Thermodynamics, electrical engineering, math and chemistry were the order of the day. All the "teachers" were excellent and spin-offs or borrowed from Rickover's nuclear world. Believe it or not, our young math prof started out with, "Men, I'm going to make math fun." Though we all snickered to ourselves, he was right, and for the first time in my lifetime, math was fun.

One dark and gloomy Friday afternoon, our class had a two-hour lecture on the "general energy equation," the heart of thermodynamics. Captain Tom Brown, sitting beside me in the front row, asked me to "wake me up if anything happens," put on his aviator dark glasses and promptly went to sleep. At the end of the session, the nuclear lieutenant commander triumphantly asked if there were any questions. I raised my hand and said that, "I thought he had done a great job, but I hadn't understood any of it." Before he could respond, Tom woke up, whipped off his glasses and said, looking at me, "Captain, I don't know what your problem is, I thought it was clear as a bell." The class erupted in a round of applause for the young instructor and everyone left happy.

Anyway, the four months would stand me in good stead because the ship guys were going crazy with a myriad of engineering problems and shipyard owners were going to the bank with wheelbarrows trying to fix them.

Carolyn and me.

Once away from the Norfolk complex with its hundreds of self-professed experts at inspections and "assist visits," life aboard ship was enjoyable. The troops settled in, the ship was clean and discipline problems went markedly down. The food was the best we'd had and the ship quite comfortable (says the Captain).

Our routine of resupplying some 150 ships never got routine. Always, there was weather, a wandering merchant coming too close, problems with our conveyors or rough seas. With up to five cargo stations and two H-46 helos transferring frozen food, aircraft engines, dry food and toilet paper to a carrier on one side and destroyer on the other, all while steaming at twelve knots, it was clearly exciting and never routine. We were doing a needed job, the results of our efforts could be seen on the spot, we got lots of attaboys and the troops felt good about the old Sylvania and themselves.

And the sea stories were never ending. As we got our fresh fruits and vegetables every couple of weeks in whatever port we were near, we would dash in to some pretty earthy dock areas far off the beaten path. On one occasion, we were backing into a narrow little berth around Naples, Italy, under the tutelage of a somewhat nervous Italian pilot who spoke little English. About this time, our navigator ran up and indicated that the water depth was only 22-feet alongside the pier. I mentioned this to our guy, as we drew 26-feet aft. His response without batting an eye, "Not to worry, Captain, it's only mud."

H-46 ready to go. Note prepositioned pallets of supplies and carrier hurrying into position.

OinC of helo det, Lcdr. Pete Peterson ... super aviator and officer.

True Faith and Allegiance

After the shipyard ordeal, we had steamed down to Cuba for refresher training — "A time to cut the umbilical to the shore establishment and get the crew together," said my Dad to me. We worked and drilled 14-hours a day and, except for not being able to hit a large barn at 1000 yards with our four three-inch gun mounts, we did OK, and day by day, the teamwork and esprit grew.

Before heading back to Norfolk, we anchored in Port au Prince, Haiti for a three-day visit to let the crew unwind and relax. At the time, Haiti had the lowest per-capita income in the Americas and it showed. Two contrasting small events: The first was a small, hand-carved wooden horse that a young street vendor was selling for $5 and for which I bargained for $2. That youngster had no doubt worked two-days steady to produce the little horse. So the next day, feeling guilty, I went back to the seller, and to his delight, gave him $3. Score one for the USA.

The next day, several of our officers and myself were invited to the Ambassador's residence and what a grand layout it was! Driving through the rancid squalor and evident human suffering of the poor city to an incredibly beautiful residential area with million-dollar gated houses was quite the contrast. Our gracious hosts were charming and friendly, but I'm not sure how the USA scored, given the opulence of this 1% high above the city.

After our first long deployment, we were assigned the task of supplying a large 30-ship NATO task force in the North Sea some 2,800 miles from Norfolk. The solitary ten days of peaceful steaming was interrupted only by the plaintive "croak, croak" of a few crickets far from their home turf of Virginia. I said to one of our marvelous and experienced officers, "We need to get rid of those crickets."

"Don't think so, Captain," he laconically responded.

"Why not?"

His matter-of-fact reply, "Crickets eat cockroaches." A lover of the Pacific who had been promised that his next tour of duty would be, "Somewhere west of San Diego," he ended up on the Sylvania in Norfolk 21,000 miles to the west.

Transiting the English Channel is always an experience — doing so in low fog and lots of shipping is an adventure. Making it safely into the North Sea, we were not sure of our position as it had been overcast, our Omega navigation gear was useless (as usual), the land so low it was difficult to get radar posits and the bottom of the sea is 90 feet plus or minus 10 feet, so bottom-contour navigation was a nonstarter. Spying an oil rig, we moved in close, got the name, looked at our latest "where-the-oil-rigs-are" pub and proceeded to our rendezvous point 24-hours away. Unbeknownst to us, the oil rig we had relied upon, had been recently moved a good ways from its charted position.

At 0700 on the appointed day, 2,800 miles from home base, we were supposed to have one very-large carrier to port (the Kennedy) and a frigate to starboard. Nothing — absolutely nothing!! This emptiness precipitated the same sort of feeling I had when I had started the first semester accounting final exam at Stanford, and which loosely translated into, "I may have been in command, but not in control."

Soon, over the horizon, hove a small twin-jet carrier airplane, rapidly wagging his wings in excitement, and shortly thereafter appears an old oiler, the Caloosahatchee, huffing and puffing at its maximum speed of 16 knots. Wouldn't you know that its captain was my friend, Tom Brown, a former attack pilot, who announced over the radio for all to hear that, "I always knew fighter pilots couldn't navigate."

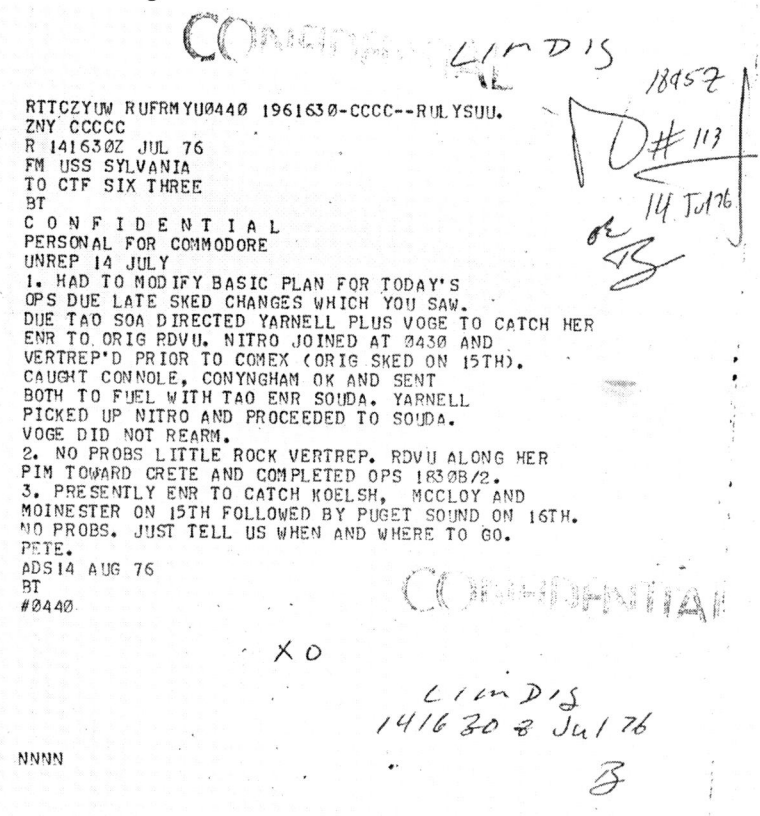

Typical update from Sylvania to our commodore in the Med. Cryptic, short, but chock-full of information.

Early on we had lots of engineering problems and had to endure the ultimate inspection — the PEB (propulsion examining board). This was the result of the Navy's awesomely poor track record in engineering safety and many serous accidents.

About 50% of our ships at the time were failing the PEB and unfortunately, Sylvania became a statistic. Everyone up the chain of command commiserated and chastised, but not much pragmatic help showed up. Our failure was not because our guys slacked off, for our engineers had really stroked it and had given it their best shot. At any rate, we gritted our teeth and the chief engineer, Lieutenant Commander Gene Razetti, rallied his troops and we did OK on the retake.

Hard working engineers far below. Chief Engineer Gene Razetti far right.

Typical message from CO of destroyer thanking us for the service with our response below. Sent by old-fashioned flashing light.

Such was the fortitude of our sailors and officers. They were right out of hometown USA with all the drug, crime, racial and social problems of the mid-'70s. Treated with care, concern and reachable goals and with an occasional dose of "nice job," they responded like youngsters have in our military for generations. A few malcontents were weeded out as fast as the system would allow, with no third chances.

Because of really significant racial problems aboard some of our overworked Vietnam ships, the Navy had undertaken serious training of those in leadership and supervisory positions. Lots of wide open "rap" sessions, treating your men with dignity and an eye toward the Golden Rule, while concurrently doing your best to reach reasonable standards of behavior and professionalism, were a daily challenge for all COs. To the Navy's credit, it was done well and today our Navy is a progressive world leader in the business of respect for all persons, no matter their background, genetics or beliefs. Our job was to fight a war at sea and win, the key ingredient of which was a cohesive crew that worked together and trusted one another!

While in Norfolk, I had been summoned to interview with Admiral Rickover for the nuclear power program. That I did not want this program is an understatement. I was slated to go to the carrier Forrestal and didn't relish the idea of a two-year regimen of a seven-day a week school house and the real demotivating (to me) specter of Rickover's style of intimidation.

So there I sat, in the large and extremely austere office of four-star (in civilian garb), Admiral Rickover. Though I was a full captain in the U.S. Navy, commanding officer of a large ship and had done reasonably well professionally, I felt like a plebe in his first year at the Naval Academy.

The Admiral did not look up, shake my hand or otherwise recognize me for several minutes. My legs were uncrossed because, "The Admiral didn't like it." Finally, he said without looking up, "Why are you interested in the nuclear program?"

My somewhat mumbled reply was something like, ". . . because it has the potential to lead to command of a nuclear aircraft carrier, sir."

Without looking up or expressing any interest, he asked, "And for how long have you been interested?"

"Three weeks, sir." Well the old admiral finally looked at me with the most incredibly cold and unfriendly eyes, and in one motion, rose from his chair, planted his hands and with absolute and total finality, screamed, "Three weeks!!"

I had never in my entire life seen anyone so absolutely angry and so totally out of control. For a moment, I was fearful for the admiral's health. Soon, a follow-on question concerning my MBA credentials at Stanford elicited an equally forceful response, for unbeknownst to me, he had no use whatsoever for any study not directly connected to engineering or science. With severely-contorted facial expression, the admiral managed to make the three letters of MBA last ten-seconds apiece. End of interview. I wasn't asked to come back. Whew!

We COs had lots of priorities — engineering, people, operational, training, discipline, inspections and on and on. Sometimes, it was kind of hard to figure out what the high command really expected. Periodically, goals would come from CNO, the Commodore, the type commander and so on. One day, four-star Admiral Isaac Kidd, Commander-in-Chief of the Atlantic Fleet, came forth with what he expected from his fleet.

It was the most refreshing message I had heard in a long while. Finally, here was a leader who dared say in bold letters that it was the job of every sailor in the Atlantic Fleet if called upon, to fight a war at sea and win! That one message to me characterized the raison d'etre of the U.S. Navy, because indeed we had been mired in an ever-tightening spiral of administrative hype. Way to go! What a guy!

One day, Admiral Kidd summoned his captains-and-above sea-going commanders to his headquarters for a day-long seminar to discuss "War at Sea." His part of the program, after being introduced by his Executive Assistant, Frank Kelso, was to lead off with a ten-minute introduction. Two-hours later, jacket doffed, tie askew and large mid-section drooping over his tensioned belt, he concluded: "When the balloon goes up, you guys will not have the benefit of all the sophisticated shore-based intelligence and guidance, because the first to go will be our satellites and that therefore you had better know the capabilities of the Soviets' and yours' cold." We all went back to our ships imbued with a renewed sense of urgency and priority.

I was relieved mid-way through our second-major deployment two weeks late because the new CO didn't show up on the appointed day. It was the best change of command I've ever had, for the ceremony was just like the old days: No band, no guest speaker, no chaplain — just "assemble the crew at quarters and read your orders." We did though, have a "three cheers for us guys" and felt good for having done so.

EPILOGUE I

Unedited memo to my commodore back in Norfolk upon departing Sylvania that provides an unvarnished glimpse into the vagaries of commanding a U.S. Navy ship of the line during some turbulent years of the mid-'70s.

I write this as my days on board Sylvania come to a close after eighteen months of living, breathing and eating this fine ship and crew. My ebullience is not due to the closeness of my departure nor what the future may hold, but rather to offer you my observations of this world of the surface Navy and the U.S.S *Sylvania*.

We have been through much and taken all the system can throw at us. From shipyard to Gitmo to loadout to Sixth Fleet to the North Sea and, as

King Tut, Logs and Sylvania

I write this, some 600-miles west of Rota, Spain, again to the Mediterranean and the Sixth Fleet. We have steamed together, my crew and me, about 40,000 miles, serviced hundreds of ships and shore stations, got our share of "attaboys" — and a few "getwithits." We have been successful.

I say "we" because of our very fine people that have made us so. This brings me to my first point: Even though we experienced a high rate of turnover (65% and all department heads), to watch our men perform and win — often times in the face of tough odds — has been a daily dose of inspiration. I have never worked with a finer group of department heads, officers or chiefs. Collectively, they were my strength and wisdom. They were universally proud, hard working, interested and producing. They wanted to do a top-notch job. And our petty officers and youngsters — excepting the 5% we kicked out — are super. Admittedly, some may have been rough on the outside, but deep inside our men did take pride in their ship and did grow in maturity and responsibility. I enjoyed talking to our new guys and telling them that I wouldn't trade any in our crew for anyone else in the Navy. An overstatement to be sure, but not by far.

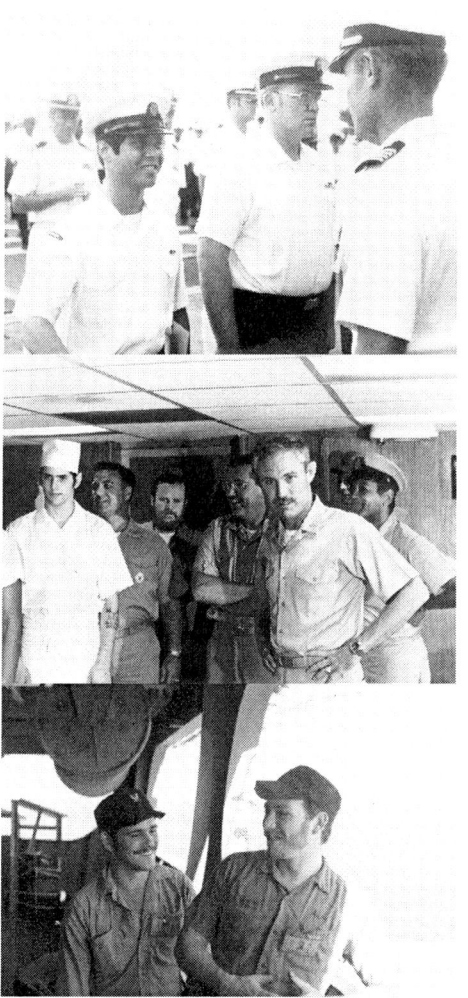

Some of our fine crew, right out of Hometown, U.S.A.

Yes, we did get inspected often — a big subject amongst my contemporaries. I felt strongly that the inspections were worthwhile and beneficial to the command. We never received a "bad gram" as the result of not doing well on an inspection or assist visit. The inspectors were universally sincere and interested and helpful.

My view of the outside world of staffs with whom we interacted: Our approach was to attempt solutions at the departmental level and minimize long and complaining philosophical messages up the chain. The personnel folks in Washington were responsive to our occasional people problems and were reasonably successful in helping us rid ourselves of the bad apples. Our supply people very effectively liasoned with their counterparts. The engineers established early-on a fine rapport at the squadron and tycom level and in most instances, message traffic was proforma. I was, in general, pleased with the responsiveness of the "system" to our problems with but a couple of caveats:

As regards overhauls: Sylvania had an overhaul at a civilian shipyard in the Norfolk area. We were a month late in completion and about 25% more than the original contract due to emergent growth and a contractor that dragged his feet on numerous occasions. At no time was the contractor liable for liquidated damages nor was he allowed additional time for completion by the Navy; he simply did not meet the deadline. Time is money, the same as a civilian ship and we need to be far tougher in dealing with contractors in the civilian sector that do not meet completion dates.

Secondly, and closer to home, I have long felt that the management of ship's force discrepancies aboard Sylvania to be weak. We never seem to get ahead of the game. We have a tendency to operate out of our back pocket and react rather than plan ahead. As a gross generalization, we would work off as many items as possible prior to an inspection and then start working on the next inspection. Once away from the Norfolk waterfront, though, the ship and crew seemed to operate smoothly, plan ahead much better and concentrate on our mission vice preparing for the next inspection.

Thanks for all you and the "system" have done for us. The result is a combat support ship better able to do its mission.

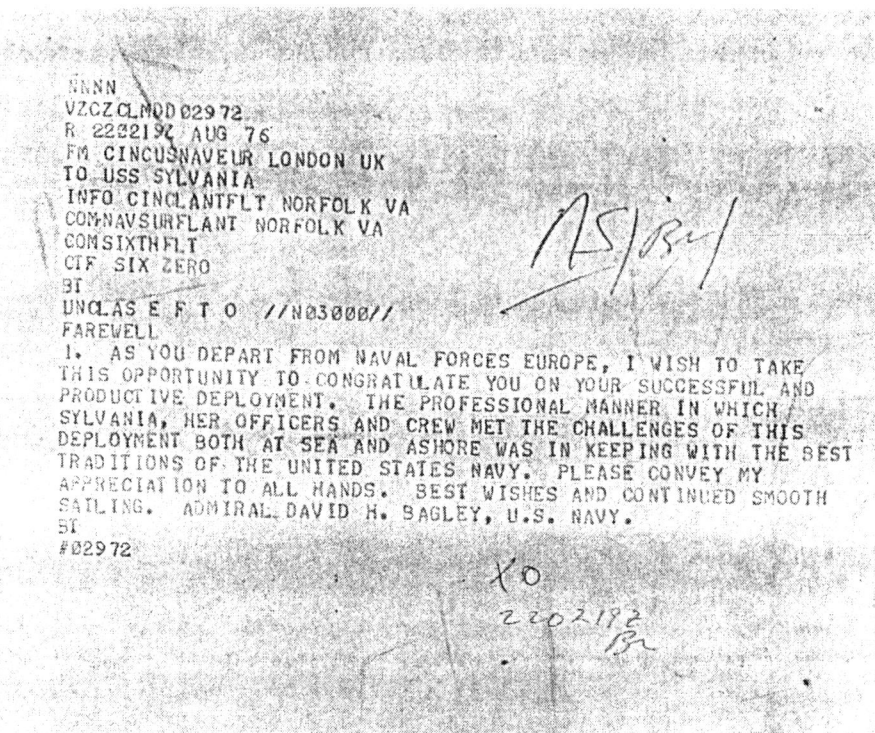

Sylvania sailors got lots of these attaboys. This from four-star admiral not atypical.

May 11, 1976

Capt. P. B. Booth
Commanding Officer
USS Sylvania (AFS-2)
FPO New York 09501

Dear Sir:

Our hats off to you, Sir. Thank you very much for the message that my husband has reported aboard and hope he will measure up to your high standards. I'm particularly grateful to you taking the time to write a postscript which proved me wrong about my notion that the highest ranking officer would not take the trouble of doing a most wonderful thing that could happen to the wife of a little man in the ship. You made us feel involved and valued.

Hope so too that we get a housing and move to Norfolk soon. My son and I are both excited to get there.

Reiterating my deepest appreciation to you, Sir.

Respectfully,
Mrs. R. R. Ganugao

Poignant letter from the wife of one of our troopers.

EPILOGUE II

- **Gene Razetti** became in overall charge of about 130 logistics ships after two successful at-sea commands of his own.

- **Admiral Kidd** continued to cut a wide swath in matters strategic and to get to the heart of what's important. Sadly, he passed away, the collapse of the Soviet Union and the Cold War a result of real sailors like him.

- **King Tut** completed his U.S. tour and has a sea story few of his predecessors can match.

- The **U.S. Navy sailor** continues his incredibly talented and unselfish service to the worthy cause of his country. To most of those minions who served with me on Sylvania, I commend and thank you for a great job during some tough times.

- **Tom Brown** commanded a carrier, rose to flag rank and today teaches school in San Francisco, hopefully without the aid of dark glasses.

- **Haiti** is still the poorest nation in the Americas, has its periodic coups and the U.S. ambassador still lives high above it all.

- **Admiral Rickover** finally retired, his legacy of bringing the Navy into the nuclear propulsion forefront a monument to his persistent attention to the minutest detail.

- **Frank Kelso** became the Chief of Naval Operations and retired under the sad umbrella of Tailhook 91.

- **Phil Moaney** retired from the Navy, having risen from boot seaman to lieutenant, leaving a legacy as the finest officer I have ever worked with, and an inspiration to the black community he represented, only to pass away soon thereafter.

- **Sylvania** continues to ply the oceans of the world and provide its lifeline of food and spares to the sea-going Navy under the aegis of civilian mariners.

FIRST IN DEFENSE

The carrier Forrestal, shooting down our own, some tough times, shoal water ahead, hip-hip hooray, more real sailors and keeping the admiral waiting while I slept.

We had a wind and current at our stern and shoal water two-miles ahead. The 78,000-ton aircraft carrier Forrestal was headed fair for an anchorage near Norfolk to take on ammunition. I quietly and conservatively ordered, "All back 2/3s" to the four huge 27-foot propellers in order to slow the ship and let go our 67-ton starboard anchor. I waited a couple of minutes while watching the ultra-slow indicator dials confirm that indeed the giant screws were digging-in astern.

Not much was happening, and at the rate we were going, the only way to keep from furrowing a new deep-water channel into the inner-Norfolk harbor, was to stop the ship. So, I ordered "All back full," with a bit more assertiveness in my voice high up on the bridge of my massive new command. I also took the precaution of calling down to the engineer's inner sanctum far down in the ship in main control on the intercom with a, "Dave, (the Chief Engineer), I need some backing power, NOW!"

His somewhat frustrated reply, "We're trying, Captain."

True Faith and Allegiance

So went my introduction in 1977 to my third tour on the U.S.S. *Forrestal*, CV-59, the first of the so-called super carriers. Over a thousand-feet long, she displaced 78,000 tons at a draft of 36 feet, was home for 5,500 sailors, officers and aviators and could chug along at 33 knots (37 mph), given a moderately clean bottom. Just out of a soul-wrenching, two-year overhaul, she had the latest of everything — new catapults, updated ammunition spaces, a star-wars electronics suit and even, a totally new dental clinic.

We stopped OK, albeit with a slight increase in our resting pulse rate and a couple more entreaties into the squawk box to Dave far below. It reminded me of a deja vu five-years earlier on the same ship coming in to anchor in the Bosphorus with a five-knot current. As a resident fighter squadron commander, I was standing behind the then commanding officer, Dutch Schoultz, who was showing me "The right way to anchor a big ship." Dutch had some good speed coming up the very-crowded ship channel, but was getting too close to an anchored merchant ship directly ahead of us. "Give me all you've got astern!" he calls down on the same squawk box to his chief engineer, as the merchant disappeared under our bow. We missed dumping our anchor on the unsuspecting merchant by yards and, though you couldn't tell it, Dutch's pulse rate was up a tad. I kind of thought it all routine as I respectfully kibitzed with my coffee cup behind the captain's big chair, my heart rate normal.

Forrestal's leadership: Russ Blatt, XO top left. Wick Parcells fourth from left top. Bud Lineberger, CAG, front third from left. Pictures are all department heads including dentist, chaplain, doc, engineer, weapons, ops, air boss, captain and so on ... too many to mention. Best leadership I've seen and all spring-loaded-to-the-enthusiastic position.

The fact is, when I took over Forrestal, the ship had just completed a major shipyard overhaul and had a crew that had precious-little sea experience. New crews are like new ships: it takes awhile to break them in and get trained up. Plus, I was a relative new guy, never having had the benefit of a carrier department-head tour. So it was with our 22-year-old "FID", First in Defense, from her namesake, the nation's first Secretary of Defense, James Forrestal.

The ship is not only big; it's huge, gigantic and formidable, all rolled into one. The most oft-asked question of a carrier skipper is, "How do you manage to run it?"

And the quick answer is, "You don't, nor do three or four or five. It's a team and it takes a team effort. The captain sets the tone, strokes the pace, outlines the objectives, offers a dose of attaboys when a job is done well, and, once in awhile, jerks some chain."

The ship is really "run" by the department heads, so called because the ship is divided into about ten of these fiefdoms from Medical, to Air Wing, to Supply, to Weapons, to Deck and so on. Engineering, for example, had over 600 men and was led by Commander Dave Pellet, a seasoned engineer and superb officer. The glue is provided by the executive officer, also a commander, who is, in effect, the executive-vice president in charge of a bunch of VPs like Dave.

Forrestal's XO was Commander Russ Blatt, a marvelous gent with a top-notch service reputation. Having served as CO of two successive twin-jet, Viking squadrons, Russ was the first S3 type to get the much-coveted, big-carrier XO slot. At least once a day, Russ and I would meet in his cabin or mine for 30 minutes or so of quiet time. The topics ranged from heavy (department head not doing his job, upcoming ammo onload,

XO, Russ Blatt and Master Chief Yogi Bair.

etc), to trivial stuff (a sailor too tall for his bunk, trashy area up forward, etc). This was one way I stayed in the loop, got off the bridge and had a chance to informally transmit what I wanted done or was concerned with.

Prior to Russ reporting aboard, we had a temporary XO in the person of Commander Wick Parcells, a former VF-102 Diamondback fighter skipper. How fortunate we were on Forrestal to have had the benefit of Wick's enthusiasm, quiet competence and even sense of perspective. Job well done, he returned to the bridge as navigator with another feather in his cap.

Daily, our department heads would make the pilgrimage to the bridge, eleven-stories above the main deck, or whenever possible, vice versa. Nothing earth shattering, just a hello and cup of coffee with an every-once-in-awhile handwringing issue.

One of the keys to rumor control is an effective command master chief, the senior enlisted troop on board whose job it was to stay close to the action and advise the captain on enlisted related problems. We had a great one: Master Chief Yogi Bair. Each night the master chief would get on TV and give the ship his version of the "Bair Facts." He would always start by a really cheerful, "Good evening shipmates, this is Master Chief Yogi Bair, with the Bair Facts." Old Yogi (he was the oldest; the second was me at 43 to start), would always have been at the every-evening department head meeting with the XO after dinner, and at least some time during the day, would have talked with me. So, he knew what was going on and the crew knew he knew, and paid attention.

From the completion of shipyard overhaul to joining the 6th Fleet in the Mediterranean Sea is about eight months, of which about half is at sea. There are two major aspects to this period: The most important is the incremental training of the ship and crew into a cohesive fighting unit. This translates into a 100% combat ready air wing with its stable of 80 airplanes and a ship that can support the wing from a supply, maintenance, hotel-services, weapons and flight-operations perspective.

Acting XO in between navigator duties, Wick Parcells.

The shore period, on the other hand, had a good-news, bad-news twist. The good clearly is that the guys are home with mama, the kids and friends and lead some semblance of a normal lifestyle. The bad is that there are 67-separate inspections or "assist visits" that need to be done. Everything, from really heavy inspections, like nuclear weapons and engineering, all the way down to the bug guys who come looking for cockroaches. Any seagoing sailor will tell you that all the inspections are most likely worthwhile, caveated by what a great pain they are. Example: cockroaches.

We had a "few" cockroaches. Well, I need not embellish the notion that two cockroaches on board ship are two too many, unless they be of the same

Two wonderful command master chiefs: Top is Ted Brooks at ship's party. Bottom is Yogi Bair.

gender. So, here comes a Ph.D. entomologist, who said he "would take care of them." What a disaster! Most of the infestation was in a large, warm, damp, low-ceilinged room three-decks below the hangar deck. It was a bug's heaven! Dr. Ph.D. did his thing in this dry-food area, released his wicked potion, and sure enough, all the cockroaches tried to abandon ship through the only way they could find — straight up to the chief's quarters one deck above! Please understand that chief's quarters on board any Navy ship are out-of-bounds for anyone including the captain and cockroaches — invitation only.

Let me assure you, Yogi and I heard about this fast, for there were a lot of roaches swarming the chief's mess; and I mean a lot!

The sequel to this came a few-weeks later while we were refueling alongside a tanker. This too, is a routine, but complex operation, because there are six, eight-inch hoses pumping a huge amount of ship and jet fuel into some 40-different tanks and under a lot of pressure. So here comes a somewhat plaintive phone call from the crew's barber shop far below and the anonymous caller says he's calling "just to let us know there are four inches of jet fuel in the shop."

Senior Chaplain Hughes. A daily dose of inspiration and common sense.

My point is not to suggest how screwed up things were, even though often times, they were in those early days out of the shipyard overhaul. But, it was all a part of transforming this magnificent ship from a shipyard monument to a fighting machine and the 19-year-old crew — who six-months before, had been in hometown USA — to learned and competent sailors. If the captain were the type to run around and scream and shout, he was positively in the wrong business. You measured progress daily, and as long as the slope was upwards, your guys were giving it their best shot and didn't make the same mistake twice, you were grateful.

A good example is the enclosed message regarding evaporators — the machinery that converted sea water to potable water and, more importantly, extra-pure water to feed the eight giant boilers that provided the steam for driving the ship at 33 knots and to the four aircraft catapults. Fresh water production was the lifeblood of a non-nuclear carrier! During the preceding extensive overhaul, the ship had had major alterations to her five evaporators. This message prepared during the workup period, though short and sweet, informs our bosses ashore that we have serious evaporator problems and that we will go to a readiness status of C4 — Navy parlance for "unable to do our assigned mission." With a total of only twelve aircraft carriers in the inventory, when one is unable to do its combat job, it's a big deal!! Underlying this simple message is the understanding that our engineering guys are doing all they can do, but need help. Though the immediate problems were fixed, the Forrestal was nagged by a continuing succession of water problems in the months to come. Along with a few other daily ablutions, I checked the percentage of potable and boiler feed water when I awoke in the morning and as the sun set.

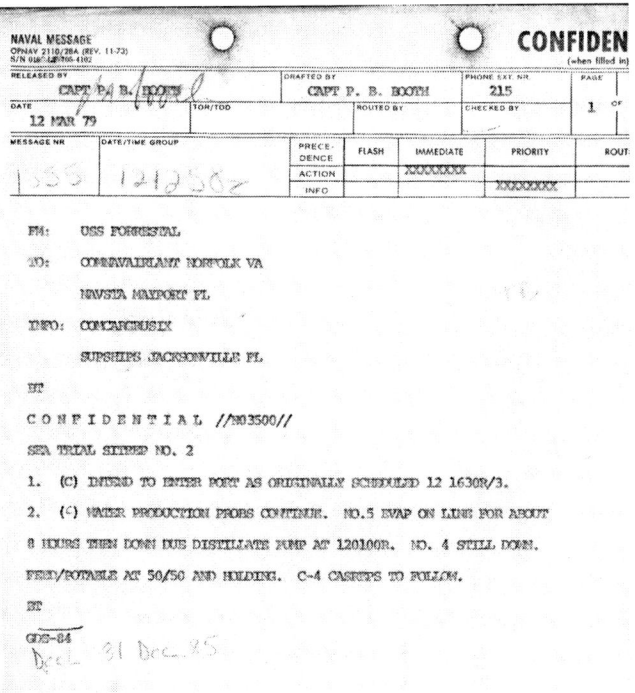

Our workups and training kept getting tougher and tougher as more and more airplanes were added. Soon, the ship started acting and feeling like a carrier. The "thump" of our four catapults could be felt about 120-times each day, accompanied by an equal number of "thump — screech," as our airplanes engaged the arresting gear and came home to roost on the big bird farm. One landing however, was a real tragedy and killed two of our guys.

It was a dark night, the launch was delayed, airplanes all over the landing area back-aft and here comes an A7 light-attack jet down the chute for landing. The pilot had the "meatball" from the fresnel lens, the deck lights and drop lights were on, but did not have permission to land from the controlling landing signal officer (LSO). I looked up from my seat high in the island and saw the flames and rolling (literally) fuselage of an A7 careening off the angle deck and into the black sea. I was confused. What had happened?

It turned out in the subsequent, very-thorough investigation, that yes, the pilot erred in not having permission to land. But, there were other serious errors as well. The lens was on — that's wrong — it's not turned on until you are ready to land airplanes. The deck was foul, but the landing deck lights were on — wrong again! And, there was no LSO on station even though airplanes were in the groove. Finally, the approach controllers deep within the ship, monitoring their electronic paraphernalia and controlling the hapless A7, had no business letting him get inside a half mile, without an acknowledgement from the LSO.

I regret that the last link in this series of human mistakes and oversights, was the captain, who should have had the presence of mind to note more closely, the imminent approach of the A7 and the clear unreadiness of the deck to land anything. A lot of folks, led by their captain, were emotionally down and you could feel it throughout the big war ship.

The video replay of this accident, vividly shows the airplane over the ramp, about to hit the folded wings of an A6 bomber and the pilot ejecting. The pilot, a much-decorated combat veteran and XO of his squadron, survived by microseconds and went on to contribute much to the Navy.

Early on, we had what I considered to be an unacceptably high unauthorized absentee (UA) rate — folks that just didn't show up for work and left his shipmates to do his work and stand his watches. I got the idea of calling the parents of each one to see if they knew the whereabouts of their son, from my friend Jerry Tuttle, the innovative skipper of the Kennedy, another large-deck carrier. Parceling out the names, a few of the senior guys, including myself, started calling one night. I was looking for Johnny Jones and got a little girl on the phone in Jackson, Tennessee. I asked, "if Johnny was there?"

She said, "Who's this?"

I said, "Captain Booth, Johnny's captain on the Forrestal."

Excusing herself, she returned to the phone with, "Johnny says to tell you he's not home." Johnny not withstanding, let me tell you that we managed to solve the problems of many of our wayward shipmates and, in most cases, help them back to the ship.

One day while moored in Norfolk, the Eisenhower came alongside our pier. What a beauty — it was the brand-newest nuclear carrier in the fleet and boasted every bell and whistle known to the seagoing world. I had lunch one day with her captain, Bill Ramsey, and as he proudly took me around, I marveled at his hand-picked and nurtured crew, his new piping and spotlessly-clean hangar deck. The ship had been crafted with care and pride by a great builder of ships. My next-door version, was 22-years old and had taken some really tough hits and hard miles in her venerable hide. For a few minutes, I envied Ike's captain, who had such a marvelous ship just starting out on its three-or-four decades of service. But, I went back to my old Forrestal and almost kissed her grimy hangar deck, how proud I was of her. I wrote the "I like Ike" skipper a nice and complimentary note, even though he was my brother-in-law.

USS DWIGHT D. EISENHOWER CVN 69
CAPT. William E Ramsey
13 SEPT 1977
USS FORRESTAL CV 59
CAPT PETER B. BOOTH

    Severing ties with our home base in Norfolk, we steamed ignominiously down to Mayport to join the U.S.S. *Saratoga* in sunny Florida, ignominious only in the sense that instead of a bunch of airplanes, we had about 1,000 cars on board so that our crew would not have to make their way back to Norfolk and then drive south for 15 hours. Super idea on someone's part.

    Except for the fact that most of the family types became instant geographical bachelors, I think the vast majority of our troops welcomed the move. After all, it was Florida and try as it might, Norfolk just didn't have the pizzazz to compete with Florida's reputation. The real fact was that the ship was at sea a very large proportion of the time and "home port" was more in name than in reality.

    Shortly after arriving, I got a call from Marv Reynolds, the base CO, who had greeted us on arrival in Mayport with a huge grin, bigger handshake and a "We're here to serve you all — let me know what I can do for you." Well, I thought, he was going to ask me for lunch, but not so. The call was about our 40-man Marine contingent, who each morning, went running in combat gear about Marv's base, replete with a large red Forrestal flag. This morning, according to an irate base CO, the Marines stopped dead-center in the main intersection to do —you guessed it — calisthenics! Leave it to the Marines. I ended up having Marv for lunch along with a spring-loaded-to-the-apologetic position, Marine detachment CO.

    Parked right in front of us in our new homeport was Forrestal's sister ship, the Saratoga, the second in our class of carriers and commanded by a good friend of mine, Ed Martin, an attack pilot who had spent the Vietnam war as an unwilling guest in the Hanoi Hilton. Ed and I had lots in common; both carriers were relatively old ships, both going through the convoluted shore-inspection cycle and both having frequent bouts with things engineering that weren't working right. Ours was the result of a recent and less-than-sterling effort from a major overhaul and Eds' from not having had an overhaul in five years. One of our prime jobs was to filter the myriad advice of well-intentioned, shore-based desk sailors who swarmed aboard in search of their particular area of expertise. Bottom line is that Forrestal and Saratoga got along great, traded lots of ideas and parts and really worked to help each other out.

> B-12   Times-Union and Journal, Jacksonville, Sunday, January 2
>
> ## Commanding Forrestal like running small city
>
> **By WILLIAM E. MARDEN**
> **Times-Union Staff Writer**
>
> At 44, he is the manager and leader of a small city with more military firepower than many small nations. He is a young man to hold his position, but is almost the literal "Old Man" of his command.
>
> Capt. Peter B. Booth, who commands the USS Forrestal — its 5,000 men and women of varying races and creeds and professions and its awesome instruments of warfare — is also a man who gets around a lot.
>
> Last year during the Forrestal's Mediterranean cruise the ship logged more than 80,000 miles, frequently under the observation of Soviet ships and aircraft that were interested in its military maneuvers.
>
> The Forrestal — its men, machines and mission — were the subject of Booth's talk to the Jacksonville Council of the Navy League of the United States at its January membership meeting in the Officers Club at the Jacksonville Naval Air Station.
>
> As Booth's slides and statistics made clear, the Forrestal is a small, sea-going city with all the problems of many small cities — and some others that are peculiarly its own.
>
> During its cruises, the city's citizens, mostly young men, must be fed, supplied with entertainment, medical attention and the other amenities of life. In addition, the ship itself is one large mechanism that needs fuel and parts while at sea.
>
> The logistics of supplying that population can be mind-boggling. As an example, Booth pointed out that 19,000 meals are served every day on the 24-year-old aircraft carrier.
>
> In addition to traditional medical services, the Forrestal also has an expert tooth maker for dental work. Look for anything that most cities have and the Forrestal will have it also.
>
> Booth said he wasn't worried about another, more drastic, move away from tradition as women begin to go to sea on Navy ships.
>
> "There are some problems, of course, but in general I don't see any real problems," he said.

A few months later, Saratoga was to relieve us in Rota, Spain, and early one morning hove into view out of the gloom to anchor about a mile from us. I heard Ed call the bos'n on Sara's foc'sle on his radio, directing him to "let go the starboard anchor." By this time, the old Sara maru was really throwing some backing power to her four big screws in order to get some sternway on and thereby set the anchor. As the ship gathered sternway, it was apparent to us eavesdroppers that the anchor was not about to leave the ship. Ed, in his normally calm voice, restated his desire that the starboard anchor be let go, to which the Bos'n replied, "I'm trying Captain." Where had I heard that?

First in Defense

At dinner that evening with Ed, I asked him "How come you all are drawing 39 feet and we are only 36 feet?" I mean we had identical everything — airplanes, fuel, people, stores, ammo and so forth. Our drafts should have been identical. Interestingly, the answer came when the Sara finally did get to a much-needed overhaul: dozens of void spaces that are normally empty, were full of sea water and heavens knows what else! The old Sara, as it turned out, had been dragging around a lot of dead weight for a long time.

Docking a carrier was always a challenge and generally one picked a time when the winds and tides were favorable. Even when conditions were perfect, we usually had at least six big-Navy tugs. And we always had a ship's pilot who was extremely familiar with his harbor. Mayport was no exception and, though close to the sea, was guarded by a narrow rock-lined jetty.

Returning from sea one day, we were standing off the breakwater a couple of miles waiting for our helo to bring the ship's pilot. Due to the fog, however, the pilot had to take a boat out to us and we had therefore arranged for boarding over the fantail. I asked the XO to let us guys on the bridge know when he was aboard so we could get moving, as the tide was starting to turn in the St. Johns River. We got the word, cranked on 15 knots and started up the narrow river. The pilot came on the bridge a few minutes later, shook hands and promptly keeled over, totally passed out! Things got a little hectic. Visibility was poor, the river was moving, we were committed to the Mayport basin and the pilot was flat-out on his back. To compound matters, we passed the word for "medical emergency on the bridge," the word got out that "the captain had passed out," the resident admiral was in high warble and I was busy minding our 78,000-ton store trying to stay in the center of the channel. Turning into the basin, awake came our pilot friend who had not the slightest notion of what had happened, took charge and did a very nice job of berthing us. As it turned out, the climb from the boat to the hangar deck (three stories) and the long trek from hangar deck to the bridge (about eleven stories) was too much for our substantially-overweight pilot.

One day, while inport in Mayport and the Saratoga at sea, in comes the U.S.S. *Independence*, another sister aircraft carrier, with Captain Tom Watson at the helm. Tom was one of those super guys, highly decorated, gobs of experience and an overall real pro. At a formal party that night, Tom and I were huddled, talking about ship stuff including problems with our 137 heads, most with a large number of commodes, sinks and showers. We each had a team of shipfitters (plumbers) roving around the clock to keep the old pipes cleared out and fixing balky johns. Anyway, along comes this nice elderly lady whose perception of a carrier captain is one who sits on a tall throne, counting his perks and being attended to. "What are you two carrier Captains talking about so seriously?" she says.

And, our reply in unison, "Stopped-up johns." So much for the stereotype.

His name was Tuttle — Jerry O. Tuttle, Captain, U.S. Navy and Commanding Officer of the aircraft carrier Kennedy, one of our newest. Jerry and I had served as squadron commanders onboard Forrestal some five-years before, he in A7 attack jets and me in F4 fighters. Both our carriers were in the Med with the 6th Fleet participating in a very-large, multi-national exercise code-named National Week. The name of the game of this particular NATO war game was, "Don't get sunk by submarines," so both of us were doing max knots and really-random courses to prevent that unwanted "through-the-periscope" photo signifying a hit by a sub. Well, the Kennedy was "sunk" by an unknown sub and ordered out of action. Poor Jerry, he was fit to be tied, because he was probably one of the best operators the Navy's ever had and hated to be out of the fray.

At the exercise debrief on board Kennedy, the fleet arrayed throughout the anchorage, Jerry and I sat side by side on his hangar deck while the Italian lieutenant commander sub CO, proudly showed his carrier picture from the podium and described how he had sunk the Kennedy. Jerry just went under his seat in mortification. Everyone applauded for a job well done, the sub skipper took his bows and we all returned to our ships.

A month-or-so later, I received a large, crystal-clear photo of Forrestal taken through the periscope of an Italian submarine dated the same day Jerry and Kennedy were ordered to the sidelines. It was with heavy heart that I copied the picture and sent it to Jerry with some opportune forwarding remarks of endearment. C'est la vie. Sorry about that Jerry.

As great an operator as he was, Jerry was also the consummate detail guy. Witness the saga of the Kennedy laundry. I had heard the miracle he had wrought with his laundry and because ours was totally out-of-control what with missing bags, late returns and lost skivs, I paid him a visit during an anchorage in the Med. Jerry proudly showed me his operation. I mean the troops looked good, the place was spotless and the laundry was collected in the morning and returned to the division or squadron that evening. Why was due to a typical Tuttle approach to problem solving — hit it with a sledge hammer. He took a squadron executive officer who was medically grounded, made him officer-in-charge of the laundry, gave him carte blanche to fire any one of his 100 people for any reason and told him if he didn't like the replacement, to send him back too. Not surprisingly, the malcontents and loafers that the divisions sent to the laundry for temporary duty were no more and within a matter of weeks, the laundry prospered. We copied his play book verbatim and got the same results. What a guy. What pragmatic leadership!

Ten years after first writing this chronology, I attacked a clutch of thick file folders that had not seen the light of day for 25 years. Therein lay the day-to-day inner workings of running a large carrier: water problems; too many unauthorized absentees in port; cleanliness about the ship; retention of our top sailors and pilots; trying to save fuel; personal appearance; conduct ashore; supply support for our 80-or-so airplanes; safety; general ship needs; dodging errant merchant ships; enough flying for our airwing and so on. And for every problem I saw, there were a bunch more down in the trenches of the departments and divisions and squadrons. But just as in any organization, the leadership works to keep the troops pumped up, the enthusiasm level high and the standards maintained.

The converse to the many problems were the large number of memos and notes from me to the department heads and sailors complimentary in nature ranging from total minutia (heads in good shape) to high availability in one of the fighter squadrons. The "atta boys" far outnumbered the grumps. So the name of the game was to constantly improve across a broad range of measurable and subjective criteria and not get wound up when things did not go right. My Dad would occasionally remind me "to keep my eye on the ball," the ball in the case of an aircraft carrier being one of combat readiness — read the ability to launch deadly strikes and defend the ship against a myriad of threats, 24-hours a day for months on end.

The point here is that leadership and enthusiastic involvement, can make all the difference. We had a V4 division on Forrestal of about 100 men that had to be the worst group on the ship. These were the guys that managed the care and feeding of our four-million gallons of jet fuel and who had the most dismal berthing area, the highest mast rate, messed with drugs the most and just looked terrible. So, we took a really sharp P3 patrol plane lieutenant commander assigned to operations and made him the V4 division officer a la Tuttle. Not long after, I climbed down a long vertical column that went down to a jet-fuel pump room deep within the bowels of the ship. Laying on their backs, fiddling with a pump, was a chief, a young petty officer and my lieutenant commander division

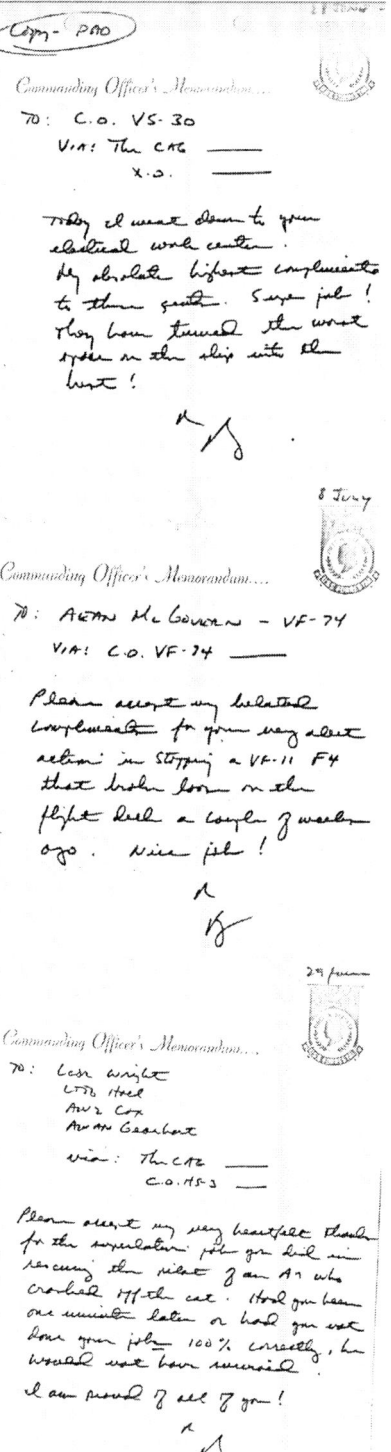

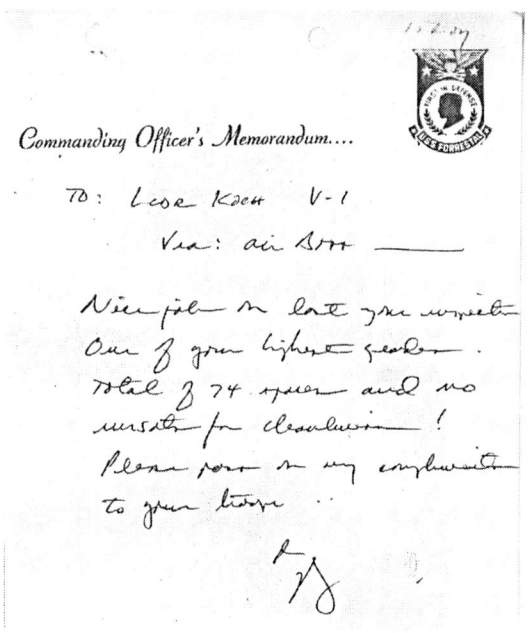

Typical short attaboy for a job well done. In this case, these are the flight deck guys (around 100) with a bunch of spaces to care for.

officer. I flat guarantee that in several weeks, all the indicators had turned positive and V4 was getting attaboys from everyone. Just goes to show that good, enthusiastic leadership does in fact, make a difference. Way to go guys!

We spent hundreds of hours alongside logistics ships taking on ship's fuel, jet fuel, stores and ammunition. Everything we consumed, we took aboard at sea. Usually these evolutions were scheduled after 14 hours of flight operations and went well into the wee hours, so fatigue probably had something to do with my less than total enthusiasm for these alongside evolutions. And, while it wasn't hairy or dangerous, it did take very-close attention to detail on the part of a lot of folks. In the old days, the salts would regale us new guys of how they rolled into the refueling slot at 25 knots, waited 'till the bow crossed the stern of the oiler, ordered all back full, and then coasted into the evolution speed of 12 knots. I guess I'll never be an old salt, for I was always conservative and took my time to do it right. More ships have been dinged and people hurt by hot dogging a multi-billion dollar national asset, than in some of our wars.

We still had fun though. One sunlit day we were coming alongside the Detroit, a large, fast, fleet oiler and ammo ship, commanded by a friend of mine from 506 days in the Pentagon, Herb Hope. Herb was also senior to me by a couple of years, wanted to be a carrier CO and would have been spectacular in the role. Herb also had a very bald and shiny dome. As we approached, he was regally sitting in his chair on the port bridge wing and would not grace us with a look backwards. So, I sent him a quick "CO to CO" flashing-light message, the essence of which was to, "Please put your hat on, your head is blinding my conning officer." We looked down from our perch some three-stories above Herb, as the Detroit's messenger reluctantly delivered our request. The top of Herb's head turned several shades of red, he waited a few minutes as befitted his status, knew he had been had, and, with a big grin, looked up, raised his hat and gave all of us a big thumbs up. Herb, I should note, had been in one of the A4 light-attack aircraft back aft, when the Forrestal had its really bad fire back in 1967 off Vietnam, and nearly lost his life.

Alongside Detroit taking on fuel, ammo and stores. Large destroyer (963 class) on Detroit's starboard side. An unusually clear day in the Med.

Like all carriers, we had a phenomenally talented air wing and great aviators. Our two fighter squadrons, VF-11 and VF-74 — I had served in both — flew the F4 Phantom. About once a week I would fly the F4, the A6, the S3 or H3 helo, the latter three from a co-pilot position. The perspective outside the confines of the old Forrestal was absolutely incredible. Looking down from six-miles overhead, one could imagine the beehive of activity: chow, problems, sleeping, pay, fixing, watches, et al.. The job of the big ship was flying airplanes and there was no better way to put the icing on the cake than to see it all from the air.

VF-74 F4 Phantom on bow cat. Cat officer is giving the signal to launch.

Our sophisticated stable of high-tech airplanes were the raison d'etre of the Forrestal, so combat-ready machines and mission-honed pilots and flight officers were the top goal of our ship. A constant and perennial problem area were spare parts. Take VF-11 for example: with twelve jets, two were not flyable due to parts shortages totaling 31 separate items.

Bomb farm abeam the island. Our raison d'etre ... combat readiness.

Keeping the troops informed takes many paths.

First in Defense

PPS - Get this out to D.O.s/CPOs.

UNITED STATES SHIP FORRESTAL
LETTER OF COMMENDATION

10 May 1978

The Commanding Officer, USS FORRESTAL takes pleasure in commending

JAMES M. KEPPER
AVIATION ORDINANCEMAN SECOND CLASS
UNITED STATES NAVY

for outstanding performance of duty as described in the following

CITATION:

As AIMD Assistant Police Petty Officer your performance has been outstanding. Your exemplary leadership and managerial skills have greatly improved living conditions for the 96 men berthing in your compartment. Your dedication to duty, performance and concern for your shipmates reflect great credit upon yourself, USS FORRESTAL and the United States Navy.

Short + to the point. No B.S. necessary

P. B. BOOTH
Captain, United States Navy
Commanding Officer, USS FORRESTAL (CV-59)

TO: X.O. + D.H.s + MCPOC
1. AO2 Kepper did a good job
2. Chief/D.O. writes up short "attaboy"
3. YN types onto nice certificate
4. D.H./D.O. present at quarters
5. ∴ RECOGNITION!!! PK

"25" Philosophy — Letter we all be what we can to promote recognition for jobs well done. 95% below to to 10% from Sup!

Commanding Officer's Memorandum...

Cdr Reaff —
Jim —
I think you did an absolutely first rate job on air ops the past few months.
My compliments for a job exceptionally well done. I could have asked for no more.

VIA: DCSD

Lots of staffs and folks throughout the Navy system worked hard to get us what was needed, but by any reasonable measure, the supply support was simply lousy and a source of constant frustration within the ship and up the chain of command. Poor supply support simply meant the combat readiness of the ship and air wing was compromised. End of sermon!

```
                         Commanding Officer
                         USS FORRESTAL  CV-59

                                              4 July 1978

    Dear Admiral Anderson,

         Please allow me to join with the many who have expressed
    their condolences over the death of your son, Pat.  His loss
    saddened me and all who knew and worked with him.

         On the morning of the day of his death, he had for the
    first time, conned the ship in the approach phase to alongside
    the USNS RIGEL.  My words to him after he was relieved were
    simply "nice job".  For indeed it was one of the best approaches
    any one of us had made.

         His performance in this evolution was indicative of his
    approach to his day-to-day duties.  Thorough, smart, interested,
    quiet, professional: all are words to describe a particularly
    brilliant young man.  We in FORRESTAL will miss Pat.

         I know my words are inadequate.  I just wanted you to
    know that we greatly respected Pat and sorrow at his loss.

                              Sincerely,


                              P. B. BOOTH
                              Captain, U. S. Navy


    Admiral George Anderson
    2510 Virginia Avenue NW
    Apartment 1102N
    Washington, D. C. 20037
```

Sad letter to Admiral Anderson. His son, Pat, was a talented A7 attack pilot.

One day, we got word that a VF-74 Phantom was down about 75-miles away, the pilot being Sam Bonanno, or "Banana", as he was called by his RIO. Soon, both were in the helo and recounting a story unique in the annals of Naval Aviation, for Sam had been shot down by his own leader, an Air Force pilot on exchange duty with the Navy. "Captain Air Force" had just completed a really-standard intercept with Sam as the simulated enemy aircraft. In this case, the "train like you fight" philosophy was taken too far, and the Air Force launched a live, heat-seeking Sidewinder missile up the tailpipe of Sam's Phantom with catastrophic and predictable results. Though a fine officer, obviously super pilot and a former Thunderbird, the captain was pulled from the squadron by his Air Force bosses and sent to a more serene stateside staff job. I suppose it went down in the record books as plain, unadulterated dumbness.

First in Defense

Another dumb one, this time on my part, came in the protocol arena. The admiral on board, Dutch Schoultz (a former Forrestal CO), and I were to visit the hierarchy of Marseilles, France, upon our arrival. It was a big deal, as we were the first U.S. warship to visit since WWII. Well, we knocked-off flying at midnight, dodged our way through lots of coastal shipping traffic until mooring alongside at 0800. I was really tired —Tuttle called being a carrier CO "an endurance contest" — and promptly lay down and fell asleep. So here comes Dutch over to my in-port cabin, replete with sword, medals, choker whites and red face. It was one of the fastest uniform races I've ever had and I am here to tell you that I was one embarrassed cookie. In the Navy, one doesn't keep admirals waiting, ever.

Everyone looked forward to port visits. While underway, it was de riguer to pack 32 hours into a 24-hour day and night and most of the crew worked at least 12-hours a day. In the Sixth Fleet at this time, we would spend about 60% of our time at sea training, working with other countries and participating in giant combined exercises. The pace was generally frantic to above. The visit to Marseilles, France was a winner and somewhat different.

Instead of anchoring out a mile or so and having to contend with boating for the crew's liberty and the vagaries of Mediterranean weather, we moored inside the harbor. It was quite an evolution for they had never had a vessel as large as a carrier enter. We had three French pilots on board, one of whom spoke passable English. Anyway, we made it fine. The crew really enjoyed the week as did the local folks who thought it a big deal. Lots of visitors and oohs and aahs. The headline in the local paper the next day in large bold print was "C'EST FORMIDABLE." The conduct ashore was almost perfect in spite of good beer, lots of money and a bit of time off for our guys.

USS FORRESTAL CV-59
Marseille, France

JUNE 1978

MARINE A MARSEILLE

L'AMIRAL

21st of June, 1978

Dear Captain Booth,

We got accustomed to see "Forrestal" in the harbour or in the roads', and to meet you and yours officers... We are a little disappointed now when you are gone away...

But the beautiful photograph we received yesterday will remind us of your visit in Marseille, and sunset parade, and kind hospitality aboard...

My wife and naval officers in Marseille fall in with me to sent many thanks for your kindness and we make ardent wishes for "Forrestal" having an happy navigation.

We should enjoy to see you again and we say good luck to "Forrestal" and her captain.

My best regards to cor Blatt.

Sincerely

contre-amiral THÉOLEYRE

Commanding Officer
USS FORRESTAL CV-59

To the people of Marseilles

Because there were so many people of the city of Marseilles who contributed so much to our very successful port visit, I take this opportunity to thank you all for a most pleasant stay. On behalf of the officers and men of the FORRESTAL, I would like to extend to you – the people of Marseilles our very sincere appreciation for your gracious hospitality and warm welcome.

We accomplished a great deal of work on our ship. But we also gained many friends. We shall not soon forget the people of Marseilles that made it all possible.

We hope one day to return. For all of you who made our visit such a great success, We thank you for the opportunity to have visited your fine city.

P. B. BOOTH
Captain, U. S. Navy
Commanding Officer

First in Defense

One of the carriers we had operated with in the preceding at-sea period was the French Clemanceau, homeported in Marseilles. Their skipper was Captain Jacques Compredon, who invited Russ Blatt and me for lunch at his country retreat about 60-miles inland near the sleepy town of Aix en Provence. Not too exciting, but a relaxing day doing something different with some nice folks. Bottom line is that the friendship between the United States and France was reinforced at many levels from the newest young sailor to the captain and admiral; and our guys got a chance to unwind and see the world!

Back at sea with the Sixth Fleet in the Mediterranean Sea late one night, we had a small hydraulic fire forward in one of the bow catapult machinery rooms and because it was a class bravo fire, we went to general quarters. On board at the time as the guest of Rear Admiral Schoultz, was a writer for the *New York Times*, Drew Middleton. A portion of the article he wrote follows:

> The night before there was a small fire forward. The iron clamor of the bell sounding general quarters was followed by the clatter of hundreds of feet on the way to stations. The sailors came down the passageway, young, alert, running hard toward the fire.
>
> In the quiet of his quarters after the fire had been put out, Rear Adm. Robert F. Schoultz, commanding Carrier Group Two, listened approvingly as Capt. Peter B. Booth, the skipper, complimented the crew on its professionalism in an emergency.
>
> "Sometimes at home you get sore when people say this generation won't work, won't fight," the admiral said. "You saw them. You saw the way they work on the flight deck and in the engine rooms. These are good boys."

Like all carriers, the bridge of Forrestal had gobs of folks on duty underway including helmsmen, lookouts, officers of the deck, navigation team and so on — about 20 in all. By definition, it was always quiet and at night, very dark. Late one night, in poor and blustery weather, we were trying to catch our last airplane, worried about a merchant ship which we figured would pass ahead by only a few-hundred yards and listening to the fire brigade on the radio attempting to sort out the cause of some persistent smoke deep within the giant ship. Though not particularly atypical on a carrier bridge, this scenario generated a slight increase on the tension meter. About this time, Russ Blatt, the XO, walked onto the bridge, surveyed the situation, and announced in a voice just loud enough for all to hear, "Captain, you may be in command, but you're not in control."

We caught the airplane, the merchant passed astern and the smoke went away. So ended another routine day in the life of an aircraft carrier.

The late '70s were tough times for the Navy: funding constraints, post-Vietnam syndrome, an ominous and persistent Soviet threat and supposedly, lots of people problems. But still, the seagoing guys did their thing and did it well, despite the gloom and doom from the pundits one may have occasionally been exposed to. Thus the epilogue of this tale is an article I wrote for my high school alumni magazine back in 1979. This is the way it was, with no embellishment. It was the same aboard Ike, Kennedy, Independence, Saratoga and all the rest.

Group of officers and sailors from AIMD: Don't know what the occasion was, but here is the Forrestal's chain of command from captain to department head to command master chief to division officer, chief, leading petty officer and on down. What incredible talent! Winners all.

EPILOGUE I

USS FORRESTAL — A MICROCOSM OF OUR NATION'S YOUTH
(Written for the St. Paul's School Alumni Magazine in 1978)

At five minutes before midnight, I walked onto the bridge. The only sound was the far-off steady clank of the anchor chain finding its way into the ship, sparkling-night lights of Naples, Italy but a thousand-yards away. The officer of the deck, a 23-year-old ensign, requested permission to get underway. Promptly at midnight, the anchor was aweigh and the aircraft carrier Forrestal was underway. Quietly, and with a confidence that belied his age, the ensign gave orders that brought the ship fair on course and headed for the open sea at twenty knots.

Below the ship's bridge and throughout the 1,000-plus-foot length of this magnificent ship, the night and watch crews went about the business of readying the ship for routine flight operations. Meals, laundry and watches took place alongside youngsters preparing their sophisticated stable of 80 aircraft for flying at first light.

Our plan was to be underway early so that we could fly our airwing all of the following day and into the night, then transit south at high speed to enter the Straits of Messina (between Italy and Sicily) at 0400, rendezvous with our fuel tanker in the Ionian Sea, take on 3,000,000 gallons of jet and ship fuel and then, at 1200, fly our airwing until 0100 the next night.

First in Defense

An atypical day? Hardly, for we did this six times during one deployment as a part of the U.S. Navy's ever-present and powerful Sixth Fleet in the Mediterranean Sea. Evolutions such as this are routine and normal in our Navy of today. And what makes it all possible, and the purpose behind this article, is the young ensign as OOD, the mess man preparing meals, the plane captain working on his airplane, the young fighter pilot practicing his deadly avocation and so on.

As Forrestal's captain, I would often be asked what I thought of our people who made our Navy go. My response, having worked very closely with a goodly cross section of America's youth, was that "90% were great, 5% OK and 5% we kick out."

It sometimes seems to me that we lose sight of America's average young man and portray him as a gangster, dope pusher, drop out, long hair, or whatever. I would not begin to suggest that we don't have our problems aboard ship, but I am here to suggest that — given he receives a fair shake leadership-wise, an occasional pat on the back, concern, some compassion, genuine guidance and a good hard kick in the rear if he goofs — the average guy on a Navy ship or squadron is an absolutely spectacular individual! Allow me some perspectives that may give you a feel for my enthusiasm.

On board Forrestal, I had a very modest daily goal, which was to get off the bridge, out of the cabin and tour around the ship for at least two-hours per day. One day, for example, I set out to explore the angle above the main deck and made the following seemingly uninteresting observations: Nice talk with our new waist-catapult officer and his very competent chief; talked with a group of V2-catapult guys, who said they had no complaints, said I didn't believe them, finally got one big-strapping guy to gripe about the chow, asked him how many complete meals he ate per day, said six, I said it can't be too bad and he agreed; nosed into the flight-deck lighting shop and talked to a really squared-away guy who was packing and going back into civilian life, and said thanks to him for all he had done; he said, "thanks for thanking me" and meant it; discovered a head that was a disaster; unhappy; talked to a young engineer who said with a smile, "We'd have a great ship if no airplanes to contend with."

"ANNOUNCEMENTS"

MENU OF TODAY:

BREAKFAST: Grapefruit, fruit, pineapple juice, hot farina, eggs to order, scrambled eggs with bacon, ham, corned beef hash, french toast, maple syrup, toast, butter, coffee, tea, milk, breakfast pastry bar

LUNCH: Beef rice soup, crackers, beef liver with onions, gravy, beef pot pie with biscuit topping, green peas, salad bar, assorted dressings, dinner rolls, dessert bar, jello, coffee, tea, milk

SEEDLINE: Soup De Jour, crackers, frankfurters on bun, tuna salad sandwich with sliced tomato, potato chips, sauerkraut, dessert bar, salad bar,

SUPPER: Stuffed pork chops, green pepper ring, gravy, potatoes, sauerkraut, green beans, salad bar, assorted dressings, dessert bar, strawberry gelatin, rolls, coffee, tea, milk, softdrinks

OK, I could go on and on, but the bottom line is that an aircraft carrier is a complex animal — put sophisticated planes on it, it becomes even more complex and throw 5,500 guys from admiral to recruits, all 50-states, the spectrum of ethnic and religious backgrounds, young, old, Ph.D. to high-school dropout, black, white, etc. and it almost defies description.

But what made all this happen, is the guy who eats six-meals a day, the sailor who is getting out, but works his tail off anyway, the catapult officer working with his troops at 2300 in the evening and so on.

It's every plane captain, mess cook, pilot, baker and storekeeper that made the ship tick. As went our guys, so went the ship!

We would have discipline problems for sure and once in awhile, something serious. But, almost all of our problems were handled at non-judicial punishment (captain's mast) in which the max punishment is restriction, fine and/or up to three-days brig time. We had a few, mostly new people — who three-months before had been 18-or-19-year-old civilians — who would occasionally "test the system."

In two areas, we were particularly tough — drugs and respect for a sailor's superior petty officers and officers. Drug cases were mostly marijuana. The danger here is that an aircraft carrier is a dangerous piece of machinery — millions of gallons of fuel, thousands of tons of high-tech weaponry, many complex aircraft and demanding machinery of every description. So for this reason, we absolutely could not allow any use of drugs or alcohol. If a man was caught (not unusual), he would receive the max I could levy against him. I never heard any complaints, simply because he knew he was dead wrong.

Once in awhile, despite our best indoctrination, a youngster would suggest to his petty officer or chief or officer where he could "get off." The result from the system was predictable, fast and generally maximum. I would say that in practically all cases, the young man was most apologetic and conceded that he had learned a good lesson.

Conduct ashore was always stressed to our people because each one of them in a foreign land was indeed an ambassador of the United States. All it took was one guy out of a 3,000-man liberty party to blemish the reputation of the ship or even the nation. In one full deployment all throughout the Med, our rate of minor incidents ashore was but two sailors in 1,000. Not a bad commentary on our youngsters, particularly in view of the fact they generally had a pocketful of disposable income and had been at sea under arduous conditions for several weeks.

I pointed out earlier that perhaps the key to success with our young people were our leaders. Everyone on board in a leadership position was and is expected to "take care of his people." I don't mean to coddle, protect or baby, but to have genuine concern for his charges as individuals. Today, all of our junior officers and senior petty officers are required to attend a two-week leadership school which emphasizes the principals of counseling, human motivation, participative management and job satisfaction.

Let me illustrate the point that if our men are to produce, then the leadership of the organization must directly and visibly care about them and respect them as individuals: One day I was doing a long zone inspection and first on the agenda were the helicopter squadron's berthing spaces up forward and right between the bow catapults and below the flight deck. These spaces were always squared away, not a rack had a wrinkle, not a speck of dust anywhere — really sharp!

Well Commander Barry Spoffard, their CO was there. He didn't have to be, as it was the day after getting in from an extended at-sea period. He pointed out to me quite forcibly, that in the summer and particularly when the catapults were firing, it got very hot in the compartment and his guys sometimes had trouble sleeping. I asked him what could be done about it and he had his stuff together. He stated exactly what A/C unit was to be installed, how much chill water was required, how much headroom, etc. I mentioned that we would have to fit this into the "priority list," which is a euphemistic way of saying, "We'll file it for consideration." Much to my delight, he recognized my non-response for what it was and started all over again. Result: The air conditioner was promptly installed.

To me this is style, and a fine example of a leader fighting for his men and really taking the time and effort to act in their best interests. A big deal? I think not. But let me tell you that Commander Spoffard was widely respected throughout his command as a concerned leader. The results were that his squadron out-flew, out-performed, flew safer and had a higher record of retention than any other squadron on the ship. Why? Because his people reciprocated to his style of concerned and pragmatic leadership.

The point that I am trying to make is that our young (and old) Navy people are as smart, as competent, as hard working, have as much fun and learn as much as any past generation. They are indeed a microcosm of our society from the captain on down and it's not just on the Forrestal that I see this — it's every outfit I've been associated with.

Morale, attitudes, spirit or whatever you want to call it? Well, as you might expect, it varied. Sometimes, when we had been at sea for a long time and the weather was poor, I could sense that the guys were down. We just had to work a bit harder at keeping the bubble pumped up. But mostly, the attitudes were positive, and often times surprisingly so.

The enclosed picture of one-half of our airwing and crew was taken during a personnel inspection while at anchor in Souda Bay, Crete. We had come in for three days — no liberty, just a chance to slow down, clean the ship, repair aircraft, have a flight-deck cookout and a not-very-often personnel inspection. The setting was lovely — clear skies, a gorgeous bay and the mountains of Crete to the south, topped by snow this glorious summer day. I selected a group of about 300 men to inspect at random and how proud I was of them! They stood tall, hair was trimmed, uniforms pressed and chests out. My group was not atypical. I stood on the back end of an airplane with our Battle Group Admiral and offered an old-fashioned three cheers for "us guys." You could hear it all the way to Athens!

Crew at inspection while anchored in Souda Bay with mountains of Crete in background, three cheers, Admiral Schoultz with air boss and CAG to right.

Two or three times a week I would get a letter or phone call from off the ship bragging about "our" guys. One, a letter from a civilian shipyard worker who had lost his wallet read, ". . . it was returned to me by RMSN Mack Burnwell. The wallet contained my personal papers and $68, all of which was returned. I have thanked the young man, but thought perhaps you would like to share my pride in the caliber of one of our Navy's men."

And another from a lady who found a wallet belonging to one of our crew who went to her home to retrieve it and wrote, ". . . a nicer representative of the U.S. Navy than this young gentleman I have never met. Not only was he a charming person, but we were so delighted to hear good cheering words about the Forrestal and "our" Navy. This young man most certainly exemplifies your fine crew of enlisted men and officers."

And on and on and on it went, for our crew really did shine.

Why do they do it? Why does our shipboard sailor work 12-hours a day, seven-days a week (at sea) and still come out smiling? Why does that young lieutenant launch in his $27-million airplane off the front end of the ship in absolute blackness? How does the crew of the carrier Nimitz stay pumped up after 105 consecutive days at sea in the Indian Ocean?

I'm not sure I have the answer. Certainly it's not pay, plush living or easy work. The mystery is not explained by economics. I do think though, that it has something to do with pride, being a part of a tough and competent team, having a worthwhile mission, being recognized for doing a good job and knowing they're on the first team. And, I would submit too, that a liberal dose of patriotism and pride in this great country of ours plays a part.

There are two bottom lines to this short tale. One is my effusive enthusiasm for the ability, competence, "can-do" attitude and generally spectacular performance of our sea-going Navy officers and men in spite of a tough, demanding, no-nonsense environment, low pay and long hours.

The other is that from my experience there is nothing automatic about this sort of sustained performance, but rather it is the result of concerned, competent and knowledgeable leadership at all levels, a leadership that enforces the standards, sets reachable goals and shows absolute and genuine concern for their people.

I would submit that in the great majority of our Navy we have these ingredients, we have the esprit and that it is our people that make us the number-one Navy in the world and a Navy that our country and you can rely on.

EPILOGUE II

- **Tom Watson**, the Independence CO, went on to flag rank and continued to serve his nation and Navy with great distinction. After retiring he became CEO of a major corporation.

- **Russ Blatt** completed a highly successful tour as Forrestal's XO and later commanded a major naval air station in San Diego.

- We hosted some great flag officers aboard Forrestal, but **Dutch Schoultz** was the best, simply because he had been there and done it all.

- **Jerry Tuttle** continued up the ranks with a focus on war fighting and no-nonsense, practical leadership by personal example. Good guy!

- **Sam Bonanno** is now a captain for Fedex. Sadly his Air Force **leader** was killed in a Stearman bi-plane at a low altitude while serving as a shuttle mission specialist.

- **Dave Pellet**, our chief engineer, did more for his country and Navy than most Americans do in a lifetime. Thanks Dave.

- **Wick Parcells** continued his magnificent service to his country, became the first skipper of the U.S.S. *Theodore Roosevelt* and attained flag rank.

- To the **Wives and Parents** of our 5,000 plus men: Thanks for the love and understanding. Without your support, our collective tasks would have been inestimably more difficult.

- To **Yogi Bair** and to **the thousands** of hard working and sacrificing officers, aviators, and troops of the great ship Forrestal, were we together today, I would offer a "hip, hip, hooray" and a "tip of the hat and pat on the back" for the incredibly tough job you all did so honorably and well!

EPILOGUE III

Some ten years after writing this chapter, I happened across some old files and papers which had gathered dust and roaches in an old cruise box chuck full of faded memories. Most of these were files that any CO collects

First in Defense

when he departs a command. In my case I had never looked at them until recently. One aspect any ship CO can relate to is the constant amount of correspondence from concerned parents or families inquiring about their son or loved one. Though burdensome in a large seagoing command, most all COs would take the time to personally respond. The one below is not atypical and even today brings a lump to my throat. The parent, though barely literate, expressed his love for the Navy he had served in during WWII and for his son, who was a barber on Forrestal. My response, though routine, tells it all.

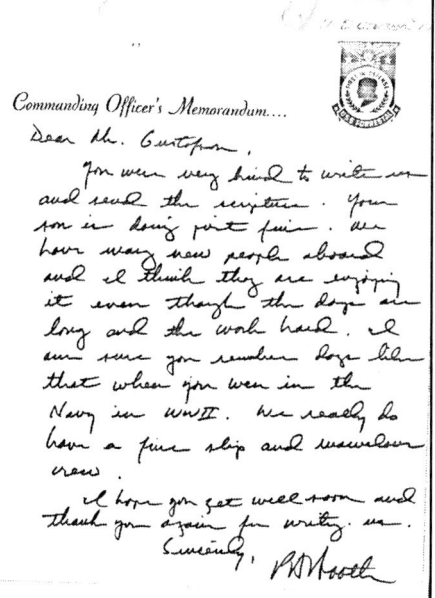

> VETERANS ADMINISTRATION HOSPITAL
> 10701 EAST BOULEVARD
> CLEVELAND, OHIO 44106
>
> SEPT 27
>
> DEAR SIR:
> I AM BURTON GUSTAFSON FATHER. MY BOY IS A BARBER ON YOUR SHIP. FOR THE LAST 10 YEAR I HAVE BEEN IN A WHEELCHAIR. MY BOY DONE ALOT FOR ME HE MY ONE & ONLY. HIS WIFE IS GOING TO HAVE THERE FIRST BABY IN DEC OR JAN. I WAS IN THE NAVY IN W.W. II LIKE IT ALOT. WAS DOWN & SAW THE SHIP IN JULY SURE LOOK GOOD. ~~I DO NOT KNOW~~ HOPE YOUR SHIP & ALL THE MEN BEST OF LUCK. HOPE SOME DAY MAY GET THE HONOR OF MEET YOU. MY GOD BE WITH YOU & YOUR MEN,
>
> R Gustafson

> Commanding Officer's Memorandum....
>
> Dear Mr. Gustafson,
>
> You were very kind to write us and send the scripture. Your son is doing just fine. We have many new people aboard and I think they are enjoying it even though the days are long and the work hard. I am sure you remember days like that when you were in the Navy in WWII. We really do have a fine ship and marvelous crew.
>
> I hope you get well soon and thank you again for writing us.
>
> Sincerely,

EPILOGUE IV

I find it hard to finally end this chapter, for yet another sliver of life at sea crept out of the thick folders of Forrestal remembrances: the families that I and so many of my ilk left behind to man the homefront, tend to schools, fix balky lawnmowers, pay bills, work with Navy Relief and find money for expensive braces. My Carolyn and the girls were no different. When Forrestal changed homeport from Norfolk to Mayport near Jacksonville, they stayed back on Summerset Lane with occasional 15-hour car treks with some other wives for visits when the ship was in port and a couple of inport periods when deployed with the Sixth Fleet in the Mediterranean. Below are two telegrams which don't even come close to expressing the gratitude and love of the seagoing sailor for those left behind. (One might return briefly to the third page of this meandering tale as to whom these vignettes are dedicated!)

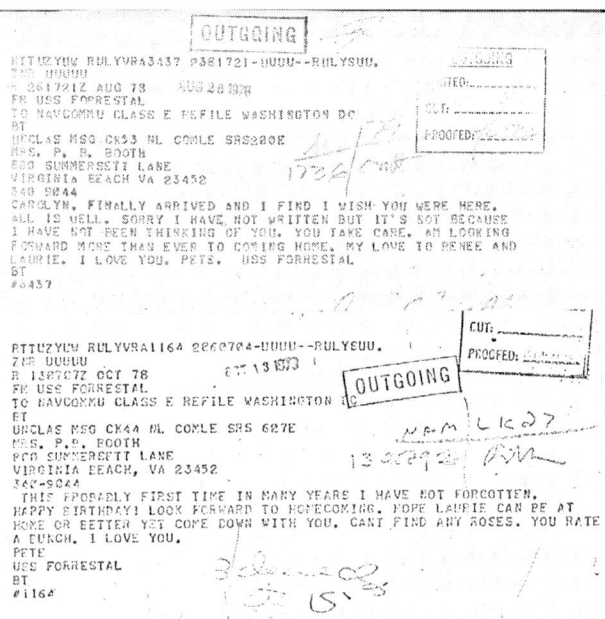

Carolyn welcomes us home to Mayport.

STAFFER

Battle group training, soviet subs, real deep in ours', whales, McKee, Waller, P3s and the passive sonar equation.

My first day on the job as Chief of Staff to the Commander of the Third Fleet, included lunch with Vice Admiral Kin McKee, the three-star head guy. Without serious preamble and before my first bite, he asked what I knew about the "Passive Sonar Equation." Well, he could as well have questioned my knowledge of the breeding habits of the Mongolian Tiger Moth. I had not the slightest notion as to the answer and told him so while munching my sandwich. Anticipating my response, he reached beside his chair and proffered a four-inch-thick tome titled — you guessed it, "The Passive Sonar Equation."

Kin McKee was one of those guys who's done it all and can do anything else. Innately smart, charismatic, and hard charging, he was the Navy's (world's) premiere submariner. His blackened coffee mug bore the name and logo of "Dace," a nuclear-powered fast-attack submarine he commanded that went places and did things few of us mortals or Tom Clancy ever dream of. Along the way he had been the head of the U.S. Naval Academy in Annapolis. He was the boss of our 100-person staff and owned half the Pacific Navy from the West Coast of the U.S. to the international date line. His job was to seek out every at-sea Soviet submarine in the Pacific and to train up each large battle group of ships enroute to his compatriot, the 7th Fleet, in the Western Pacific. My job was as "XO," or chief of the staff, which loosely translated, meant execute the admiral's program and provide him the necessary staff support. Our product bottom-line was knowing the whereabouts of Soviet Pacific subs and effective battle group preparation for warfighting. Heavy stuff!

Because the best sub-hunting platform is another submarine, my boss arranged for a 48-hour ride in an older fast-attack nuclear sub for me under the command of a mini-McKee, Commander Karl Krupp. I've done lots of intense things, but this experience is near the top. After departing Pearl Harbor, Karl took her down to 1,000 feet. I am here to testify that I've never heard such creaking and groaning in my life on a sea-going vessel! Dinner that evening in the tiny wardroom, took my eyes on a dance from the depth gauge to the "bubble" and back. The depth hovered at a thousand feet most of the time. Once, however, it went below and the XO very casually excused himself. We settled lower, accompanied by a higher up-angle and more complaints from the old hull. The junior officers loved my discomfort and kept up a cheerful banter of JO talk throughout. The XO returned with a nonchalant smile, the depth gauge back to normal.

VADM Kin McKee and staff ... all smiling. Leo Profilet to Admiral's right.

The sub was typical I suppose, of subs everywhere. Most of the crew were on a six-on and six-off routine. Hot bunking, wherein two guys on different watches used the same bunk, was more the norm than not. The old ship was spotless — you could eat off the deck plates. Morale was sky high. These sailors were good and you could tell it.

In my tiny little bunk above the Executive Officer's, I lay with both eyes wide-open listening to the strange sounds about me, feeling the 1,000 feet of the Pacific Ocean not more than four-inches from my right shoulder and trying not to think of the 7,000-feet below us. Walking casually into the wardroom at 0200 (to check the depth gauge), there were three junior officers studying the emergency procedures for "what to do if you are going down and you really want to go up, but the machine is not doing what you want it to do." This was a far cry from my previous incarnations wherein I was the master of my own destiny in the cockpit or on the bridge — at least 98% of the time.

Back ashore, I was host to an obscenely big office with one of those desks that could convert to a double bed in an emergency. Outside were a covey of helpers and assistants. We were housed in an old two-story, WWII building in the middle of Pearl Harbor on an island named after an early Army aviator. In the basement, however, were some of the most esoteric and advanced command-and-control and sub-hunting facilities in the world. As a staff, we functioned of course, 24-hours a day and seven-days per week.

Our sub-hunting job was incredibly serious business, because at any one time, the Soviets had four-to-eight, nuclear-propelled, nuclear-tipped, missile-firing subs on patrol in our area, with a great many highly-accurate, nuclear weapons targeted on the United States. Some of these missiles had a time of flight of less than twelve minutes, so the name of the game we played was to know the position of all these subs, all the time. A tall order!

To do this job, we had lots of sophisticated assets at our fingertips including subs such as Karl's, big P3 four-engine patrol airplanes, an expansive underwater sound system and most importantly, a vast array of intelligence sources.

I'm convinced that the smartest folks in the Navy reside in the intelligence community. By smart, I mean plain, unadulterated brain power. McKee called them "gumshoes," so called because they sneaked around looking for any source possible to make their case. Each day, key staff members got together in our highly-classified "Puka" and the gumshoes would recite their litany of heavily-digested bits and pieces of an incredible puzzle.

Flag Sec, Chief of Staff, McKee, and aide, Randy Bogle.

There was many a weekend and middle-of-the-night rendezvous when a few of us would gather at the admiral's behest, to brainstorm a "missing" Soviet missile-shooter.

Typical of these Intel guys, was Mary Anne Avcalade. Mary Anne had been in the Navy about six years, worked some 60-hours a week normally, and more if we had some tough problems. She lived to find Soviet subs and she was good at it. Her briefs to the admiral were always stimulating and the result of very meticulous work on her part. She was also smart and a good acrylic artist. She was not atypical of the sort of folk we were blessed with on our somewhat oversized staff.

When Kin was skipper of Dace, he had a reputation as the best hunter of Soviet subs in the Navy — kind of a modern-day Baron Von Richtofen. Without embellishment, our admiral was naturally prone to use our highly capable subs in the "find-Soviet-subs" scenario. One day in the puka, things were tense, because one of our subs had lost the object of his mission. Kin turns to me and says, "Get Thunman!" Thunman being the two star in charge of all Pacific submarines and the second-best sub hunter in the world. Summons such as this didn't wait for the Ford Island ferry and the two star took my place in the puka within a few minutes. I doubt if the combined five stars gave any guidance to that sub CO, for sub skippers were traditionally, extremely autonomous, but I am here to testify that there was little conviviality between my admiral and the admiral that took my seat that morning!

The every-hour Ford Island Ferry passes the Arizona Memorial. Our quarters to right back in trees.

The living was deja vu. It was like a time warp going back to WWII. About forty families lived on Ford Island, all nestled in amongst the banyan trees and plumeria bushes of decades past. Having moved from our home on Summerset Lane in Virginia Beach, Carolyn and the girls would make our own flower leis from the backyard bushes. Ours was a sprawling, one-story, linoleum-floored, no-air-conditioning, five never-locked doors to the outside and a many-windowed house that catered to the soft breezes and fragrant airs of Pearl Harbor. The views to the mountains beyond were breathtaking. That's the good news.

The bad news was that Ford Island was indeed, an island, the only connection to the mainland being an old ferry. It ran each hour from 0600 to 2200. Because schools, shopping and the real world of 1980 were across the harbor, the ferry became an intrinsic part of our life support, albeit a sometimes pain in the neck. Despite an occasional annoyance, it was always sobering and inspirational to cruise within fifty yards of the Arizona Memorial, the eternal home to 1,177 sailors since December 7, 1941 and the symbol of our nation's entry into World War Two.

My mom and dad visit Carolyn and me on idyllic Ford Island.

One day, my boss announced he was going off to a neighboring island for a few days to "work on a speech." The occasion was the every December 7th ceremony on board the Arizona. By normal speech standards, it was a small affair, as only some 200 could attend and there was no TV. Nonetheless, in typical McKee fashion, he attacked this small duty with gusto.

It turned out to be the most awesomely-phenomenal speech I had ever heard, most of this nature having the common ingredient of being totally boring and occasionally specious. Not McKee's. He started out, "This is a special day for a lot of special folks, many of whom cannot be with us today." And on it went. You could have heard a pin drop. It was vintage McKee, and I suppose, that of a few others of his ilk. No big bonus, no accolades, no medals — just a good Naval Officer doing the best job he could, by putting forth a non-self-serving 115%.

In the "believe it or not" category, we also dealt with whales and archeological digs. The unoccupied Hawaiian island of Kahoolawe, just south of Maui, had long been used as a bombing and gunnery target complex by the Navy and Marines. It also had the dichotomous distinction of being the ancestral home and burial grounds of many Hawaiians. And finally, just offshore in protected leeward waters was the ten-thousand year breeding ground of the great Pacific Humpback whale. Can you believe it? What a mixture.

Although the bombing had long ago been cut way-back, the clean up of thousands of rounds of unexploded ammunition scattered in and amongst the digs will be a never-ending job. One of our missions in life was to walk the fine line between whales, digs and the need to train an increasingly sophisticated military in the Hawaiian area. The walker of this line for Admiral McKee was Leo Profilet. Leo had the patience of Job, was good at explaining the Navy's side of the issue and was a senior Captain of great experience. His tenure as a seven-year POW in Vietnam, plus his own natural abilities, went a long ways towards smoothing the waters and he became a favorite of both sides of the fence, due in large part to the force of his own awesome credibility.

On the training side of the ledger, we spent a good deal of effort in orchestrating large, multi-dimensional training exercises for our battle groups. There were lots of tough hurdles for these guys such as sub threats, large air attacks (often times using Air Force assets), working in total electronic silence, using clandestine intelligence sources and for the carriers, hitting targets in excess of 1,000 miles away. I guess I was particularly sensitive in these areas having been closely exposed to several years of generally unimaginative, colorless and sterile, multi-national exercises in the Med. Making them realistic and worthwhile was the name of the game.

I had read one of Patton's books, the "Patton Papers," while on Forrestal and was struck by the apolitical and no-nonsense approach of the general. On one occasion, prior to WWII, he was the commanding general of the Army's attacking forces in the big, annual war games in Louisiana. The "war" was supposed to start, according to the rules, at 0600 on day X. But Patton, not one for the conventional, commandeered every vehicle and truck he could get his hands on, mustered his troops and by 0100 on day X, had surrounded the defending forces and captured the extremely irate and more senior opposing general, while they rested up for the big "battle." Defenders cried foul, umpires were befuddled, Patton was the winner and the peacetime Army was in high warble. But, Patton prevailed with the dual thesis that, "... the enemy won't tell you when he's going to attack" and further, "The job of the Army is to win battles, no matter what it takes."

Using a piece of this mind-set, one of our battle group commanders, Rear Admiral Bill Ramsey, snuck out of San Diego early with his force including a big carrier, some subs, a bunch of surface ships and in total electronic silence. His battle group was supposed to run a gauntlet of attacking ships and aircraft, all of which were asleep awaiting the 0600 start. We didn't get in a lot of training, but to me it was the ultimate in progressive war-fighting thinking and the sort of attitude that will tip the balance when and if the bubble goes up.

Reinforcing this attitude on the door to my "perky" office was a hand-done, small sign I put up with scotch tape with words to the effect of, "If its got something to do with winning a war at sea, come in." It was clearly corny and kind of trite, but was one-small step towards getting our staff to think in a warfighting framework. The reality was, that if we had to go to war, it would not be with months of warning and preceded by massive buildups and preparation. We had to be ready to go — and win —with what we had now (similar to the message of Admiral Isaac Kidd not too many years before when I was CO of a supply ship). If given the go order, our strategy was to strike with massive carrier-based force at the northwestern-Pacific underbelly of the Soviets. Win was the name of the game!

> **"IF IT'S GOT SOMETHING TO DO WITH IMPROVING OUR READINESS AND ABILITY TO FIGHT A WAR AT SEA ---- COME IN"**

Kin McKee was relieved by Vice Admiral Ed Waller, a man of equal intellect, same number of admiral's stars and who would also become a superintendent of the U.S. Naval Academy. There the similarities ended, for Ed was a P3 patrol-plane type and who, in the highly technical world of Anti Submarine Warfare (ASW), was known as the "Father of the P3." As Kin McKee knew subs, Ed was the world's quintessential aviator-ASW authority.

One day in the puka, we had recommended a considerable force of P3 aircraft and sonobuoys (small underwater devices that listened for subs), be employed against a Soviet boomer we had lost. Expecting a "Roger that" concurrence from our new boss, I was kind of concerned when the admiral asked, "What's the weather in the area?" Well, it was typical north Pacific winter weather — very-high winds and towering seas. Ed says matter of factly, ". . . too much ambient noise from all the wind and high seas." He was, of course, dead right. It would have been a waste of very expensive and scarce assets. Such was the common-sense approach that this remarkable officer brought to our staff.

VADM Ed Waller and staff ... all smiling.

It was my second flight in a big four-engined P3 and one of their typical "take off at 1800 and land at 0600," 12-hour flights. The target was a Soviet Yankee-class, nuclear, missile-loaded sub a thousand miles from Pearl Harbor. The talented boss of about forty of these big and expensive machines, Captain Danny Wolkensdorfer, had called, and asked if I was interested in a ride against a "real target." This was of course, a great opportunity to see our P3 guys in action on a routine mission, and I jumped at the opportunity.

And what a magnificent flight! Sun setting in the west on take off, three-hours enroute, let down in gloomy, dark and bumpy weather, flying as low as 200 feet over the turbulent Pacific Ocean and prosecuting the unknowing contact to absolute perfection. Were it wartime, the big patrol plane would have shed one or two of its deadly homing torpedoes and scratch one sub and several nuclear weapons targeted on the U.S. west coast. As it was, we tracked him, listened to some on-going noisy work (with a hammer, no less) and, after a few hours, handed the sub over to our relief. On landing, the sun was just starting its westward trek in the east above the Hawaiian mountains.

Aide, Chief of Staff, Admiral Waller and Flag Sec – Note map of Pacific Ocean – our domain.

The mission commander was a non-pilot, an NFO, whose expertise was the highly-complex world of the sensors, computers and weapons and who directed the actions of the pilots. To his 17-man crew, this mission was normal and routine. It may have been in the middle of the night, on a Saturday, on his kid's birthday or on Christmas. No difference. No big deal. These guys were pros and extremely good at their chosen profession.

```
                                              25 September 1979

Commander Walter D. West III
Commanding Officer
Patrol Squadron FOUR
FPO San Francisco 96601

Dear Commander West,

     Just a short note to say thanks for a super flight with
your crew 5, lead by LCDR Schindler. I was absolutely impressed
with the entire conduct of this flight which took off at 1830
and landed at 0630 last Wednesday.

     The mission was conducted superbly and with a very fine
sense of professionalism. But what was very apparent to me
(and not reflected on the post-mission reports) was the sparkle
of enthusiasm, absolute beautiful crew teamwork and total dedi-
cation of this crew.

     Please extend my compliments and thanks to all.

                                  Sincerely,


                                  P. B. BOOTH

cc:  COMPATWINGTWO
     COMPATWINGSPAC
```

Copy of letter I wrote thanking the crew for a most professional flight.

Staff duty was interesting and guys like myself learned a lot, but it was terribly slow moving compared to the pace, excitement and challenge of previous tours. Part of it was the shore-based environment. It was comfortable, no doubt. But the other three equivalent fleets in the Atlantic, Mediterranean and Western Pacific were all based aboard ship and lived and worked in a sea-going framework. In my judgement, we could have done our job as well with a lot less folks and no civilians had we been in the more mind-stimulating environment of a gray-hulled ship.

So, any chance I could escape to the real world of ships, airplanes and sailors, I'd grab at it. The 963 Spruance class destroyer was reasonably new to the Navy and, one day, I got the opportunity to go visit one. Compared to my 2,250 ton destroyer duty on the old Buck, this beauty was 8,000 tons, had all the latest electronics, missiles and sub-killing homing torpedoes and four-huge gas-turbine engines driving two big variable-pitch screws.

True Faith and Allegiance

Landing aboard in the ship's helo off Hawaii, I went to the bridge, met the captain (a commander), who indicated he "was doing 5 knots and would the chief of staff like to see 33 knots?" I thought to myself, he's just like a fighter pilot — got to show off. The ship had but one 747-sized jet engine going at idle, the other three shut down. The OOD, went to a console, pushed three buttons, advanced the two throttles forward, and, within four minutes, we were at 33 knots. On the good ship Buck, it would have taken several hours to get up enough steam and work up to high speed. "Mighty impressive," I said to the young captain and meant it. As a side light, the ship was spotlessly clean, the troops stood tall, they smiled with an easy confidence born of having their stuff together and they were ready for any task their skipper might have ordained. They were on the first team and knew it!

```
                                      17 September 1979


Commander Fred Triggs, USN
Commanding Officer
USS DAVID R. RAY (DD 971)
FPO San Francisco 96601

Dear Fred,

     Many thanks for the opportunity to ride your ship the
other day.  Needless to say, I was impressed.  I wish I
could have stayed longer.

     Your crew looked good, the ship looked good, but most of
all there was a sparkle of crisp professionalism throughout.
Your guys were smiling and seemed spring loaded to get on
with the deployment.  Keep the bubble pumped up.

                              Sincerely,



                              P. B. BOOTH

P.S.  My special thanks to LT(jg) Bob Peranich for the tour
of the plant.  He was super proud of the plant and of his
people.

cc:  COMDESRON 9
     COMNAVSURPAC
```

Copy of letter to destroyer CO with copies to his bosses up the line.

After 18-months of pleasant living, good school for daughter number-two and an interesting hiatus from sea duty, I was promoted to flag rank and the specter of more staff duty, this time back to the Pentagon on the Navy staff. I took with me a good appreciation for subs, P3 patrol planes, integrated-fleet operations, a far-better understanding of the power and limitations of intelligence, a great post-graduate education in ASW from two smart vice admirals and the notion that I didn't relish being a staffer.

EPILOGUE

- **Third Fleet** did manage to disengage itself from the shore-based syndrome and move aboard ship, shedding a goodly number of folks and becoming leaner in the process.

- **Kin McKee** went on to relieve Admiral Rickover as the overseer of anything nuclear in the Navy, is now retired, uses the same Dace coffee cup and is still spring-loaded-to-the-go position.

- **Bill Ramsey** survived the unthinkable of not abiding by the rules, went on to three stars and is now retired having become an expert in the space business.

- **Danny Wolkensdorfer** made flag officer and was a key player in the continued high-tech development of ASW.

- **Ed Waller** retired, and for many years continued his high-stakes work as one of the world's foremost authorities in finding enemy subs.

- **Karl Krupp** became the head of a sizeable chunk of the Navy's Atlantic submarine fleet as a two-star admiral and passed away some years later.

- The creaky old **sub** commanded so ably by Karl, was long ago relegated to the scrap heap.

- **Mary Anne Avcalade** may rest secure in the considerable contributions she and her ilk made over the ensuing years to snooping out the whereabouts of Soviet submarines.

- **"Thunman"** went on to three-star admiral, headed up the submarine force for the entire Navy, retired, and continued in the field of education.

- **Captain Leo Profilet** retired from the Navy, his selfless contributions to his nation and Navy far beyond the norm. Sadly, he passed away not long ago, his legacy one of sacrifice, contribution and service to his nation and Navy

PENTAGON REVISITED

Plans, policy, xerox machines, Foley-san, Army tanks, B-52s and an inside look at a five-sided building that feeds on itself.

I was on the phone with a friend of mine trying to concentrate over the inevitable "clank, clank, clank" of the large Xerox machine nearby. My friend asked me "What's with the noise?"

My matter of fact reply, "The Xerox machine."

That's the way it was that fall of 1981 in the "E" ring of the 4th deck of the Navy side of the Pentagon. I was wearing the regalia of one-broad stripe and a thinner-one as well as the two stars of a rear admiral (lower half, that is). That's the good news. The bad news was that I was only "frocked," a euphemistic Navy way of saying rank, but no pay. I was and would continue for the next year, to be paid at my "non-frocked" rank of captain. Can you believe it?

Well, at least we were wearing uniforms in those heady, early-Reagan years instead of posing as clandestine Naval Officers in civilian garb.

My new job was kind of hard to describe, as it was more of a "Let's expose him to senior-level issues of the Navy and the defense establishment." My title was Deputy Assistant Director of Strategy, Plans and Policy working in the larger office of the Assistant Chief of Naval Operations for Strategy, Plans, Policy and Operations. It sounds convoluted, but recall that the Navy's headquarters staff supporting the Chief of Naval Operations (CNO) is divided among functional groupings such as aviation, subs, surface ships, R&D, strategy, logistics and budgets. All of these fiefdoms were headed up by three-star admirals who in turn reported to the CNO, the Navy's top admiral.

Our world included heavy dialogue with the Navies of other nations, working closely with our sister services and the Joint Chiefs of Staff, addressing policy issues such as length of deployments and overseas home porting and the articulation of overall Navy-operational strategy. Though my responsibilities were minimal and my authority somewhat less, it was the most horizon-broadening tour a guy in my position could have and a spot in which many super-savvy folks had preceded me. My charter was to learn as much as I could about a lot of complex issues as well as the mores of the five-sided building as fast as possible. It was almost like a senior level junior officer's journal!

Perks? Most flag and general officers had a respectable office, as befits such reasonably senior status. But, because of a recent staff shuffle, it would be several months before I escaped the xerox room. I did get a half-decent parking space some three-blocks away and felt fortunate for little things. And, it was fun to touch base with the many small and large power centers I had known in my previous Pentagon incarnation of six-years before.

My immediate boss was an incredibly-smart and savvy ex-submariner, turned jack of all trades, Art Moreau. A master wheeler and dealer, Art really had a handle on the myriad of issues associated with the Joint Chiefs as well as the Navy's strategy and policy formulation. In those early-Reagan years, the money flowed like melted butter and guys like Art were instrumental in ensuring the Navy got its fair share, read, "50% for the Navy and the rest for the Army and Air Force." Fourteen-hour work days were the norm for Art.

Soon after I arrived, I found myself representing the CNO on a large global-war game down in the super-secret innards of the building and sitting amongst some powerful and veteran Air Force and Army two and three stars. I sometimes felt uneasy, because I was wearing two stars, but I was only frocked and only a one-star frockee to boot. The Navy had been disguising one stars as two stars forever, so I figured I could hack it.

Well, the "war" was heating up and the Army guys, whose focus is 99% on the central front of Europe, wanted more naval forces to protect the massive amount of shipping across the Atlantic that would make the war sustainable. They knew well, that without the ships, the war in Europe would soon turn into the greatest retreat in history. So, the Army heavy, backed by his Air Force buddies, proposed moving the bulk of the naval forces in the Pacific to the Atlantic, the so-called "swing strategy." This is anathema to the

Navy, simply because our overall maritime strategy called for taking massive battle group striking power to the Soviets in not only the Atlantic, but in the far-northern reaches of the Pacific. So here I was, fighting the "Pentagon war," trying to stick up for the Navy, but slowly and surely getting eaten alive by the Army and Air Force "Pentagon cowboys." (Loosely defined as those who spend a disproportionate share of their career in the Pentagon halls vice out in the field, mud, cockpits and deckplates).

Calling a "time out," I placed a plaintive "What do I do?" call to my mentor, Art. In moments, he strode to the podium, world map at his back, turned on the charm and proceeded to give the assemblage the benefit of a 15-minute tutorial in naval strategy and why it was clearly not in the best interests of anyone to swing the forces. All agreed. Passing the baton to me, he smiled again to all and marched out as deliberately as he had entered. What a guy!

Art's boss was Vice Admiral Sylvester Foley, an older clone of Art's, an attack pilot of some repute, former carrier skipper, smart, great sense of humor, a fine sense of his own unimportance and a master at working with the other services. Foley-san was his call sign, attesting to his vast experience in the Pacific theater. He was too, as good an operational leader as he was in the corridors of the Pentagon and had, in years past, been in my job.

Foley-san's boss was Tom Hayward, the Navy's Chief of Naval Operations and a combat-experienced aviator cut from the same bolt of cloth. Art, Foley-san and Tom were all hard-working, incredibly smart, charismatic and enormously effective in leading the Navy. Compared to their civilian counterpart in the larger corporations, these guys worked as hard or harder, but got paid maybe five-percent as much with no golden parachute should a job be done in mediocre fashion. What a team, and not atypical of the leadership extant on the Navy's top staff.

To balance the picture, I've got to include the CNO's boss, by law, the civilian Secretary of the Navy and a younger, political sort of guy, named John Lehman. On the surface, Lehman was the perfect "SecNav." His self-proclaimed job was to restore the Navy to its position of preeminence, a dominance somewhat diminished in recent post-Vietnam years. He rode the coattails of a president elected by a landslide majority, much of his platform hinging on a military-rebuilding plank. Coaxing the Congress into buying off on Navy programs was 90% of his job description.

My introduction to Lehman came at a meeting he had called of the CNO and his covey of three-star deputies, including Foley-san, who asked me to come with him. As we sat there exchanging small talk, I noticed that the appointed hour had come and gone for the SecNav's arrival. Finally, after keeping the Navy brass waiting for some 25-minutes, he shows up and has his aide get him some coffee. Not only did he not ask anyone else if they would like coffee, he didn't offer an explanation or apology for his tardiness. The icing on the cake however, was the meeting's substance, a long discourse by

Lehman on what his agenda was to be for the Navy and how he intended to do it. From the sidelines, I muttered to myself, "He'll never last." How wrong I was!

NEAC was the mundane acronym for National Emergency Airborne Command Post, a star-wars Boeing 747 converted to the president's airborne command center for use during a nuclear crisis. Within this airplane were some of the most sophisticated command-and-control technology in the world, which would enable the president to communicate with his nuclear forces and hopefully survive a nuclear exchange. Because our office dealt with policy regarding the control and safeguards of our substantial nuclear arsenal, I arranged for an "orientation flight" in the big machine.

NEACs after landing at Andrews while in a hover from my helo.

Dressed in an old Navy flight suit and armed with a briefing of the president's black book of nuclear codes and options, I jumped in a helo on the Pentagon helo pad just below my fourth-floor office and flew to the awaiting 747, already poised in position on the Andrews AFB runway, its two outboard engines idling. Several tommy-gun wielding Air Force guards were strategically arrayed outside. The giant self-contained stairway was swallowed into the airplane, and, as the door closed behind me, the inboard engines were starting and before I was seated, we were rolling.

The practice scenario was beyond belief and even today generates a higher resting pulse rate than any night-carrier landing I've ever done. Here's how it went, all simulated of course: Tensions between the Soviet Union and the U.S. had escalated to the level at which there was some remote possibility that a nuclear attack on the U.S. could occur. Should the Soviets launch, the president (me) would have to decide if to respond and if so, which of several response options to employ. By this time, of course, our 1,000-Minuteman ICBMs were on the highest alert, every flyable B-52 was airborne and headed north to their "go, no go" point over the Arctic tundra and our fleet of missile-firing submarines were in position. The highest state of national defense readiness, DEFCON 1, was in effect.

A colonel retrieved me from my perch in the relative comfort of the cavernous cockpit with an, "Admiral, we're ready to commence the exercise."

As the practice scenario unfolded, our first indication of real trouble was the infra-red satellite detection of missile launches from the Soviet ICBM fields far north in the frozen wastelands of the Soviet Union. Seated in a large, leather-bound chair facing a brace of enormous projection screens, I had at my disposal, several staff advisors, a dozen telephones of various colors and an overwhelming desire to be somewhere else, like the cockpit. I asked to speak to the Strategic Air Command (SAC) head guy in Omaha. "We're cut off, sir," says the anonymous talker.

"Well, get me the Chairman (of the Joint Chiefs of Staff)." Same response. All communications were lost except those reserved as a last resort to order the fire commands to our nuclear triad — B-52s, subs and ground-launched missiles.

An anonymous voice intones, "Estimate 29 minutes to first impact, sir." followed by, "More launches from submarines 1,200 miles off the east and west coasts." And so it went, a routine periodic practice of our procedures, communications and responses to the unthinkable, a full-scale nuclear exchange with the Soviets.

The clock wound down: "17 minutes to first impact, sir." I had to make a twofold decision under enormous duress (and this was only practice, a fact my being seemed not to accept). First, was whether to launch the 1,000 Minuteman missiles and commit the B-52s and second was to select the targets to be struck. If we hunkered down and allowed the Soviet missiles to hit first, we would, of course know for a fact that the warnings from our satellites had been real, but we would for sure lose the ICBMs, as most could not withstand being hit and still launch. Furthermore, if the B-52s were recalled, it was doubtful they could find a safe place to land.

"We" opted for the "LUA" option; that is, launch under attack, and, at the last moment, committed our B-52s and ICBMs, but held the SLBMs (sub missiles) in reserve. I wasn't comforted by the colonel's notion that, "That's what we would have done, Admiral."

Back at the office, everyone wanted to know why my flight suit was soaked with sweat on this cold, gray, Washington day.

Our Navy had long affirmed the policy that we would sail our ships anywhere in the world as long as we remained in international waters and, in general, 12-miles offshore. Many nations challenged this notion with outlandish claims of up to hundreds of miles of "territorial waters." We always responded by making it a point to conform to accepted international law and, in fact, operate in these forbidden waters. One of these was the Gulf of Sidra and a "line of death" ordained by the emotionally unstable Muamar Qhadafi. I had penetrated inboard of this fictitious line on many occasions as a pilot aboard Forrestal, and later, on both the Sylvania and Forrestal.

However, in 1982, old Muamar was getting real belligerent, so another long-standing and routine exercise was scheduled into the waters south of the "line." This was not a clandestine move by a long shot, as announcements went out to the international community broadcasting our intentions for another "Naval Exercise." Foley-san set the policy, backed by a personally-briefed president.

One day while on these routine ops some 100-miles north of Libya out in the Med, here come two Libyan jets, armed to the teeth, one of which launched a missile against two of our F-14 fighters led by Commander Hank Kleeman (an old VF-102 squadron mate). Hank and his wingman promptly shot both of the hostile jets out of the sky in less than one minute. They did not have to ask permission to do this, nor did they, because the rules of engagement always included a broad caveat — "A commander retains the inherent right to self defense." Hank and his guys did right. No question!

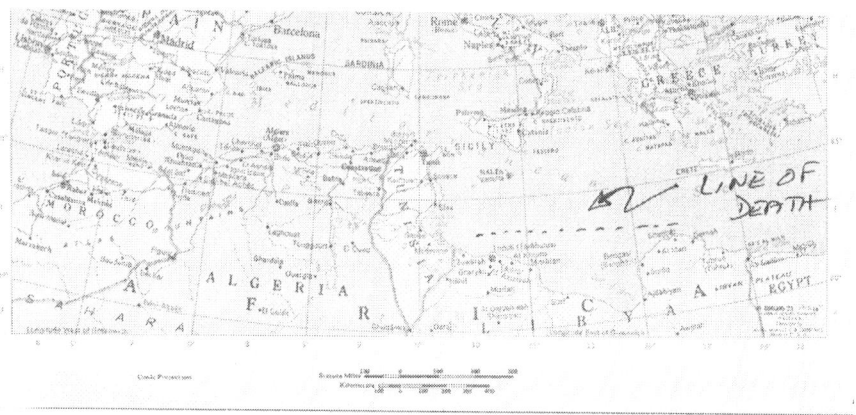

One perennial hot spot was saber-rattling Lybia and the line of death.

The aftermath of this, however, was a small, but persistent myth in the press and Congress, that it was a setup and we had somehow bent the rules and so on. Nothing could have been further from the truth.

One of the more vociferous of these folks in the Congress was a very young New York representative, Tom Downey. So, Foley-san dispatched me on a "Tell Mr. Downey what really went on" mission. Off I went in my sharp blues; we had a great visit and dialogue. Mr. Downey was most appreciative and thankful to have gotten the straight word and escorted me to the lobby of the Rayburn House office building, where I was to meet my car. Standing there with my host, many people came up to us and said, "Good to see you, admiral," and "How's everything in the Navy, admiral?" and so on.

Mr. Downey, consummate politician that he was, had not even been noticed. So he said to me, "I'd like to be an admiral."

"No way," I replied.

Somewhat plaintively, he asked, "Why not?"

"Because you're not old enough!" I responded politely, all the while smiling to the many folks who wandered by.

One of our Navy's major problems in the early '80s reflected a growing awareness of drug use amongst our troops, not unlike the country as a whole from which we drew our recruits. So one day, Tom Hayward assembled all his Washington area flag officers and announced a major goal of "Zero Tolerance" in the drug arena. His message: "We're going to educate and help those that need it and hammer those who persist in drug use." And further, "We're going to eliminate drug use in our Navy and make the Navy the model the rest of our nation can emulate." Seated with my flag-officer contemporaries, all recently from the fleet, we looked at one another and silently agreed there was simply no way a zero-tolerance policy would work. We'd be out of business.

But Admiral Hayward was a smart and tough cookie. Soon we started the controversial urinalysis program, the first samples coming from a few resident senior guys on the Navy staff. Finally, we had a tool to use along with the education and help side of the drug issue. New recruits were not allowed in the front doors with a positive sample, chiefs and officers who tested positive found themselves wearing civilian clothes in record-short time and any others caught, had but one more chance. Soon, "Not in my Navy" tee shirts were sprouting and the peer pressure changed from one extreme to the other, all in less than two years. Much of this enormous success story accrues to the credibility and personal involvement of a combat-seasoned, charismatic and no-nonsense leader named Tom Hayward.

The services were riding tall in the saddle. Defense outlays were way up, pride in country and flag was fashionable and retention and recruitment quality were sky high. One of my quick trips was to Orlando to be the recruit reviewing officer for some 500 newly-graduated men and women sailors, and was it ever an eye-watering experience! Those kids were bursting with good feelings about themselves and the prospects for the future. How proud I was of them and what they represented.

Though the pot got bigger, the competition for available dollars was awesomely intense within the services. The Air Force wanted big bombers and transports, the Navy new fighters, subs and carriers and the Army more of everything. We fought the paper battles in the fortress of the Joint Chiefs of Staff, for it was the paper that drove most of the essential programs and budgets. It's the one part of my job that I disliked the most. It was not atypical at all to spend weeks "arguing" over the inclusion of one or two phrases in a key strategy document. The "swing" issue of moving ships from one ocean to another was a good example. But Art and Foley-san were masters at wearing down the opposition and getting the Navy's way.

The guy who got his way the most, however, was John Lehman. There was a saying around Washington, "that if you put Lehman in the same room with the Army and Air Force secretaries, he would come out with 80% of the defense budget." And it wasn't far from the truth. Lehman had the President's ear, was brash to the extreme and the Congress loved him. He dealt from an articulate and knowledgeable power base. But he also delved deep into things traditionally the domain of the ranking Navy brass more so than any secretary in modern naval history. Like him or agree with him or not, from a macro perspective, the controversial Lehman was the right man for the Navy at the time.

The SecNav was no chair-borne bureaucrat by a long shot. A reserve commander as a bombardier-navigator in the A6 bomber, he kept his flying skills honed with frequent forays into fleet aviation, trips to subs and a highly-visible presence throughout the Navy and around the world. His mannerisms varied from a boyish and contagious smile to a tough guy from the wrong side of Philadelphia. The troops loved him; the admirals were tolerant.

I continued my occasional meanderings out of the Pentagon, one of which was at a confluence of strategic folks at the Strategic Air Command (SAC) headquarters in Omaha. One of the many Air Force generals there asked if I would like to visit a SAC base. By now the answer should be obvious, so I called Carolyn and got permission to extend the trip for a couple more days.

Arriving at Ellsworth Air Force Base, an absolutely desolate, but functional enclave in the prairie land of South Dakota, I was met by a radio-wielding, small-sized Air Force colonel, the wing commander of a stable of about 30 giant B-52s, Peewee Lambert. Old Peewee took me all around the base, got me an eight-hour flight in a B-52, had me over to his home for dinner, woke me at 0430 (he wanted to show me something), and all in less than the allotted 24 hours. I mean he was something else and the epitome of, "It's not how big you are, it's how tight your spring is wound."

But the real trip was in the monstrous B-52. Parked near eight, fully-fueled and nuclear-weapons-loaded, five-minute alert sister ships, we took off in the big eight-engined jet and did a little of everything — low-level bombing, refueling (I tried, but couldn't hack it), F-15 attacks, instrument approaches and navigation. The aircraft commander was an Air Force captain of high repute named Bill Weller and who, at age 28, was younger than his big machine and who led his six-man crew with a maturity and competence typical of the officer corps of the services' first teams.

We landed in a heavy rainstorm with about 70,000 pounds of fuel (enough for five or six Phantoms on take off) in a severe crosswind and Bill handled the huge bomber with its castering-main landing gear like he did his little sports car. Those Air Force guys took on a special meaning to me, because the entire base reflected Peewee's enthusiasm and total commitment to a job that has to be done perfect the first time. I sent Peewee and his wife a nice note, thanking them for the superb hospitality and a rare glimpse by a Navy guy of SAC at its finest. What a team. What eye-watering professionalism!

B-52 crew in rain following eight-hour flight. Captain Bill Weller, the aircraft commander, in center; wing commander, Colonel Peewee Lambert to left with instant radio; to his left the two navigator/bombardiers; enlisted tail gunner to their left. Once again, the best of the best. BUFF in background.

One of my Army buddies was a new brigadier general named Don Penzler. Don was a tanker, very-operationally oriented, and, like most senior-Army types, extremely well educated in at least three years of service graduate-level schooling in the art of war and diplomacy. He was kind of in the same category as I was, "New guy who needed seasoning in the bigger picture, so assign him to the Army staff and expose him to the real-world system." He with his one star and me with my two, and both of us getting paid as a colonel/captain. I loved it; he tolerated it.

That winter, Don and I were our service's representatives to a major joint exercise in the Florida panhandle on the sprawling Eglin AFB complex. We flew in an old Huey helo from site to site, getting briefed, looking important and asking the right questions of our gun-toting, helmeted and camouflaged Army and Air Force brothers-under-arms. Because these guys didn't see much Navy blue, they would always go out of their way to show me what they knew I didn't know.

As Don and I winged our way over the treetops enroute to yet another canned briefing, I announced that, "I'd like to see a real tank instead of all those colonels and briefing rooms."

Within micro seconds, Don was galvanized from total boredom to instant general, grabbed the mike from the two Army warrants piloting the helo, glanced at a grid map, pointed to the ordained spot and hardly heard the "No way, sir" from the pilots.

Now a helo has a different connotation to a senior Army guy than most folks. To Don, a helo is not a machine that flies through the air; it is generic jeep, car or truck — simply a way to get from A to B and nothing more. Few Army aviators got away with saying "no way," particularly with a "war" going on and even more so with an impressionable Navy guy in tow. Sprouting full-general plumage, Don emphatically points to a small clearing the size of a destroyer helo pad nestled 60-feet down from the tall pines. With a "whoop, whoop, whoop," and flying tree branches, we descended to the tiny landing spot. Don tells the pilots to "get lost and come back in 30 minutes."

Right then this really big tank rumbles out of the trees and brush. I clamored aboard, and in retrospect wished I had brought my camera. That state-of-the-art MA1A, gas-turbine powered, incredibly-accurate five-inch-gun machine, was formidable and truly awesome! I could have stayed there all day. The four-man crew, led by a lean, cigar-chomping sergeant, were super proud of their tank. Old Don was like a rejuvenated kid in a candy store. He loved it. So did I.

The flight out of the clearing was kind of exciting because in addition to the "whop, whop, whop," was a more authoritative "WHOP, WHOP, WHOP." The helo vibrated a bit more as we fluttered down to a clearing some two miles from the tank. Stopping the rotors, all got out to sagely stare at the slightly-pockmarked rotor-blade leading edges, including Don, who wasn't too complimentary of Army aviators at the moment. Anyway, off we went to continue our orchestrated tour of the Eglin war and eventually back to the big building in Washington, armed with a new-found knowledge of tanks, generals and briefing rooms in the boondocks.

All this Army and Air Force exposure was kind of provident, for increasingly, our naval strategy hinged with that of the other services. Indeed, naval forces were not necessarily controlled by the Navy, but rather were operationally controlled by large joint commands, whose head could be a Navy, Army or Air Force four star. We had of course, been operating this way for years, but the pace and intensity had quickened in recent times. This was due, at least in part, to some joint operations that had been poorly executed, the most notable of which was the abortive rescue attempt for the hostages in Iran. I have to admit that this interaction caused me to do a flip flop of my perceived Army and Air Force stereotype. These folks were as smart, as dedicated and as professionally competent as any Navy guys I had known or worked with.

I would occasionally see my old aviation buddies in OP-05, the offices of which were some quarter-mile down the Pentagon's "E"-ring corridor from mine. Because our offices were up near the CNOs', the resident officer in charge of naval aviation, Vice Admiral Wes McDonald, would ride his three-wheeled bike, complete with tiny little bell, and try to entice anyone to hop on the back and ride with him to the CNO's conference room. Never had any takers. Only the charismatic Wes could get away with such ridiculous antics.

Foley-san would get called to the White House periodically, mainly to the National Security Council offices (NSC). One day, he suggested I go visit and find out what went on, so I called a friend of mine, John Poindexter, a rear admiral who had been selected for flag rank about the same time as had I, and who was the number-two guy in the NSC.

John was a hyper-talented surface-warfare officer. Kin McKee, one of my previous bosses at Third Fleet, paid him the ultimate McKee compliment, "There's a real sailor!" Very smart, John had spent a lot of time at sea as well as in the Navy's geo, political and strategic inner-sanctums. We had an informative visit including lunch in the White House mess and a nice talk with John Nance, a retired former-Forrestal skipper who had had John's job several years prior and was now a special assistant in the NSC.

What impressed me the most however, was the absolute aura of enormous power that permeated that big house. I mean it reeked! You could feel it! What the president wanted from a military perspective, he got. Us military folk were always respectful of the high command and their bidding was our command. As Commander in Chief, however, the president was the supreme honcho. John didn't need to talk about it and did not, but to me, the connotation of presidential desire — whether specific or not — was clear: "Make it happen."

During this time, Big John Lehman continued to strut his wares. The Navy increasingly gained the support of the Congress and the people of the United States, largely due to the efforts of the SecNav. He was brassy, bold and never, ever, gave up. But more and more he was getting into the internals of the Navy that by all rights and tradition, he ought to have steered clear of. Only Lehman could have gotten away with it.

The fact was that the Navy was riding tall in the saddle. Symbolic of this high road were the three large carriers on the building ways in the Newport News shipyard in 1981 — the Lincoln, the T. R. Roosevelt and the Washington. Lehman says, "Who could cancel a carrier with those illustrious names?" Concurrently, he had outlined ambitious plans for a so-called "600-ship Navy," a goal widely accepted as reasonable and doable. The Navy's maritime strategy received wide acclaim for its "Take-the-fight-to-the-Soviets" theme. And Lehman et al., had everyone convinced that the decline of shore-base access throughout the world could only auger well for the U.S. Navy and its proclivity to roam the oceans of the globe with impunity. Way to go, John!

On the heavy side of the ledger was the Iran/Iraq war and its potential for major destabilization of a region President Carter had deemed, ". . . to be in the vital interests of the US." There were few who were not convinced that should Iran succeed in blocking the Persian Gulf, Japan's reliance on oil would cause her economy to stumble and thus adversely influence the economy of her number-one trading partner, imbalanced though it might have been.

But the scariest issue of all was the long-standing Soviet quest for access to the gulf region through Iran and/or Afghanistan. Throughout all this, seapower was widely accepted as the way to maintain stability and project power if necessary. This translated into enormously long and sustained deployments into the Indian Ocean for the Navy. During this time, the Nimitz battle group spent one period of 105 days at sea without ever seeing land, much less dropping the hook. Submarines would routinely deploy from Charleston, cruise underwater to the Indian Ocean 8,000-miles distant, and return six-months later with only one-short port visit to show for it. One carrier was deployed from its home base in San Diego for over ten months. Tough as this was on the troops at sea, there was no alternative, for a lack of presence and resolve on our part, could have created a vacuum for the Soviets to fill. Trying to grapple with these toughies, was a part of the 4th-deck-E-ring Pentagon action back then.

28 May 1981

Dear Admiral Booth: [Pete]

    Your recent presentation to the 1981 Naval Reserve Flag Officers' Conference contributed significantly to its success. Our goal was to update the flag officers on current procedures and issues within Navy and Defense and on the world situation as viewed from the Pentagon.

    Your remarks were enlightening, thought-provoking, and appreciated by all.

    On behalf of our Naval Reserve Flag Officers, thank you for your participation and support.

                     Respectfully,

                     Cricket

                     C.A.E. Johnson, Jr.
                     Rear Admiral, U.S. Navy Reserve
                     Deputy Director of Naval Reserve

Rear Admiral Peter B. Booth, USN
Deputy Director Strategy, Plans,
   and Policy Division (OP-60)
The Pentagon
Washington, DC 20350

A reminder of a trek to New Orleans to stand in for my boss once removed, Sylvester Foley, to give his hot-spots brief to fifty or so reserve flag officers. I remember it well, as it was after lunch and one rather portly soul was sound asleep in the back of the room.

But there was a lot of routine stuff as well. One of these was a visit to Halifax, Canada as the Navy representative to an annual Canada/US defense treaty meeting. This was a far cry from the cockpit and deckplates, but these important and continuing relationships needed to be nurtured and sustained.

Our Canadian hosts were most gracious and hospitable. In and amongst visits to military sites, most notably, a P3 patrol-plane base, we had discussions and dialogue on the upcoming purchase of F/A-18 fighters, increased participation by Canada in ASW patrols and a continuing exchange of officers between our countries. No earth-shattering issues, but the net impact of dozens of such relationships throughout the world added up to a host of military and economic power and silver bullets in the reserve slot. These were interesting excursions from the norm and, once again, I came away impressed with the professionalism and competence of many of our allies.

On a personal note, the issue of pay was hitting home. We had one daughter in private school, one in college, four cars in various stages of disrepair and a modest townhouse we had bought which soon sprung a leaky roof. Carolyn worked some in a nearby bank and I still wasn't getting paid any more; In fact, I had taken a pay cut as I was no longer drawing flight pay. We had arrived in Washington from Hawaii in mid-September, schools had already started, we were anxious to find a home and ended up buying (by cashing in most of our chips), a three-story townhouse two miles from the Pentagon.

The foregoing is not an atypical scenario for a Navy guy with 25 years of service. If on the fast track, a lot is expected of you, both personally and professionally. This translates into long-work weeks and many moves. Adequate cash flow for most families, is a real issue.

Back at the "Five sided wind tunnel," the building continued on its inevitable course and speed of zero. Each day on its seven levels, there were thousands of meetings, hundreds-of-thousands of phone calls and an enormous amount of incoming messages from around the world. Should some enterprising soul have had the wherewithal to cut a vertical cross-section through its center, it would have been far more fascinating than an ordinary ant colony, although the similarities would be many. I sometimes felt, that if all communications external to the Pentagon were severed, it would take several weeks for anyone to realize it, so frantic was the intra-Pentagon activity level.

Don Penzler summed it all up somewhat irreverently from his deep-underground office. I was gazing out my office window overlooking the broad expanse of Arlington Cemetery and mentioned to Don, "What a gorgeous day it was."

"You have a window?", says he.

"Yeah, it overlooks Arlington Cemetery."

His matter-of-fact reply, having been a building resident for two years, "They're the only ones around here that know what they're doing."

True Faith and Allegiance

NOV 2 0 1981

Dear Admiral Suanzes

    This is just a short note to belatedly express my very profound appreciation for your gracious hospitality and the hospitality of your Navy during our visit to Madrid a month ago. I had delayed writing until the issue regarding ASW equipment for your frigates and LAMPS helos had been resolved. I am delighted that it was resolved in your best interests. Clearly you and your Navy have a great capability and strategic awareness and could effectively utilize this equipment.

    I would also like to offer my sincere thanks to you for the "sailor-to-be" LLADRO statue. We have him in our living room at this moment beside the tall "sea captain". Many thanks.

    My offer to have you over for dinner when and if you return to the United States still stands.

    With great professional admiration, I remain,

                Sincerely,

                P.B. BOOTH
                Rear Admiral, U.S. Navy

Vice Almirante D. Saturnino Suanzes
2nd Jefe de la Estado Major de la Armada
Cuartel General de la Armada
Montalban 12
Madrid 14, Spain

Typical low-key thank you note to our hosts in Spain. I hope the Lladro statue was under the legal limit for a gift!

EPILOGUE

- **Foley-san** went on to four-star admiral and command of the Navy's Pacific fleet, retired to further service as a super-grade, senior civil servant in the Department of Energy and eventually as president of his own company.

- **Don Penzler**, the irreverent tanker, is whereabouts unknown.

- We sold our **townhouse** for less than we bought it, having finally fixed the leaking roof after three tries. Twenty years later, it's worth three times as much!

- **Art Moreau** rose to full admiral and died while on active duty, his selfless contributions to his country continuing to the end.

- **Tom Hayward's** legacy of zero tolerance was an awesome success and the Navy's program became the model for the rest of the country.

- **Peewee Lambert** made general officer and I remember him well for his pragmatic and total commitment to combat readiness.

- **John Lehman's** legacy of a 600-ship Navy was good on paper, but became the victim of real-world funding realities.

- **Bill Weller**, I hope, is a SAC heavy-weight by now, and, if he's still flying the BUFF (Big ugly fellow, in polite vernacular), he's still younger than the big airplane, airplanes that are still on fully-loaded alert at many forlorn bases around the world and South Dakota.

- **Hank Kleeman's** shoot down of Muamar's finest, was repeated by Navy fliers some years later with the same results. Hank managed to survive a mess of night-carrier landings and combat, but was killed in an F-18 landing accident due to a landing-gear malfunction.

- **Tom Downey** is still "just a congressman" and never made admiral, though by now he's probably old enough.

- **John Poindexter** went on to three stars, became the head of the White House NSC and defended his presidential boss with honor. Continuing his total service to his country, he continues orchestrating sensitive issues at the highest level of the government.

- **The Pentagon** continues its course and speed of zero. My former office overlooking Arlington Cemetery was the bulls-eye for the 9/11 terrorist attack.

- After four decades of Cold War, the **Soviet Union** finally imploded thanks to the Poindexters, the Foley-sans, the Moreaus, the Kleemans, the Penzlers, the sergeants and even Big John, the untold heroes who manned the front lines during some tough times.

LOTS OF WINGS

Escape to reality, training the best of the best, the Blue Angels, getting your mind right and the will to win.

Boarding the twin-engine, prop-jet Navy trainer at Andrews Air Force Base near Washington, I noticed that the pilot had longer than reasonable hair, though a nice welcome-aboard smile. An advanced flight student, she was to fly me to Corpus Christi, Texas, the headquarters of the Naval Air Training Command, under the watchful guidance of a veteran instructor pilot. After takeoff, the three of us, me ensconced in one of the back seats, proceeded to Dulles, whereupon one engine was feathered and we commenced a series of single-engine maneuvers, including a bunch of landings.

Never having been truly exposed to the rigors of multi-engine training, much of which is simulated engine-out procedures, this was an anomalous experience for me as was the "she" side of the cockpit. After an hour and a half of some "not so comfortable from the back seat" riding on my part, off we headed for an Air Force base some 300-miles distant to gas up and shoot a few approaches for training. The practice approaches and final landing were right at the minimums — one-half mile in solid fog. And so the flight went — seven hours all told — of latter-stage instrument and emergency training.

She did well. And, not only did I get a free flight, the Navy got one more of its 3,000 student aviators closer to winning their wings of gold as full-fledged Naval Aviators.

Long before, I had harbored one of those secret dreams along the lines that if I ever made admiral, the one job I wanted was to be the Chief of Naval Air Training. The reason was simple: The Naval Aviator had always been the best aviator in the world whether he be a patrol plane type, a helo pilot or fighter driver. I recall being asked by a local TV personality in Corpus what my number-one goal was to be. "Why, to maintain the extraordinarily high quality of aviator the Navy has always been known for, of course!" More so than any school or regimen, excepting perhaps the Naval Academy, the 18-month program leading to designation as a Naval Aviator, sets the tone and pace for his entry into the fleet or Marines. This was action, it was dynamic, it was impressionable people and a guy like me could make a difference, I thought.

Our job was to produce 1,500 pilots and 500 Naval Flight Officers each year, for the Navy, Coast Guard and Marines and even a few foreign countries such as France and Saudi Arabia. The turf was six widely-separated training air wings, the training aircraft carrier Lexington, the Blue Angels, 1,200 instructors, 900 airplanes of seven types and some 14,000 folks altogether. Our official boss was the head of the Navy training in Pensacola, Florida, a three-star admiral. Our unofficial boss was the Navy's leader of naval aviation in the Pentagon, also a three star.

I got the word while in my by now "perky" office high in the Pentagon's "E" ring from Lando Zech, the top personnel guy for the Navy, who simply asked if I would like to be the Chief of Naval Air Training or CNATRA, as in Frank. I couldn't believe it! It wasn't that I disliked the Navy staff as much as it was that I had had three years in two large staffs and I just did not like being a staffer. It was hard to make a difference, most of your time was spent in incredibly useless meetings and non-productive work and low-key politicking was the rule rather than the exception. It seemed that the harder you shoveled, the bureaucratic tide washed it all back in and you were right back where you started. More often than not, your only internal satisfaction was in knowing you had done the best job you could muster. "Keep plugging," was a Pentagon virtue.

We soon set some reachable and crystal-clear goals — Safety, Quality and producing the numbers needed for the helo, patrol plane and jet cockpits for our customers.

In the not-too-distant past, Naval Aviation and safety were a contradiction in terms. Safety was a total disaster in the '50s and '60s. We lost lots of airplanes and pilots. Back when I was a student pilot in the late '50s, the Naval Air Training Command lost or seriously damaged some 100 aircraft each year. In recent times, however, flying just as hard, with the same mix of aircraft and the same number of flying hours, we lost six machines. Why this incredible success story in such a short time?

Lots of Wings

Former Chiefs of Naval Air Training: John Disher, Wes McDonald and Ed Martin at the Blue Angels' end-of-the-season air show at Pensacola.

    The pragmatic reason, was that the Navy and Marines were no longer the beneficiary of thousands of inexpensive fighters and trainers. An F-14 would cost $30M and a P3 patrol plane, $66M. One jet pilot cost the taxpayers over a million bucks to train. Despite the 25% of our national budget that went to defense, the competition for available dollars was intense. So, "Don't lose airplanes" was the name of the game. Safety had become a driving force not only in the training command, but throughout the Navy. Our job was to keep instilling this safety credo into the instructors and get the young student aviators off on the right mind set, while concurrently and most importantly, doing so without compromising the aggressiveness necessary to win in the air. After all, we weren't training airline pilots; we were nurturing and developing future warriors!

    The approach was easy. As aviators, we had lots of rules and regulations, most all of which were well known, widely publicized and studied and reasonably broad and flexible in content. Compared to other military aviators throughout the world, Naval Aviators always had a long leash. We hammered hard for each guy to operate within this box of rules, most of which were common sense and all of which we, the users, could change if they didn't make sense or were overly restrictive. Good examples that had bitten us many times over the years, some from my occasionally tarnished past, were flying too low, inadequate flight planning, shaving the 12-hour-bottle-to-throttle rule and a host of others. The days of "kick the tire, light the fire and brief on the emergency radio channel," were long gone.

    A really sad example happened to one of the Blue Angel pilots while on a non-show flight. He was taking one of the maintenance troops up for an orientation ride in the two-seat variant of their A4 Skyhawk and severed a one-inch-thick power line across a small river with his vertical tail, his canopy just missing it by an inch. Though the damage to the airplane was fixable and they made it back OK, they came within a hair's breath of killing themselves and losing an airplane. The catch was, the wire was but 120-feet above the river. Why were they that low, an altitude clearly well below that authorized by Navy and Federal codes? Furthermore, the orientation ride had a zero need to be that low. The entire training command, of course, knew about this clear violation. What to do?

After a thorough investigation, the pilot involved was grounded and the Blues continued the season with five vice six demonstration aircraft. The pilot could well have lost his wings, but did not. The decision on my part to yank him from the team, was tough. In private, I had tears in my eyes, for clearly, the young pilot was the best of the best. But, if safety was to be effective and not just more rhetoric and paper, action had to follow deed.

Quality was more amorphous than safety and production and took constant attention to detail and attempts to improve the process. If the particular training flight called for five spins, four loops and ten landings, then do five, four and ten, not something less. Don't cut a hop out of the syllabus just because a guy is doing well. Fact was, our customers were the folks in the fleet, so we stayed close to them. The quality axiom of producing a good product and staying close to the customer was a given in our business and, whenever a new guy had problems in the fleet, we would go to great lengths to find a correlation with his training as a student aviator.

Our handpicked staff guys responsible for standardization and quality – Navy, Marines and Air Force – unconstrained talent and enthusiasm.

A good example of this was the Navy's perennial loss of expensive airplanes due to loss of control, like stalls, departures and spins. Although taught in the very early stages of pilot training, the average fleet aviator wouldn't see another spin in a lifetime of flying, particularly inverted spins. So, we started a three-hop, out-of-control (OOC) series of flights for the jet guys. Both inverted and upright spins were taught, the former of which to most, myself included, got your attention real fast. But, once you've done one, it's like any other learning process — you know what it feels like and you practice.

But the real thrust of improving this aspect of the quality process, came with the notion that once the jet started behaving in a way that you're not commanding it to do (departs from controlled flight), neutralize the controls. Though my test-pilot friends might not agree, I would opine that 99% of all airplanes flying today, will recover from such uncontrolled flight, if the pilot doesn't mess with the controls and aggravate the situation.

The maneuver selected to demonstrate this given of aviation was the "Lumsckavok," defined as a random tumbling of the aircraft about all three axes. It goes like this: Get about 350 knots at 15,000 feet in your twin-jet T2 "Buckeye" trainer and go straight up. Once in the vertical, relax the G load and start an easy roll. Then, when the airspeed bleeds down to 100 knots (still in the vertical), put the stick hard to the far-left-front corner of the cockpit and concurrently jam in full right rudder. The result is a total out-of-control situation in which the machine simply tumbles at random and completely unpredictably. Key to this, of course, is to neutralize the controls after the departure from controlled flight.

After a couple of these, it becomes a comfortable maneuver, not withstanding the flip flopping. Because the airspeed is so low, there is essentially no G load, so you kind of sit and float. Soon, gravity asserts and the little airplane starts downhill. And, the most important lesson, the airplane being an airplane, is that its nose will seek the ground, the speed will build up and all the pilot has to do is ease back on the stick to regain level flight. From departure to straight and level will take 35 seconds, plus or minus five. The result: More confident, capable and trained aviators for our front-line forces.

About once or twice a year, we would invite our customers, the head fleet and marine aviation guys, to come for a couple of days to Corpus to talk under the umbrella of quality. These guys were all flag or general officers, most of whom knew one another, so the dialogue was priceless and the aviation talent in one room, awesome. The patrol plane guy for example was Danny Wolkensdorfer down from his headquarters in Maine, the fighter jock, Skip Furlong from San Diego, and the A7 light-attack czar, the highly-decorated Jim Busey. Some twelve in all. All flew their own aircraft and the sight of the fleet's best on the Corpus Christi ramp brought many an envious student aviator out for a look see.

But, when it came time to leave it was reminiscent of the Keystone Kops. Jim Busey mounts his steed for the trip back to California, closes the canopy, notices he has no oxygen, can't get his canopy open and sits there and roasts in the 100-degree Texas sun. Skip taxis his big F-14 to the runway, only to return dripping buckets of red hydraulic fluid. And Danny is sitting in the left front seat of his big P3 for an hour and not moving. Wandering over, I looked up at him in his perch 20-feet above me, motioned for him to open the door, walked up to see what the problem was and was informed by the gritted-teeth head of the Navy's fleet of 200 P3s, "We're waiting for one of our crew who's still at the beach."

Bottom line is that quality was a big deal. We had and were producing the best aviators in the world. But the name of the game was to do better. In most situations, "better is the enemy of good enough," but not for us. We knew that to win and prevail in the air, we had to be the best and couldn't afford the luxury sitting on our hands. Thankfully, we had many senior types visit our far-flung operations and reinforce the "win-in-war" credo. Good example was an excerpt from a note to me from Admiral Sylvester Foley who was just taking over the Pacific Fleet after a visit: ". . . My intent out here is to reemphasize combat systems and readiness to go to war. Too much tilt toward material and engineering and not enough on how to fight."

A typical every-three-month wing commander's conference, this hosted by wing three at Chase Field near Beeville, Texas. To my right, CNATRA chief of staff, Ken Dickerson, to my left, Les Jackson from Kingsville, Arv Chauncy, our host, and Jimmie Taylor, inbound to the Kingsville job. To a man, incredible leadership!

I tried to describe "what I did" for some visiting civilians one day as, "Management by wandering about," a la the style of Wal Mart's Sam Walton. My focus was to ride above the minutia, let our extremely competent troops do their thing without being "nit-picked" and to conduct myself as I was — a leader concerned for his people, but who was committed to reasonable standards of performance. Our civilian secretary, Jo McKenzie, would block out two days each week for informal visits to each of six wings (or bases) and when the Lexington was underway. On these visits, I would hang out with the maintenance troops, visit supply, poke into barracks, fly at least once, listen to squadron and wing commanders, talk and listen to instructors, jog about three miles, have a small social and, in general, get a once-every-two-months, in-depth look at each operation. It was kind of a 50/50, transmit the safety, quality message and listen to what the troops and their leaders had to say.

Force Master Chief Bobbie Graves, our senior enlisted. We were blessed with extraordinarily inspired leadership throughout.

All the helo action was over at Whiting Field near Pensacola. I flew the H-57 helo with some phenomenal instructor pilots, including one of the squadron skippers, Commander Clyde Lassen, a Congressional Medal of Honor winner on my 1968 combat cruise on America. I worked on these hops too — hovering, cut guns, square-box patterns and, my nemesis, full autorotations to touchdown. But, it soon became apparent to me that I was really doing some mediocre work — I mean flat out half way. One of my consistent messages to the troops was something about ". . . mediocrity is not in the naval aviation game plan," and here I was, a living testimonial to the "kick the tire, light the fire" attitude of yesteryear.

One of my IPs at Whiting Field, a USMC captain, who went on to fly the president in Helo One.

So, with great reluctance, I went to talk to the squadron CO, "OB" Powell, a veteran helo pilot who had done and seen it all. I explained I wasn't doing too well (a fact he was well aware of!), and "Did he have any ideas?"

Much to my surprise, he smiled broadly with a "Yes, sir." His unadorned message: "You can't expect to come up here every couple of months, hop in a machine that basically doesn't want to fly and do it well. You've got to study and put some effort into it." And how true were those words. I returned to Corpus armed with a thick H-57 manual and the next time, had my mind right and did OK. Commander "OB" Powell was typical of the kind of great leadership and talent we had on the deckplates.

Wing commanders at NAS Whiting hosted by super-helo pilot, Jerry Hatcher in front center. From left; Hal Berson (Lex CO); Les Jackson (Former Kingsville); Jim Ryan (Schools Command); Ron Horne (Meridian); Jerry Goodman (Corpus Christi); Dave Page (Beeville – under 1401); Charlie Ward (Pensacola); Bill Mooberry (my Chief of Staff); Jimmie Taylor (Kingsville); Missing, Hoss Pearson (Blue Angels).

As the job of CNATRA entailed a lot of travelling all over the U.S., I usually took a stock, but absolutely beautiful TA4 Skyhawk, single-engine, two-seat jet trainer reserved for the use of the head guy and his staff. Because it was expensive to operate, I would almost always take a student pilot along in the back seat who was in the instrument stages of training. We could then write the hop off as a full student-training mission, I would get a chance to instruct and teach plus get to where ever it was I was going.

ENS MARK BURNS, USNR
VT-21
NAS KINGSVILLE, TX 78363

CHIEF OF NAVAL AIR TRAINING

29 October 1983

Dear Mark —

Enjoyed the flight with you. You did a fine job. Overall you seem to be a very confident aviator — you fly the airplane smoothly and precisely. You'll do good in the fleet providing you <u>work hard</u>, <u>learn hard</u> and <u>listen hard</u>. See my write up of flight — provided for your info.

Take care — good flying in the fleet!

Peter Booth

Short note to student pilot after we flew together.

Initially, everyone was kind of antsy about "the admiral flying with an ensign student" under the premise that the poor guy would be too tight to function. But, in over thirty or so such flights, we never had a problem. I'd always ask the guy over to the quarters on returning to Corpus for a beer or coke and, in our sweaty flight suits, debrief the flight. The word got around, as it did on all flight instructors, that in this case the old guy was OK.

From my perspective, these were great hops. Most went like this: One hour to brief the weather, route, emergencies, get acquainted, preflight and man up. The student pilot would put a "bag" or cover over the back seat which totally enclosed the aft cockpit to the point where he could see nothing but the inside of that tiny enclosure with its banks of friendly instruments and blinking lights. Once cleared for takeoff, we would go to full power, check the engine gauges and, with the stick forward, start the takeoff roll. At 60 knots, I would say, "You've got it!" and let go of the controls. At 140 knots we would be flying and my guy would do it all including several approaches enroute down to 200 feet. On the final one, I'd take over at minimums, he would "pop his bag" and dead ahead at a half mile was the friendly destination field. A flight like this, reasonably well executed, was a confidence builder and an excellent learning experience for the nights and bad weather ahead on our fleet carriers.

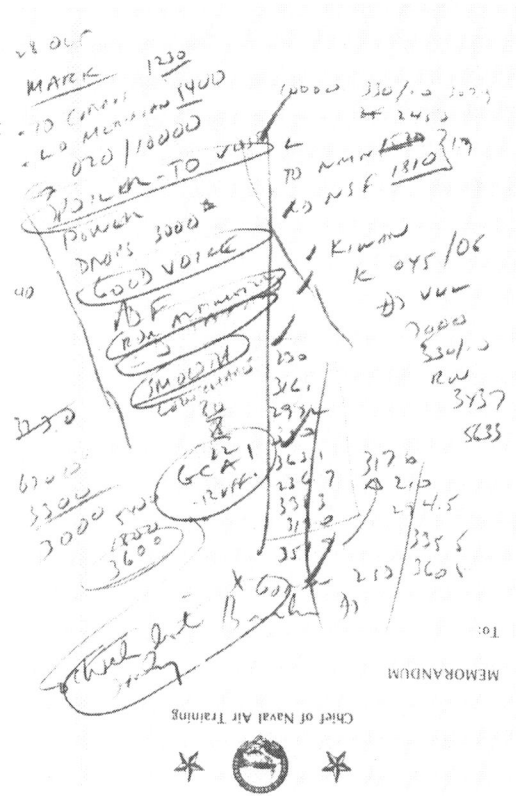

Notes from flight with Mark on cross-country.

One such trip took me to the El Centro desert and the winter training home for the Blue Angels preparing for their next season. Me and my "stud" did our thing and, as I am wont to do on occasion when the weather is good, had taken along my "Rand McNally Road Map" to identify rivers, towns and the like that were not on our navigation charts. Rolling into our spot with the Blues' pilots lined up in greeting, I pointed to my atlas with a thumbs up and big grin. They loved it.

Lots of Wings

On that trip I flew in the back seat with the Blues' number-four slot man, a big, confident and outstanding aviator, Lieutenant Commander Scott Anderson. And what a hop! I had always been a fan of the Blues and for a few hours long ago, had been in the running to be their head guy when they had Phantoms.

Anyway, old Scott did all the obligatory maneuvers and I was totally relaxed back aft. That is, until the big guy got to the part of the routine where "six aircraft cross over one point all together." Out of the blue, he yanks on six Gs and I went out like a light, a first for me. Just getting my wits about me at 10,000 feet, Scott jerks me off to sleep once again. Lots of laughs over a cold one that night, but not at the time!

The best of the best. Big guy who put me to sleep is number four to my right. Leader, Hoss Pearson, to my left and Doc to my far right.

We pinned on lots of gold wings in my three years, like around 6,000. Whenever I got a chance, I'd join in the weekly ceremonies, my contribution being a short speech. Most of the times, the girl friend, Mom, Dad, sister, et al. were there for the great occasion and always the new aviator would feel ten-feet tall.

The gist of my five- or ten-minute pep talk was: 1) "Great job. You guys have a right to feel good about yourself because for every twenty that apply to be a Naval Aviator, only one will stand here today." 2) "You are at the absolute bottom of the Naval Aviation ladder and you've got to keep applying yourself and work hard." And 3) "The name of the game is to win. There are no awards for second place or runner up. And, as so aptly put by the Red Baron of WWI fame, 'Your job is to shoot down the enemy and anything else is rubbish.'" Way to go guys!

True Faith and Allegiance

CHIEF OF NAVAL AIR TRAINING
16 March 1983

Dear Ensign Chase,

What a great pleasure it was for me to have participated in the pinning on of your wings last week in Meridian.

As a reminder, I want you to remember what I said there in the chapel. Aside from the fact that I was so proud of you all that I could bust, I want you to remember:

- First is that you have succeeded in a tough and demanding regimen where many others have failed.

- Second is that you all have a great deal to learn. You are at the bottom of the naval aviation ladder. Work hard and study hard to master the aircraft and weapon system you will be flying.

- Third and most important is to remind yourself daily that the bottom line of your job will be, if called upon, to win in war. You must be ready at all times. Anything less is unacceptable.

Super job. Keep charging. Have fun.

With my very best regards to you in the years to come, I remain,

Sincerely,

P. B. BOOTH
Rear Admiral
U. S. Navy

Ensign Michael Chase, USN
Training Squadron SEVEN
Naval Air Station
Meridian, Mississippi 39309

Follow-up letter to newly-winged Navial Aviator reinforcing my short message.

One really interesting every-six-month gathering was the so-called "Air Board", a conference of the twelve or so senior Navy and Marine aviation leadership, including CNATRA. One of these, held at the Navy's big test center at Patuxent River, Maryland, was to have a short guest appearance by the Secretary of the Navy, John Lehman. His subject — a discussion of the lessons learned from a poorly executed "eye for an eye" carrier air attack into Lebanon several months prior.

Well, for two hours Big John strutted to and fro across the podium, pointer in hand, lecturing to some 300 years of combat and fleet-experienced senior folks on, ". . . how screwed up things were and how I was going to get things on track," or words to that effect. I really felt compassion for Dutch Schoultz and his three-star Marine cohort, and even a twinge of embarrassment, so abrasive was this civilian head of the Navy. Though I had little association with him, the perception in the fleet was that the guy ought to stick to working with the Congress and the American people and let the pros run the operation. Too bad! But the facts were that Lehman had the Navy on a role and was daily in the press and on the TV about his "600-ship Navy." So, in general, the senior leadership acquiesced and tolerated his style.

Big John in my Dad's old pre-WWII leather flight coat – Lord of the Seas?

While continuing to fine tune our safety and quality goals, one of our chief problems was retention of our cadre of instructors, particularly the carrier guys. Problem was, that as high as the Navy was riding, the strain on our fleet was tough — long carrier deployments were the norm and sometimes the endless shipboard training was not overly stimulating in the far reaches of the Indian Ocean. At the same time, the economy was picking up with the Reagan euphoria and airlines beckoned, as they usually did in good times. Married, with a growing family was the norm for these 27-year-old lieutenants who, upon leaving the instructor ranks, would most often end up on U.S.S Carrier as catapult officers, navigators or airplane handlers and facing the same tough at-sea regimen. Unfortunately, many opted to leave for the airlines, despite the best efforts of a concerned leadership.

Symbolic of these instructors were two aides with whom I had worked closely, Craig Luigardt from the patrol plane community and the other, an F4 fighter pilot, Ernie Wattam. Both had served for a year or two in the trenches as instructor pilots before suffering the ignominy of becoming my aide.

Craig was a smart, confident former-P3 pilot who had been a top instructor pilot in the local T-28 primary training squadron. He checked me out in the T-28, my favorite flying machine of all times and was the embodiment of someone who absolutely enjoyed what he was doing. He loved flying and working with the new guys and was superb in the role. He also sailed his little boat like a maniac (Win!) and was the first person I had known who wore a real Rolex watch.

Because of my close association with Craig, I learned much about the subtleties of our multi-engine pipeline, about one quarter of our training job. This type of flying was as different from jet carrier work and the world of helos as driving a truck compared to a sports car.

The big thing was engine-out work, à la my first encounter some months before. I mean these guys would chop an engine in a heartbeat. The reason was simple: In any more-than-one-engine airplane, if you lose one engine, the situation can be handled safely with one very large caveat to wit: it must be done correctly! Ergo, practice and more practice. Old Craig could fly the twin-prop jet transports we had on one engine as well as he could two. But, it is demanding, and after eight or so of these low altitude "emergencies," I was ready to head for the barn and a cup of coffee.

In three years we had two particularly tragic accidents in this pipeline. One involved a young student who was having problems handling the loss of an engine. Because he was due for a check ride the next day (we surmised), his instructor was giving him some extra practice. As I recall, he crashed on his 14th landing attempt, the accident board concluding that he had put in the wrong rudder when the instructor chopped one of his engines in the landing pattern.

When the very thorough accident and JAG investigations got to my office some two-weeks later, no one had spotted what to me was obvious. Fourteen landings is too much at one time, particularly for a guy having trouble to begin with! Craig agreed with me. But what bothered me the most, was that the accident board, the squadron CO and the Wing Commander had not picked up on the fatigue aspect. What happened, never should have. The leadership, paid 99% for executing common sense and prudent judgment, dropped the ball and was just as much at fault as the harried student and over-zealous instructor pilot.

Another doubly-tragic accident, shortly after I arrived, was the loss of two T-44 aircraft and six pilots, including two highly-experienced instructor pilots. While practicing landings at a tower-controlled outlying field, the two machines simply collided. But, once again, it never should have happened. The weather was perfect, a tower operator was working the pattern, radio comms were all good and all were conforming 100% to long-established course rules. How could two brightly-painted aircraft come together and crash? Maybe the pilots were not as attentive to lookout doctrine as they should have been and maybe there was a hint of complacency due to many years of routine operations at this particular field. Or perhaps it was due to a tower operator who was legally correct, but didn't do anything when he saw the airplanes too close to one another. What a shame. And what a loss!

As all of our 400 jets were old, tired and expensive to operate and maintain, the Navy had agreed to replace them with the British "Hawk" trainer aircraft. So Craig and I flew to the UK to find out more about this soon-to-be Navy trainer. My host for this short visit was to be an RAF brigadier general, Kip Kimbal.

My first flight was at the large British Aerospace plant and field about an hours drive from London, on a cold, rainy and low-overcast day. Clamoring in up front, the experienced company test pilot in the back, off we went into a solid 400-foot overcast, soon to be on top at 15,000 feet and witness to a glorious sun. What an incredible little airplane! It flew like a Cadillac and handled like a Corvette. What a delight. Stalls, spins (yes), loops and a bunch of landings in the rain and low visibility. Notwithstanding that it was almost too easy to fly, I said to myself, "We've got a winner."

Following a rainy initial hop in the British Hawk outside London with company test pilot. What a wonderful flying machine!!

I also got a chance to fly the little machine from an operational British training base in the north and went up with a hyper-active, spring-loaded and mustachioed lover of things aviation, an RAF instructor pilot, this time in gorgeous weather. This hop was to be an advanced low-level flight and I mean low (all legal and expected in this case). Once again, I came away mighty impressed with not only its flying qualities, but the low operating costs, easy maintainability and extreme reliability.

The return trip on an American Airlines DC-10 was a real kick, as it turned out. Coming over, we had flown first class, compliments of a friendly station chief in Corpus. The fully-loaded return was just the opposite. Stuffed in beside a big Craig and another large-sized fellow, I got set to endure the eight-hour marathon-trip home. But along comes the flight attendant who wanted to know, " Could I get you anything, Admiral?"

"I'd like to visit the cockpit, please."

"No way," says she rather emphatically. But, shortly, she returned and whispered, "The Captain has invited you to the flight deck." So up I went to the front office of this magnificent machine with 350 folks aboard to be greeted by three ex-Navy pilots! All they wanted to talk about was naval aviation, carriers and airplanes and trade a few time-worn sea stories, mostly having to do when they were students in the Training Command. What fun!

A more serious sidelight occurred upon arrival in Dallas late that night, to American's big simulator-training facility. Because we had very substantial simulator investments in the Training Command, and were using them more and more, I wanted a first-hand look at what the airlines were doing.

Here's how it went: Senior American captain in the left seat for his every-six-month proficiency check, fully grossed-out DC-10, night and low overcast, the lights of the partially-obscured runway stretching ahead. The captain rotates at 168 knots, the instructor fails one of his three engines, the airplane is committed to fly and the big machine realistically lumbers into the sky until reaching 200 feet. Soon, the airplane starts down, the radar altimeter intoning, "pull up, pull up, pull up," and the debonair captain is sweating. At 100 feet, the instructor quietly suggested that "you'll need some more right rudder, Captain." The captain complied, the amount of drag producing spoiler and aileron hanging out on the starboard side was reduced and the big airliner started to gain altitude. The moral of this story is not that the pilot screwed up, which he did, but rather, 1) He'll never make that same mistake again and 2) simulators are great for realistic training.

About once every six weeks, the U.S.S. Lexington would set sail from Pensacola. Usually, I'd climb into our little TA4 jet and go visit, having had the benefit of one or two sessions in the "bounce" pattern at one of our many outlying fields under the watchful eyes of the Landing Signal Officer or LSO. I would usually tag along as number four with an instructor leading his two studs and one old guy out to the ship some 75-miles off the beach.

Like many other phases of naval aviation, day carrier landings in the calm waters of the Gulf of Mexico are no big deal to someone of my experience. But, as in all flying, it has to be approached and conducted with professionalism. Flying by myself in this case, I'd manage to remember to drop the hook, put the fuel where it's supposed to be, get the correct radio channels, fly as sharp a number four as I could and, in general try not to screw up. And always, I would limit myself to two landings, enough, I reckoned, "to get my mind right." That shiny airplane would then go to Ensign "Jones," who, with heart pumping, would go off to test his mettle on the playing field of catapults, arresting gear and LSOs.

Station commanding officers at top and wing command master chiefs below. Absolutely awesome leadership!

What an inspiration to be out at sea and on the Lady Lex. Commissioned in 1943, with an illustrious combat record in WWII and crewed by 1,500 men and women sailors, it did its job with class and pizzazz. When the sun set, our guys would watch the night work of the fleet A6s and A7s and wonder if one day, they too would be out with the fleet and the most uncompromisingly-demanding flying in the world.

And too, it was a chance for me to chat with the skipper, let the troops know what was going on from my perspective and wander about. As it had been two consecutive staff jobs for me, I had had limited opportunity to talk to real sailors and feel the deckplates, so I relished these occasional visits at sea. To look eyeball to eyeball with a young LSO, or engine room 19-year old or the ship's Master Chief Petty Officer, and tell them what a nice job I thought they were doing and get a sincere, "thanks" in response, made it all worthwhile.

Back at Corpus, we dealt with a myriad of issues and problems common to any large organization. Budgets, improving the process, lack of assets, spare parts, people problems and the like, were all part of the norm. But, led by our able Chief of Staff, Tom Wimberly, (with whom I had served when he was XO of VF-74 in the Forrestal fire), our staff of some 50 folks plugged away, and little by little, we managed to stay ahead of the power curve.

One small example involved a long-standing directive from the Defense Department to wear seat belts when on military installations. In spite of the paper and rhetoric, few (except the Air Force) complied. So, we said, "Why not — a rule is a rule — let's stop giving it lip service and do it." Furthermore, we figured if we saved one life, it would have been worth it. As expected, we got some grumblings from a few who felt they were being hassled, but it worked. In one year we had four documented cases of people who were alive because they had developed the habit of strapping in, but who prior to this, had never done so.

One soggy and bumpy day, about 84 students, flight instructors and myself had a frighteningly close call in a big Navy C9, twin-engine, jet transport. We had been at a confluence of naval aviation's rite of passage at Las Vegas where the Naval Air Training Command was front and center and returning to Corpus. The weather was rotten — big Texas thunderstorms all over. I was riding in the jump seat as the two Navy reserve pilots (but also airline pilots) guided the big airplane down to an instrument approach. This particular approach had a minimum altitude of 400-feet above the water or ground and was the simplest of all approaches to fly. The C9 was in heavy turbulence, bursting thunder and pounding rain all the way down to 400 feet, but continued lower at a very rapid rate with no field in sight and no recognizable action on the part of the pilots. Along with the radar altimeter low-altitude alert, I said unbelievingly, "Pull up, pull up."

We finally landed at a local airport, no one saying much. Most of us had never come as close as this to "buying the farm." The barograph in the belly of the plane read 19 feet and had an accuracy of plus or minus 30 feet! No one knows to this day why those extremely qualified pilots allowed the airplane to go way below the 400-feet minimums. To any one of our thousands of instructors and students, busting an altitude on an instrument approach is a deadly "no-no," and one not likely to be made twice and survive. Eighty-four aviators and two "heads-up-and-locked" transport pilots learned a real-life lesson in what the minimum descent altitude really means.

One of the passengers on this flight was the wing commander from our base at Kingsville, Jimmie Taylor. Jimmie was typical of our senior leadership — hard charging, combat seasoned, good and motivational instructor pilot and a perfect role model for his charges. He was a former F-14 squadron commander and had demonstrated the Tomcat to the world at the Paris air show some years before. His squadrons, base and people sparkled, if not literally, then figuratively. Successful at the safety and quality end game, his enthusiastic and common-sense leadership set the tone for a first-class operation.

And outside the gates to our bases was always a solid and proud-of-their-guys civilian support structure. Each base employed many civilians and pumped big dollars into the local tills. Good example is Beeville, Texas, some two hours up the road from Corpus.

King Ranch deer hunt. Jimmie Taylor at left with our host top center. Sam Flynn seated. Typical Texas hospitality!

When I went through advanced flight training at Beeville some 24-years earlier, its population was 14,200; it was still 14,200. But, in large part due to the strong Navy presence, its economy was robust and balanced the oil and ranching extant in the area. So, each visit, I would manage a talk to the local Rotary or Navy League and give them the "big picture" and a few sea stories. They reciprocated with gusto by entertaining the Navy with real cookouts, dove hunts and just plain friendly Texas hospitality.

In fact, I managed to talk to a Rotary or some civilian group about once a week for almost three years. The Rotaries were always a good cross section of their communities and were an excellent way in which to get the Navy's story out to mainstream America, which I felt, was simply not being done effectively. They were pleased to get a chance to talk to a relatively senior type and hear about the incredible job the Navy was doing around the world first hand.

Carolyn and I representing the Navy at the Dallas Military Ball.

On the homefront Carolyn and I lived in 5,400 square feet of a two-story, WWII sprawling house, designed in the days when the Navy allocated people to staff them. We entertained local and visiting folks a good bit and Carolyn was inevitably the head cook, server and chief bottle washer. At Christmas, many of the staff wives would get together and decorate the old house in grand style and await the hundreds of local folks who would come to marvel at its old-style elegance.

One of our sadder jobs was to retire the venerable T-28 to the boneyard for old airplanes in Arizona. With an oft-overhauled 1,400 hp, oil-guzzling, reciprocating engine and some 30 years of getting beat up by aggressive students, these airplanes were ready for a rest. Because I loved the old machine, I "volunteered" to lead the flight along with the professional competence of a marvelous lieutenant commander, George Gardner. After an uneventful flight, the four machines landed at Davis-Monthan AFB to be met by an incredulous Air Force general, whose domain we had entered. Not only did we have no squawks whatever on the airplanes, the airplanes looked as if they had come off the factory floor. For thousands of naval aviators who had mounted and flown it, the relegation of the T-28 to the desert and civilian collectors was a sad day indeed.

Letting down enroute to Davis-Monthan AFB. George Gardner to my left and Ernie Wattam far right.

Lots of Wings

While the Marines would espouse the "few good men" theme, the Navy was blessed with an abundance of absolutely top-drawer men, in the ranks and as leaders. A good way of explaining this sometimes cliched rhetoric, is to describe a ten-day, Washington selection board, of which I was a member. The purpose of this board was to select the next couple-of-years worth of major commanders for our carriers, large bases and some bonus commands, all from a slate of folks selected for or already in the rank of captain.

```
              ORGANIZATION

  * BEST IN HISTORY OF NAVAL AIR TRAINING COMMAND

         * WING ONE - RON HORNE (VA)

         * WING TWO - JIM TAYLOR (VF)

         * WING THREE - DAVE PAGE (A7)

         * WING FOUR - JERRY GOODMAN (VS)

         * WING FIVE - JERRY HATCHER (HS)

         * WING SIX - CHARLIE WARD (VAW)

         * LEXINGTON - HAL BERNSON (VAW)

         * SCHOOLS COMMAND - JIM RYAN (VF)

         * BLUES  DAVE CARROL (VA)
                 HOSS PEARSON (VF)

              · COS — BILL MOOBERRY - EL
```

Copy of a briefing view-graph listing our leadership, not one of whom I would trade for anyone else in the Navy!

True Faith and Allegiance

What an experience! There were about ten of us on the board, all flag officers, and we would spend ten-hours a day reviewing records and making sure we selected the best of the best. It was tough, for there were literally eight highly-qualified guys for every slot. Each one of these fine officers had been in command and had jumped through a dozen hoops already to get where they were. My eyes watered at the leadership and talent we had in the Navy. Way to go guys!

Early on, I had paid a visit to a portion of our training that transformed civilian college graduates to newly commissioned ensigns. The program had been around a long time and basically involved exposing the new guys to a modicum of military indoctrination. I was horrified! Shaved heads, long runs, thousands of push ups, and four months of a mind-numbing regimen spanning the theory of jet engines to the tough, gnarly image of a Marine drill instructor two-inches from your nose. This was the real home base of the movie, "Officer and a Gentlemen," only the players weren't acting. I mean it was tough, it was close to demeaning and I was not overly impressed.

Bob Rasmussen, a former Blue Angel, Crusader fighter pilot and Lexington skipper, had done it all. As leader of this formidable entry into naval aviation, Bob set the standards and watched out for his charges. In answer to my concerns, Bob explained, "We've got to make it stressful. If we don't, and the guys crack under the real stress of combat or routine fleet flying, we will not have done our job here."

How true it was and how proud were these guys when they conquered the hurdles in their path. Time after time, I would ask those who had completed Bob's school of obstacle courses, short hair and rigorous academics, what they would change if they could. The consistent answer, "Nothing — leave it alone."

I had met Jim Stoffregen, a tall, strapping and good-looking student pilot from Chicago at his graduation from Bob's school, marking his transformation from civilian to ensign. One each, Mom and Dad, two grandparents and four sisters rounded out the admiring clan. As chance would have it, I flew later on with him in the TA4 and saw him and his family again when he received his wings at Meridian, Mississippi. Like most all flight students, he had more fun than he deserved, but he also had his sights set on being a Naval Aviator and worked hard at it. We were blessed with a cadre of some incredibly smart, self-motivating and principled student aviators from all corners of the country and Jim was not atypical by a long shot.

Bob's schoolhouse also had its self-contained house of tortures, which, on occasion, I would sample, just "to test the environment." One of these was the 9D5. The 9D5 was but one small piece of a tough indoctrination into water survival, a big deal in naval aviation. Parachute drags, Dilbert dunkers and underwater swims in full flight gear were the norm.

The 9D5, a helo, less engine and rotor blades, was a guaranteed pulse-rate generator. The "pilots and passengers" would strap in as it dangled above the deep pool. Blindfolds would be donned, and without warning, the device would drop into the water and randomly turn one way or the other as it sank to the bottom. No one was allowed to unstrap and try to escape until the machine was totally stopped, your compliance in this latter obligation checked closely by two scuba-clad divers.

On one run, I got confused while getting kicked by frantic students to my left and right, so peeked with one eye past my blindfold, got my bearings and triumphantly swam to the surface 15-feet above. "No way, Admiral," says the Navy guy in charge, "Do it again!" And I did.

Just as my first flight instructor, Lieutenant (junior grade) "H.P." Jones ("Hot pilot and don't forget it, Mr. Booth.") so influenced me, so too did our cadre of 1,200 flight instructors set the tone of the entire command. Leaders can cajole, plead, speak and jump up and down, but no matter; if the guys in the trenches didn't want to do it, it would not get done. So, to buttress the chain of command words and paper on safety, quality and teaching a "Win" attitude, I would meet personally with each group of incoming instructors at the rate of once or twice per month for a good three-hour session. Not an overkill, I preached staying in the rules box, lots on quality and recounted tales of dumb things we had done, including myself. Most often, we would get a dialogue going and garner some useful feedback about what these folks were thinking. One of those in an early class was Ernie Wattam, one of the few fighter pilots on board and a self-proclaimed great aviator.

I was out jogging early, poked in the simulator building and ran across an off-duty instructor who got his student in ahead of the schedule so he could do some extra instruction. Not atypical.

Ernie was a piece of work. In many respects, he and I were alike — similar flying backgrounds, both average pilots trying to do an above average job, and both managing to stay out of trouble most of the time. Old Ernie could smell an airplane — he would rather have flown than most anything. He was also an excellent flight instructor at the Naval Air Station in Pensacola and pretty much the top of a talented heap of compatriots.

Ernie Wattam in his element.

At a going-away party some of our guys had for Carolyn and me, Ernie, knowing my love for the Blue Angels and secret desire to have been one, organized a skit with a Blues motif, the setting being an old-sailor's home a few years downstream. Arrayed in front of us were four blue-and-gold wheelchairs, piloted by Ernie and his buddies. Hard hats, sharp flight suits, radios, heads drooping and flashing strobe lights, they paused to start the routine, as the Blues are sometimes wont to do. They could have stopped there, so enthusiastic was the response. But, alas, they did crossovers, loops and diamond fly-bys, all in ultra-slow motion. What a show!

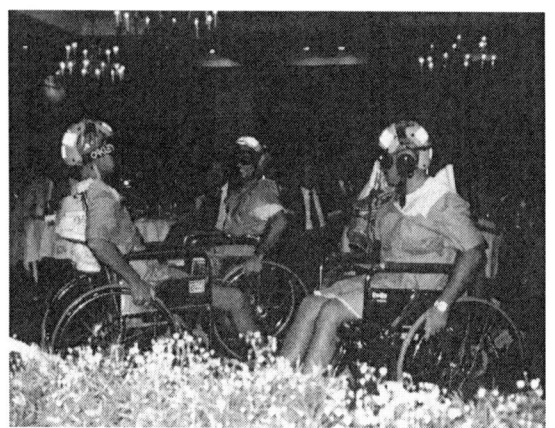

Marsha Goodman, author, Dutch Schoultz, Carolyn.

And so it went. Everyone knew that the name of the game was to "...shoot down the enemy and anything else is rubbish," but you didn't have to tell that to Ernie, Jimmie Taylor, Bob Rasmussen, Craig, Jim Stoffregen, Tom Wimberly or anyone else. They wrote the book.

EPILOGUE I

This short piece, intended for some of our local newspapers, surfaced out of some obscure, dust-ladened manila folder long after the foregoing was written. In retrospect, it seemed to capture a tiny slice of the Naval Air Training Command's persona.

PRIDE — U. S. NAVY STYLE

Last Friday, Carolyn and I drove up to Chase Field near Beeville to attend a change of command ceremony of one of our squadrons in the Naval Air Training Command, VT-25. As changes of command go (we have about thirty per year), I suppose this was routine. But was it really?

The squadron was much like all of ours — about 30 jet aircraft, 200 maintenance men and women and trains some 110 jet pilots for the Navy and Marine Corps yearly.

The setting was in a large hangar — Giant American Flag, troops in dress uniforms, wives and family, folks from town, three 15-year-old airplanes that looked brand new and the band from the Beeville High School.

But, what was particularly impressive were the people that made up this fine squadron. The Commanding Officer was Commander Ray Hoberg, a veteran of many years at sea and combat — a superb leader — who is shortly to report to the U.S.S. Nimitz for a two-year tour of more tough sea duty. The young instructor pilots, both Navy and Marine, are the best in the world. They have come from the far-off oceans and will probably return after their shore duty. The student naval aviators — all hand picked — are survivors of very high attrition in the early stages of selection and training. And the enlisted folks stood so tall you could not touch them. They took care of 30, old-and-tired jets better than I have ever seen airplanes tended to. Each morning, there would be 25 polished and ready to go.

The meaning of it all? Captain Dave Page, the wing commander, summed it up when he said that their purpose at Chase was to produce the best aviators in the world and reminded us that Lieutenant Mark Lange, recently killed in an A6 jet in Lebanon, had been a graduate not long before of VT-25.

The business of this squadron and our nineteen other squadrons, is to produce combat aviators that can hack whatever it is, whenever, and wherever they may be called upon to do it. The pride of all of them was incredible. They knew they were good — they felt good about themselves.

As did I! For these young men and women are needed by this great country of ours. We need not forget the sacrifices of these few such that we may be free. Pride runs deep.

EPILOGUE II

- The **Lexington** was decommissioned in 1991, having served her country through almost 50 years of tough service and is now a museum in Corpus Christi, Texas.

- **Tommy C. Wimberly** retired as a captain and continues to preach the Navy message as a senior member of the civilian Navy League in Texas.

- **Jim Stofferegan** flew F/A-18's in the fleet and is now in the reserves and flying for Delta Airlines.

- **Ernie Wattam** went on to command an F/A-18 squadron, retired early and is now in charge of all test flying for Boeing's military side.

- The **Naval Air Training Command** continues its incredible record of safety and still produces 2,000 of the best aviators in the world each year.

- **Skip Furlong,** one of the Navy's most gifted fighter pilots, retired and is mostly responsible for the tens of millions of dollars raised for the awesome National Museum of Naval Aviation in Pensacola.

- **Jim Busey** retired as a four star, the number-two guy in the Navy, and became the head of the Federal Aviation Administration.

- **Bob Rasmussen** retired from the Navy, is one of the nation's top aviation artists and sculptors and is the hands-on director of the National Museum of Naval Aviation in Pensacola.

- **"OB" Powell**, my helo mentor, became a captain and served as an advisor to the Navy's civilian R&D head guy in Washington.

- **Scott Anderson**, the strong-armed Blue Angel, never did apologize for putting me to sleep and is now a captain for Northwest Airlines.

- **Jimmie Taylor** went on to make flag and later became the head of the Naval Air Training Command, carrying on the traditions of safety, quality and Win.

- **Craig Luigardt** opted for the technical world of computer science at the Navy's Post Graduate School and is now a leading force in electronically tying together the Department of Education.

- **John Lehman**, visible though he was at the time, lowered his profile somewhat, his 600-ship Navy a victim of real-world funding constraints and competing priorities.

- **Kip Kimble** made three stars in the RAF, ran the Falklands air campaign and is now retired.

- The lovely little **Hawk trainer** came on line ten-years after I flew it, testimony to an out-of-control acquisition process, bureaucratic tweaking and hardly resembles the sprightly and simple machine of yesteryear.

- The **Beeville Naval Air Station**, became a victim of the DOD "cut" list and is now a booming Texas prison.

- I continue to wear the seat belt as I have each time since starting a small but worthwhile program back in 1982, and carry my Rand McNally road map on occasion when flying in our tiny airplane.

A montage of smiles, four stars, Trader John, plane captains, jets, C9 (ugh!), neighbors in town, student pilots, instructors, which captures the spirit and persona of the Navial Air Training Command.

COLOR ME PURPLE

*Purple suiters, F-16s, jumping out of airplanes
(not me), lots of generals and extreme perks.*

Wallace H. Nutting was what an Army four-star ought to look like: tall, athletic, good looking, articulate and smart. General Nutting had done it all. Because he was the leader of a large joint Army, Navy, Marine and Air Force staff, he was considered to be in military jargon, a "Purple suiter." And, because I was his chief of staff, I too was "purple."

It would take a book to describe what this ridiculously-large staff did, but at the end, you still would not understand. Its mission had gestated from one swing of the bureaucratic pendulum to another over the past couple of decades. But three things had not changed: an Army four-star general was the CINC (commander in chief), an Air Force three-star was the deputy or DCINC and a Navy two-star, the chief of staff.

Some background: All operational forces world-wide are controlled by unified commands. A good example is CINCEUR, an Army four-star, who commands all the military forces in and about Europe. When skipper of Forrestal in the Med, my ultimate boss was this same guy. The Pacific and Atlantic commands were headed by Navy admirals. The Southern Command, headquartered in Panama "owned" all the U.S. forces in Central and South America and so forth. All told there were some eight of these czars.

These CINCs reported directly to the civilian Secretary of Defense with a "dotted line" to the Chairman of the Joint Chiefs of Staff, both in the

Pentagon. Should there be a conflict, military response or whatever, the combined or unified forces under each CINC would take action down through their respective chains of command.

General Nutting's Readiness Command (REDCOM), at least on paper, was the owner and controller of forces in the U.S. One of our jobs was to ensure these forces were trained and ready to operate in the joint arena, should they be called upon to reinforce the other commands. The problem was that these forces reported to a covey of different commanders, so it was sometimes convoluted to figure out who belonged to whom.

Example: The 24th Infantry Division at Fort Stewart, Georgia. If there was a need for troops in Iceland, they went to the Atlantic Command. If in Central America, it was to the Southern Command and so forth. When in the U.S. in their normal peacetime readiness role, they really belonged to another Army four star (but a non-CINC) who owned all the Army in the U.S., unless activated by the REDCOM for the defense of the U.S. Clear as a bell, right?

Soon after reporting to the general, it became apparent to me that the Readiness Command functions could be done by other means already in place. But, I figured, smarter guys than me must know what they're talking about. So, off I went, to once again do the best job I could for the general et al..

We had moved, Carolyn and me, from our palatial quarters in Corpus Christi to a very small, one-story, one-carport house in a secluded area of MacDill Air Force Base in Tampa, Florida. Built in WWII for majors and lieutenant colonels, about 20 or so of these modest quarters now housed the base's platoon of flag and general officers of the Navy, Air Force and Army.

The Readiness Command chapter had started with a phone call from the Bureau of Naval Personnel's head honcho, Vice Admiral Bill Lawrence, who said I was to proceed to Tampa, Florida as the chief of staff to the Readiness Command. My response was a polite, "You can't do that to me!" He didn't have to say anything, but I could feel his smile through the phone, as it had been ordained by on high that my next incarnation was to be as another "staffer." "From the best job in the Navy to the worst," was my vocal assessment. My pleas to the bosses up in the five-sided building, that the job to which I had been destined, had a terrible reputation and that every Navy guy had ended up retiring, fell on deafened ears. Ugh!

So it was, from a large office to an obscenely larger one and a huge house to one of 1,700 square feet, and on an Air Force base to boot. MacDill AFB was host to one F-16 fighter training wing and two mammoth unified staffs, the second being responsible for the Persian Gulf arena and headed up by a Marine four-star. I really felt for the poor Air Force colonel who commanded the base, for it's a given that anytime you have a four-star anything, he has about eight generals and admirals under him. Furthermore, all were required to live on base, a base that hardly managed to accommodate the assemblage in the manner to which most had become accustomed.

> I am initially most impressed with the world down here at MacDill. Lots going on, as I'm sure you are aware. Some initial impressions:
>
> - General Nutting is spectacular. An incredibly talented leader.
>
> - Our ability to fight a war in the joint arena without major start-up efforts is weak. I get this at all levels, mainly as a result of exercises.
>
> - Strategic sealift overall game plan is weak or non-existent. Vis-a-vis overall goal. Boss wants long term, well defined (quantified) plan as per MAC Master Plan.
>
> - CINCs (Joint) have got to be much more involved in the PPBS system, starting with DG influence.
>
> - REDCOM trying hard to be the leader in the development of joint tactics and joint training, including several large simulation techniques.
>
> - REDCOM trying hard to find its "niche". What should it really be doing?

Feedback from Navy guys working the far-flung joint arenas was welcome. This exerpt from me to the Navy's number two in Washington, Admiral Hays, was early in my two-year tour with the Readiness Command.

I soon found that one of our primary purposes in life was to brief the hoards of folks that came to visit MacDill. They were usually very senior, from all over the world and particularly, from the Washington complex, who would swoop down in their private jets and see one Air Force base and two joint commands, all in one visit. As we didn't have any troops or ships or airplanes, what they experienced was a magnificent briefing room, a great briefing replete with pictures of tanks, fighters and ships, lots of sharp officers and usually a small social, such as a luncheon or dinner. I can truthfully report that these visitors, from the Chairman of the Joint Chiefs of Staff on down, were universally impressed with, ". . . the magnificent job you all are doing."

Our staff troops were hard working, talented and experienced. You can imagine, with a total of 19 stars, that we had more than a few colonels and lieutenant colonels. Not too many liked being on a big joint staff, but, typical of their ilk, they all put forth their best shot and tried to do the best job possible. These guys were good at their profession of arms, most all had served extensive combat time in the air or on the ground in Vietnam and all stood tall and were proud of who they were.

The key directorate on our staff was the "J3" or operations, headed by a bull-Army, infantry, two-star, Major General Bill Klein. Bill was all Army — show him the objective and he went after it like a tiger, undeterred by ordinary-folk obstacles.

Bill had limped in to my "austere" office one day not long before and I asked how come he was limping?

"Hurt it night jumping, chief."

"Night jumping?" said I. Yes, he had leaped out of a perfectly functional C-130 the night before with a bunch of our Army majors and colonels and hurt his leg. I couldn't believe a 50-year-old, two-star general, jumping out of anything, much less at night. But, alas, that was vintage Bill and lots of other senior Army guys just like him.

It wasn't a month later that Bill says at a meeting, "Got to go."

"Where you going?" I said, a bit peaked because we were in the middle of the meeting.

"Got to jump," he muttered, limping out of the room.

"Thought your leg was hurt?" I intoned.

He said, "No problem — jumping into the water, chief!" And off he went to do his monthly leap from a helo into the bay. Can you believe it? I still can't!

In the smaller suite of offices outside mine, reposed about eight wonderful people, all purple. There was a full Army colonel in an office adjacent to mine who was supposedly some kind of assistant, but I never figured out what he was supposed to do, nor apparently, did he. When he retired, we didn't bother to fill his position.

Then there was the sharp Air Force captain who handled protocol, and her assistant, an equally squared-away Navy petty officer. There were a few that I never did figure out what they did. But two I remember well.

First was Jean Kunkle, a career civil servant and my executive assistant who had to be the most organized and professionally competent secretary I had ever worked with. She had been the chief of staff's helper for the past six admirals and clearly knew her way around. About five feet ten inches in her bare feet, she was always shod in tall spike heels and had a commanding presence about her that rivaled that of Wallace Nutting. On occasion, she too had a hard time figuring out what it was we were supposed to be doing.

The other, was an Air Force non-pilot, Lieutenant Colonel Jerry Koontz. I hate to keep using the words sharp and smart, but he was. He also helped me get up-to-speed on what he thought our job was as well as a professed belief that the command should be disestablished. Jerry was not original in this notion, however, as a recently retired four-star CINC of REDCOM, had recommended just that in his change of command speech as he retired out of the job.

We had a small air force assigned for the use of the staff, mainly to support our role as organizer and runner of major joint exercises at the rate of about two to three per year, ranging from Alaska to Central America. With about ten C-12 Army Beech Super King Airs and helos (Hueys), the contingent of twelve-or-so pilots were headed by a full Army aviation colonel assisted by a major. I will categorically state that these pilots were among the best I had ever flown with! Because I was the colonel's immediate boss, they took it upon themselves to get me an AASE patch (Army Aviation Support Element), which soon adorned my well-worn Navy flight suit. I did get checked out in the two machines and managed to boondoggle a few flights with these extraordinarily fine Army warrant aviators.

One day late in 1984, the deputy, an Air Force three-star and I were enroute to Honduras via Panama in our Army C-12. In Panama, the bunkered underground headquarters of the Southern Command was the site of numerous briefings in our behalf. As were we, they were good at this particular facet of staff duty for they too were subsumed by dozens of briefings for hundreds of important folks who traveled south, in part to escape the rigors of Washington traffic, and partially in search of some modicum of an answer to the messed-up situation in Honduras and the region.

Army C-12 transport airplane enroute to Honduras. Note pilot in command and two co-pilots. Booth takes picture from the rear end.

Our high-tech machine with its plush interior and all the latest bells and whistles, was at contrast to the pock-marked and rutted airfield in a remote northern part of this economically-depressed country. Visiting an even more remote joint training facility with a Honduran major, we were invited on the return trip to his home in a small town on the seacoast. Though the setting was lovely (it had at one time been the capital of Honduras), it was a microcosm of life in much of the country and indeed throughout Central America, with a standard of living comparable to the lowest in the western hemisphere, Haiti. One-half of all 14-year-old girls were reputedly pregnant, dirt, flies and filth abounded and I never saw a youngster with shoes. Electricity and plumbing were a rarity.

The general flew us over to the capital city of Tegucigalpa where we parked in and amongst dozens of military aircraft, soon to be whisked to the ambassador's residence in a bullet-proofed car with body guards in the trailing van. Like most U.S. embassy residences I had seen, this one was opulent, well staffed and heavily guarded. The embassy itself was more fortress than office.

Because the alleged purpose of our visit was to observe "our" forces, we toured by helo the entire region including Contra base camps, Salvadoran bases, observation posts and remote airfields. The objective of all this activity was, of course, to thwart the growing menace of a communist-supplied and increasingly-militant Nicaragua. The Hondurans were anxious for the perception of neutrality, but willing to accept arms, dollars, intelligence and moral support from the U.S. Our presence, from a visible Army on "exercises," to a Navy offshore, to CIA and an Air Force in the wings, was pervasive. "Our" troops were indeed the recipient of some invaluable on-the-job training.

Early one morning, I jogged out the front gate of the ambassador's compound for my three-mile random run and again, the contrast was enormous. Shanty towns, filth and poverty abounded. Our most gracious hosts later chastised me for my adventurism, because it was "extremely dangerous out there." The notion of the "haves and have nots," was at every turn in this troubled region and I reckoned that as long as you had 50% of the population giving birth at 14 or so, no shoes, rampant disease and poverty, then all the military in the world would make no difference. At dinner that evening, my gracious hosts — Ambassador and Mrs. John Negroponte — seemed impervious to my observations. It was déjà vu Port-au-Prince, Haiti a few years before while CO of Sylvania.

US Advisor and Honduran major.

Back at our headquarters in Tampa, the staff routine continued. Old Bill in J3 would hack away at his two or three joint exercises while his two-star Air Force compatriot in J5 worked his plans and responded to unceasing paperwork, mainly in response to the latest Washington stimuli.

The J5, Lee Babcock, was a superb officer who simply was not a staff guy and constantly expressed his displeasure to me at being held hostage in this four-sided bee hive. His background, like lots of us senior types, was heavily operational and indeed, like me, he had come to this job from a top Air Force operational command in Europe. While I felt sorry for myself on rare occasion, I'd look at Lee and feel better.

Our communications guy was an Air Force, non-pilot, brigadier general, Jim Crouch, who was weaned in the ICBM fields of Montana and North Dakota and had most recently completed a tour as a wing commander of some 200 of these deadly missiles. As J6, a part of his responsibility was to oversee an elite, battalion-sized, joint communications outfit, the purpose of which was to fly anywhere and set up instant and clandestine world-wide communications, be it in a hotel room, the top of a mountain or middle of the desert. Most were jump qualified.

So Jim, taking the lead from the Army J3 and not to be outdone, announced he would like to go to Colorado Springs for jump "orientation." Unfortunately, I got a call on Saturday from Jim, who at the moment, was lying in a hospital bed, his right leg in a massive cast and starting the road to recovery from a badly broken leg. Jim didn't have to jump; he just felt that if it was required of his troops, he ought to at least sample the environment. Nothing ventured, nothing gained. Good on you for giving it a shot, Jim! Our three- and four-star bosses were unimpressed.

Every morning we would hold a "briefing" in our grand, three-story high and many-large-projection-screened theatre (different from where we briefed our VIP guests). A succession of sharp staff officers (Army, Navy, Air Force and Marines and even an occasional Coast Guard), would appear below our windowed-off perch from above and discuss weather (why, I never did figure out), where "our" forces were, their status, world-wide intelligence and so forth. The 19 stars in attendance wisely assimilated this information and would usually ask a few questions about this or that. Following, we would disperse to a succession of normal large-staff stuff. Though interesting, it was hard for me to get enthusiastic and turned on.

General Nutting with foreign VIPs.

Even though he was kind of a paper commander — more of an influence generator than a controller — Wallace Nutting loved it. His operational incarnation had been as a tanker and he was proud of it. The general was one of those talented leaders of men that by all rights ought to have had a real command or have been the Army Chief of Staff. He would have been spectacular in either role. As the Commander in Chief of the U.S. Readiness Command, even though he exercised little authority and had even less accountability, he was nonetheless, a player equal to the big guys and would spend a major portion of his time in high-level meetings with the other CINCs, the Joint Chiefs of Staff and the Secretary of Defense. So, as a staff, we were always scrambling to make sure our boss was well prepared for the conference-table battle fields.

Typical great Army pilot.

Chatting one day with my Army aviation colonel honcho, I indicated I would like to see "real" Army aviation in action with zero briefing rooms or full colonels." I wanted to see the troops in "their combat environment." Well, just like the tank general of a few years past, the colonel organized what turned out to be an eye-watering perspective of Army aviation at its best. Here's how it went:

About 2300 at night, some 50-miles west of Savannah, Georgia, in the black, wet and fog-shrouded woods, I was eating MREs with a tough-looking Army major, the CO of a 15-helicopter outfit participating in war games with the 24th Infantry Division, one of "our" forces. His machines that dark night were scattered about the fields and woods, the three-man crews in small tents rigged nearby, their night-vision devices at the ready. All was quiet. Soon, a whistle blew, and with no lights, no radios and no sounds other than the "whop, whop" of the rotor blades, 15 machines lifted eerily from their hideouts and winged to the troop pickup point, the major in the lead.

We tagged along in our Blackhawk helo, watched them load up the better part of a battalion of troops, fly some 15-miles away and drop them off, presumably in response to an "enemy" move. Never did any machine get higher than 20-feet above the trees, all were totally blacked out and no radios were in use.

I got a chance later that night to use the night-vision goggles that turned the blackest night into a dull day. It wasn't quite like a TV, but for sure you could operate clandestinely without electronics, lights, or external control.

And how impressed I was! Most of the pilots (and troops) were 19-years old, not too far removed from hometown USA and doing an absolutely superb and professional tough job. I might add that my association with the U.S. Army on numerous occasions and at all levels, reflected the same enthusiastic accolades, for they were universally spectacular. These guys were warriors, they were combat ready and proud of it — no doubt.

Color Me Purple

I had a chance to chat also with the division commander, a tough, big bear of a man, Major General Norman Schwartzkopf. We met in his command post out in the boonies, everyone dressed in full combat gear. The general launched into a longish and detailed brief of the "battle," little of which I understood. Clearly, he was a man who loved his work, was good at it and was respected by the troops.

Back at my perky office, I heard Bill and a bunch of our guys were going jumping that night, so decided to tag along. The machine, a nondescript C-130 from some national guard outfit, was to take our guys to the jump zone some 90-miles north. General Bill briefed me on all the "Geronimo" stuff, techniques and so forth and off we went, 40 guys in full combat regalia leaning forward and ready to go. Bill, like generals are supposed to do, was to be first out the door.

Meanwhile, up in the cockpit, the pilots were having a hard time finding the drop zone in the darkness, but finally got their bearings. On final approach, I went aft, captive by not one, but two straps securely anchored to the airplane. Technique? Geronimo? Forget it. The jump master said, "go," a green light came on and in less time than it takes to read this sentence, 40 troopers were drifting to the ground below, their mission almost accomplished.

The next day I asked my friend Bill about all that "Geronimo stuff?" "Got to get out fast, chief," his matter-of-fact response. I loved it.

"Our" forces also included an elite C-130 spook outfit up at Hurlburt Field in Florida's panhandle. These guys had the capability to go anywhere and drop troops, land or whatever, with no lights, no outside control and without talking to anyone on the ground. Enroute one night with two young Air Force captains at the controls and seven others, off we went, headed north. It was a flight to remember!

Our mission was to head north at very low altitude to about Knoxville, head east and south into the mountains, navigate low through the valleys, drop a container over a darkened drop point back in the Eglin complex and then land at a totally blacked-out field with no lights or electronic aides. I had not been uncomfortable in an airplane in recent years, but I was that night. At one point, not 200-feet above the valley floor, I put my face to the cockpit sidewindow and could see the mountain sides rushing past! For four hours, the big four-engined 130 rose and fell to the contours of the ground below.

The container was dropped within 100 feet of its target and the landing, in total darkness with no lights, was right on the money. Just another routine "days work" for this young Air Force combat-ready team.

About half-way through my tour at REDCOM, my general announced he wanted Carolyn and me to move into one of the four very-nice and expansive quarters next door to his. We politely declined on the premise that we had moved more than our share in the past few years, were happy in our little house and "Thanks for the offer, sir."

"It's not an offer, chief," says my leader. I guess he wanted his chief of staff, a Navy two-star, up with the big guys. By so doing, I think he felt the image of REDCOM would be enhanced. Given that I had no intention of being in the job more than a few more months, we stayed where we were, an imperceptible crumbling of the relationship, the result.

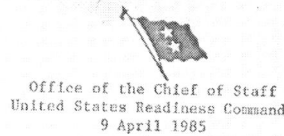

Even four-star generals like an occasional attaboy for their troops. These were two truly spectacular professional flights

General Nutting receives top Boy Scout Award with Jane.

But, that small event notwithstanding, Wallace Nutting was an inspirational leader. Not a "Pentagon Cowboy," he had spent his career in the trenches and loved his troops. At his urgings, we would have periodic formal "Dinings Out" at the base officer's club and what a sight they were. All the Army guys had unique formal wear, depending on whether your specialty were tanks, infantry, logistics or aviation. The Marines were far and way the most colorful and the Navy and Air Force resplendent in their shades of dark and light blue. The ladies of course, got all gussied up and outdid all of us.

My general would usually be the MC. A great motivational speaker, he would regale the crowd with anecdotal tidbits and occasional forays back to his younger days. What a guy. The troops loved him, the gals all dreamed and his wife Jane, just smiled. They were fun evenings and, the cost and dress code notwithstanding, were always fully booked.

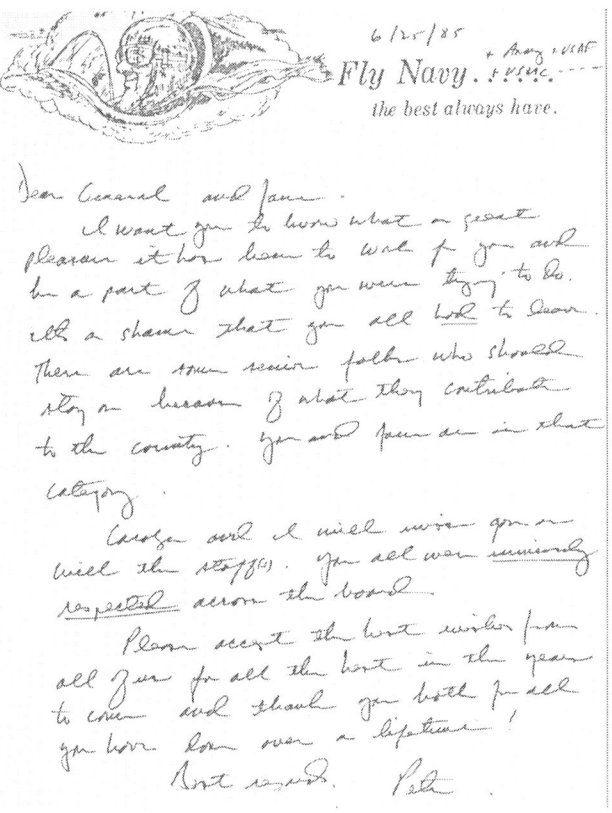

After one year, General Nutting and Jane retired from active duty.
My thoughts to them at the time in this handwritten note said much.

We flag and general officers would get together informally every two months or so for dinner or small social at one of our quarters. This meant about 16 couples due to the two large staffs on base. But we had fun and one of the reasons was that we all had somewhat similar backgrounds, ones that had been demanding, selfless and kind of arduous on occasion. The tankers would try to outdo the flyers, the intel guys the suppliers and the one or two Marines, everyone. The Army guys usually talked too loud because they had been shot at so much and couldn't hear worth two cents. There was little pompousness in this group, if for no other reason, than by the time you got to this stage, most could spot a BS artist before he ever walked in the room, his reputation an open page.

True Faith and Allegiance

General "Jake" Moore was my counterpart on the other staff. Because their area of responsibility included the Persian Gulf region, the Central Command had real troops, airplanes and ships. Why they were based in Tampa, Florida some 10,000 miles away will forever elude me. Anyway, old Jake was a piece of work. As my general was what an Army general ought to look like, so too was Jake the Marine version. Trim, fit, touch of justified arrogance and a smile that would wow the gentle ladies, he too had done it all. Jake also was not married which lent a slim air of intrigue to his being, a being that cut a wide swath. Good guy and probably a much better "chief" than I, even though our affinity for the jobs was about the same.

Jake and I would commiserate on the never-ending plethora of important visitors. It seemed that we spent 1/4 of our time preparing for VIPs, 1/4 briefing him or her and 1/4 figuring out what we could do to better improve the briefing process. The rest of the time was spent in doing what we were supposed to do.

Newly selected for Army general officer and the logistics guy on our staff, was Sam Wakefield. His title in purple, J4. Sam was a great logistician with talent oozing out all over, but only working on one or two of six cylinders. He was also a tad overweight and clearly not the sort to carry the "lean, mean" purple slogan in front of our important visitors. So one day, not having much to do either, I suggested we go and jog some during lunch. Old Sam got the hint, lost a few and we've been good friends ever since.

As one of our jobs was orchestrating major joint exercises for "our" forces, I reviewed the plans and found to my consternation, that we were using large C5 transports to airlift trucks some 600 miles. So, I said to Sam, "How come we use the most expensive airplane in the world to haul dump trucks?" No answer. We drove them this time, but I soon found out why Army guys hate to convoy large numbers of vehicles. It's simple: Lots of trucks break down, drivers occasionally take small detours and the command and control problems can be akin to pushing a wet noodle uphill. They would not buy the logic that ". . . if they broke down in practice, then they would do the same in wartime, so-why-not-find-out-what-is-wrong-and-fix-it-now?" logic.

Without question, the best intelligence I had on the staff was Jean Kunkle. Whenever her eyebrows raised, she had some tidbit to pass on. Because our senior folks, on rare occasions, would vent their spleen in front of their secretaries, the unofficial word would filter back to the front-office complex. I suppose it wasn't really rumor or gossip, but close to it. I have never been exposed to a civilian person who knew more about what was going on, than Jean. If one could write a book on being an executive assistant, Jean would be the one to do it.

Captain Linda Logan, the CINC's protocol officer, was married to Lindsey, a squared-away F-16 instructor pilot who was up one day bothering his wife. We started talking tactics et al. and I casually mentioned I would love

Color Me Purple

to fly an F-16 sometime. The next day, the harassed wing commander, an Air Force colonel and a good guy in his own right, called and offered me a ride. My instructor pilot: Captain Lindsey Logan.

The first thing any pilot notices about the F-16 is that there is no stick between your legs, but rather a small "force transducer" on the right console. It's kind of weird. But could that machine ever fly! As a Phantom was to an Indianapolis race car, the F-16 was to a Corvette. Not any faster, but incredibly agile and maneuverable. And, it was almost impossible to get into trouble with unless you flew it into the ground, so advanced was its flight control system.

```
                                            28 March 1986


Commander Gil Rud, USN
Commanding Officer
Blue Angels
Naval Air Station
Pensacola, Florida 32508-7801


Dear Commander Rud:

    I am responding to your Navy Times article requesting a demonstration
pilot for your team. I believe I have the requisite qualification.

    My background includes a lot of flight hours, most of which are in
tactical Navy aircraft. I have a lot of carrier landings too.

    I am career oriented and on shore duty and want to become a Blue Angel.
I say this because I feel you all represent the best in aviation and are
instrumental in letting people around our country know what excellence in
aviation is all about.

    I sure would hope you favorably consider this request because I love
to fly, and would make a good Blue Angel.

    Please send application to:

                    P. B. Booth, USN
                    US Readiness Command/RCCS
                    MacDill AFB, FL 33608-6001

                            Sincerely,


                            P. B. BOOTH, USN
                            Naval Aviator
```

Each year the Blue Angels send word to the fleet looking for new pilots for the coming season. I managed a few minutes out of my tight schedule to write this request. Interestingly, I got a call from a three-star friend who wanted to know if I was serious. I said I was.

Take a standard loop for example: All you do is simply pull the grip back to a G loading anywhere up to 9 (yes, nine!) and hold it there. The flaps and slats come out automatically, the rudders lock out at a preset angle of attack so you can't mess it up and the little airplane does it all for you. It's an easy machine to fly for sure. But the beauty is that rather than worrying about flying the airplane per se, your brain is allowed 100% to focus on how best to employ the total weapons system, both air-to-air and air-to-ground.

Lindsey and his wingman were as professionally a competent duo of aviators as I've flown with. It's not surprising, because only the best in the Air Force get into the F-16 to begin with and the instructors are the tops of that lot. They had their stuff together and I was grateful to have shared a unique and fascinating 1.4 hours in the front seat with them.

A couple of months later, I arranged an overnight carrier trip for seven of the wing's finest. Just as many Navy types are seldom exposed to the other guy, these aviators had seen carrier ops only on TV or the movies. I can guarantee, they were impressed beyond words with the day and night challenges of that big ship. I heard later that a couple had volunteered for exchange duty with the Navy, provided they were assigned to a carrier air wing. I suppose they too, wanted to be a part of the ultimate in military flying.

In this vast world of purple, us Navy types stood out. Much to the delight of our camouflaged-suited compatriots in arms, we would routinely wear our sharp whites one day a week. We even started a Navy Ball on the Navy's October birthday and had to turn away over a hundred folks the first time around! We may not have been on the Navy's first team, but you sure couldn't tell it.

One sad day I wrote a "Dear Admiral" to the head Navy guy in Washington. No one had burned up the phone lines asking me to go do something a bit more challenging and, indeed, I somehow managed the distinct impression that the "system" was looking the other way in my case. It was clear to me that I was to be the sixth consecutive Navy rear admiral to retire out of the job. I suppose I could have gone to Washington in the Joint Chiefs of Staff or the Navy staff, but I had come to the irreversible conclusion that staffs and Booth were an oxymoron.

So, one day, thirty years to the day I walked aboard Buck in Kobe, Japan, Carolyn and I left as we had come aboard. No bands, no speeches, no accolades and just the duty medal; and a handshake and "thanks" from the new general.

It's a typical exit line for so many standard Naval Officers — another average career for an average guy trying to do an above average job for his Navy and country.

Last Flight.

EPILOGUE

- **Linda Logan** left the Air Force so "I could raise a family."

- **General Wallace H. Nutting** retired out of the job to continue his contributions to his country in the civilian world, firmly believing in the need for REDCOM.

- **Jean Kunkle** finally retired after "training seven admirals in a row" to continue her avocation of golf sans high heels.

- **Captain Lindsey Logan** came close to becoming one the elite of the elite as a "Thunderbird" pilot and was to me, just another great young warrior putting forth the ultimate for his country.

- **Bill Klein** retired from the Army and became a top VP for the Tampa Bay "Buccaneers," his winning attitude finally rubbing off on his charges.

- **Sam Wakefield** continued to outrun me and became the head of the Army's Logistics Command as a three-star lieutenant general.

- **Gerry Koontz** retired to counsel younger officers and troops on planning for their financial future.

- **Norman Swartzkopf** went on to bigger and better, his seasoning in the swamps west of Savannah standing him in good stead.

- Ambassador **John Negroponte** continued his service to his nation and became the highly visible U.S. ambassador to the UN.

- **The Readiness Command** was disestablished a year after I left, its functions assimilated by other outfits, and its Navy chief of staff keeping the retirement string intact.

- The **U. S. Naval Officer** — and his **family** — continue his steady, round-the-clock, unadorned service to his country, a legacy unbroken for over two centuries.

FINAL EPILOGUE

This final thought was written ten-years ago and seems to capture the spirit and intent of the forgoing journals.

ATTRIBUTES OF THE INSPIRATIONAL NAVAL OFFICER

- **COMBAT**: The raison d´etre of the breed. When the time comes to confront the enemy, everything is second nature. He knows well there are no points for runner up. The name of the game is to win and anything else is rubbish. To be fully combat ready, face any adversary and win, is the Ph.D. of the Naval Officer.

- **PATRIOTIC**: Patriotism runs deep and is fundamental to the breed. Those who have gone before, heroes or not, imbue a legacy that is ingrained from the day the uniform is donned. When he salutes the colors, it is meaningful and deep rooted and sometimes, unseen tears will well up.

- **SACRIFICE**: A Naval Officer straps it on 24-hours a day, seven-days a week and sometimes for months on end. He often lives in a little shipboard cubicle devoid of family and loved ones. His family endures separation. He does his obligatory shore duty, but strives to get back to the fleet and the tough job. He worries about money, but is not driven by it.

- **JUDGMENT**: Much of his paycheck accrues to sound judgment. He knows full well the fine line between right and wrong and moral and immoral and imparts this ethic down the line to his men. He takes the heat, if need be, and resists any compromise to good order and discipline knowing that if he does, the ability of his team to win is lessened.

- **TAKES CARE OF HIS TROOPS**: He knows his men — their strengths, foibles and problems. He does not coddle nor condone mediocrity. He ensures they have the wherewithal to do the job. Respect flows both ways. "Attaboys" are in public, "chain jerking" in private.

- **FOSTERS TEAMWORK**: He promotes a sense of team destiny and success and keeps a weather eye for weak links. Knowing the immense value of listening, he fosters a climate of feedback from his team.

- **STANDARDS**: He stresses that standards seldom change while understanding that the enforcement of standards do change, depending on the malleability of the leader. The Naval Officer will do his best to meet all the standards of the world's top naval power, even though some may be mundane.

- **WORKS THE CHAIN OF COMMAND**: He keeps his boss in the loop, both formally and informally. He resists the temptation to by-pass his chain of command by putting the responsibility where it belongs. He is loyal up the chain and, more importantly, down the chain. He is honest to excess and never distorts the straight word — up or down.

- **LEADS BY PERSONAL EXAMPLE**: With a strong work ethic, he knows the action, rewards liberally, is enthusiastic and presents an up-beat and positive zest for putting forth an above and beyond effort.

- **LIKES WHAT HE DOES**: He loves his profession; he welcomes the challenges; he is intensely competitive. He may indeed question his motivation on occasion, but no matter, will grit his teeth and get the job done right. He'll feel good when he's done it. His troops will look up to him and vice versa.

Author Reminder

I hope you enjoyed this three-decade inside journal of real Americans doing the tough job 24/7 during some perilous years in our nation's short history. You might be inclined to reread the "Dedication" and "Caveats" pages before chapter one and perhaps gain an insight into the next-to-last paragraph at the bottom of the caveats page: **"They make this story and they are heroes all."**